BUSINESS, GOVERNMENT, AND PUBLIC POLICY
Concepts and Practices

Dan Bertozzi, Jr.
California Polytechnic State University

Lee B. Burgunder
California Polytechnic State University

Prentice Hall, Englewood Cliffs, New Jersey 07632

Library of Congress Cataloging-in-Publication Data

Bertozzi, Dan
  Business, government, and public policy: concepts and practices/
Dan Bertozzi, Jr. and Lee B. Burgunder.
    p. cm.
  Includes index.
  ISBN 0-13-093402-X
  1. Industry and state—United States. 2. Business and politics—United States. 3. Antitrust law—United
States. I. Burgunder, Lee B. II. Title.
HD3616.U47B525 1990
338.973—dc19   88-36766
                                                                                                CIP

Editorial/production supervision
and interior design: **Eleanor Ode Walter**
Cover design: **Diane Saxe**
Manufacturing buyer: **Laura Crossland**

Printed in the United States of America
10 9 8 7 6 5 4 3 2

ISBN   0-13-093402-X

Prentice-Hall International (UK) Limited, *London*
Prentice-Hall of Australia Pty. Limited, *Sydney*
Prentice-Hall Canada Inc., *Toronto*
Prentice-Hall Hispanoamericana, S.A., *Mexico*
Prentice-Hall of India Private Limited, *New Delhi*
Prentice-Hall of Japan, Inc., *Tokyo*
Simon & Schuster Asia Pte. Ltd., *Singapore*
Editora Prentice-Hall do Brasil, Ltda., *Rio de Janeiro*

*To Deborah
and Susan*

CONTENTS

PREFACE

This book provides an analytical framework for understanding the complex legal, political, and social forces that affect business. As we enter the 1990s, business and management must clearly recognize and understand the various elements of the public-policy and regulatory processes in order to survive and flourish. How do public-policy issues that may affect business arise? What political and social influences bear on the development of such issues? What roles do government institutions play in the development and implementation of public policy, and how can business be effective in influencing that policy? What are the forces that are likely to have an impact on the future relationship between business and government? The goal of this book is to assist students, managers, and interested citizens in resolving these questions.

Throughout the book we have endeavored to illustrate consistently the interrelationships among major subject areas. The early chapters link the public-policy process with the institutions that make and implement such policies. The chapters on antitrust policy not only provide a detailed analysis of the antitrust laws but also emphasize the public-policy aspects of antitrust and the implementation roles of administrative agencies. Finally, the chapter on business-government relations describes how corporate social responsibility is related to business regulation and suggests that the challenge of international economic competition may lead to a new series of public policies to improve American competitiveness.

We have tried wherever possible to place the subject areas discussed in this book in historical perspective. In this way the reader can assess the contemporary significance of subject areas such as business regulation, antitrust, and the business-government relationship as well as how and why these subject areas have evolved over time.

This book is intended for use in management courses that deal with (1) business, government, and society; (2) business and public policy; (3) business-government relations; or (4) government regulation of business. Such courses typically emphasize the external political, social, and regulatory forces that affect management decision making. The book is designed to provide instructors with the maximum flexibility by presenting a set of core materials on business, government, and public policy that can be supplemented by other materials suited to the needs of particular courses and individual instructors. It can be used quite effectively with supplements such as a casebook, readings books, or more narrowly targeted books that provide extended coverage of the issues raised. The book also serves as a foundation to which other subject areas may be added, such as corporate governance and business ethics. Owing to its focus on public-policy making, government regulation, antitrust policy, and business-government relations, the book also should be of interest to business managers and participants in executive development programs.

The book can be divided into three parts. The first part, which comprises Chapters 1, 2, and 3, analyzes the major elements of the public-policy process and presents a model to aid in understanding the interrelationships between these elements. Here we examine the government institutions involved in the making and implementation of public policy and discuss what business can do to influence and take part in the process.

The next part, consisting of Chapters 4, 5, and 6, provides an in-depth look at how the public policy of antitrust developed in the United States and how the forces of the public-policy process have substantially altered the direction of that policy in recent years. In this part the reader is introduced to particular antitrust laws that affect business as well as to the strategies business can employ to help shape the future direction of antitrust policy. This part thereby serves to clarify the concepts previously developed in the book, along with offering a somewhat sophisticated knowledge of an important policy directly affecting business in the United States. The relatively thorough focus on one major policy area also familiarizes readers with the complex considerations required in most other public-policy analyses so that supplementary materials and projects may be more profitably assigned.

The final part of the book, Chapter 7, discusses the future of the business-government relationship. In this regard we address two major forces, corporate social responsibility and the growth of international economic competition, which are likely to bring about a more cooperative relationship between business and government. We believe that the issues examined in Chapter 7 and in the preceding chapters of this book will stimulate thought and discussion about public-policy making and the business-government relationship.

ACKNOWLEDGMENTS

We are grateful to the following people who reviewed the manuscript: Edward Paul Fuchs, University of Texas at El Paso; J. Edwin Becht, University of Texas at Permian Basin; Richard Cuba, University of Baltimore; Bruce Yandle, Clemson University; and Raymond Raab, University of Minnesota.

CHAPTER ONE
Making Public Policy

INTRODUCTION

This chapter examines the principal factors that are involved in the formulation of public policy in American society. First we discuss how policy issues arise in American society. If managers are to be effective in influencing the formulation of public policies affecting business, they must understand how policy issues arise and how such issues can be identified early in the policy process so that appropriate corporate strategy can be developed. The remainder of the chapter deals with policy analysis. In order to help you understand why certain issues eventually become public policy while other issues do not, we will develop a model of the public-policy process that identifies the principal factors influencing the making of public policy. The model also analyzes the process by which these factors operate upon one another in order to influence the making of public policy.

Why Study the Public-Policy Process?

Why is it important for business managers to understand the workings of the public-policy process? The vast array of regulatory legislation affecting business that has been enacted by Congress over the past fifty years provides the answer. The impact of this legislation on the corpora-

1

tion has been enormous — in terms of the cost of doing business and the loss of freedom to carry out its business functions as it sees fit. The following examples of regulatory legislation (each of which is an example of a public policy) illustrate the point: the Social Security Act of 1935, the National Labor Relations Act of 1935, the Taft-Hartley Act of 1947, the Securities Act of 1933, the Securities and Exchange Act of 1934, the Civil Rights Act of 1964, and the Clean Air and Water Acts of the 1960s and 1970s. The number of regulatory public policies affecting business grew especially rapidly from 1962 to 1976. Table 1-1 illustrates the extent and impact of these public policies on American business. If business had been more sensitive and aware of the emerging issues of race and sex discrimination in employment, of air, water and noise pollution, and of health and safety problems in the workplace, to name but a few, it could have been a much more effective participant in the public-policy process of the 1960s and 1970s. The public policies that emerged during that period might well have been less costly, more efficient, and generally less burdensome, since these regulatory policies would have benefited from the practical input that the affected businesses could provide. Moreover, business would have benefited in the long run by developing a cooperative and socially responsible image.

Business managers need to understand the public-policy process in order to be able to influence the process in the best interests of the corporations they represent. Such an understanding should enable business managers to identify issues important to the corporation early in the policy process and to view them as an opportunity and a challenge rather than simply as a threat. Managers who ignore issues in the public-policy process (for example, proposals to increase controls on biotechnology firms or proposals to protect the privacy of consumer, employee, or investor records in computer data banks) often do so from lack of knowledge about what is happening and a belief that they have no control over the process. Understanding coupled with participation can help managers overcome these kinds of reactions.[1]

Public Policy Defined

What exactly do we mean when we use the term *public policy*? The public-policy literature offers many definitions, most of which are too abstract to be practically useful. The following definition is a good starting point:

> Public policies are those policies developed by governmental bodies and officials. (Nongovernmental actors and factors may, of course, influence policy development.) The special characteristics of public policies stem from the fact that they are formulated by what David Easton has called "authorities" in a political system, namely, "elders, paramount chiefs, executives, legislators, judges, administrators, councilors, monarchs, and the like." These are, he says, the persons who "engage in the daily affairs of a political system," are "recognized by most members of the system as having responsibility for these

TABLE 1-1   Extension of Government Regulation of Business, 1962-80.

YEAR OF ENACTMENT	NAME OF LAW	PURPOSE AND FUNCTION
1962	Food and Drug Amendments	Requires pretesting the drugs for safety and effectiveness and labeling of drugs by generic names.
1962	Air Pollution Control Act	Provides first modern ecology statute.
1963	Equal Pay Act	Eliminates wage differentials based on sex.
1964	Civil Rights Act	Creates Equal Employment Opportunity Commission (EEOC) to investigate charges of job discrimination.
1965	Water Quality Act	Extends environmental concern to water.
1965	Cigarette Labeling and Advertising Act	Requires labels on hazards of smoking.
1966	Fair Packaging and Labeling Act	Requires producers to state what a package contains, how much it contains, and who made the product.
1966	Child Protection Act	Bans sale of hazardous toys and articles.
1966	Traffic Safety Act	Provides for a coordinated national safety program, including safety standards for motor vehicles.
1966	Coal Mine Safety Amendments	Tightens controls on working conditions.
1967	Flammable Fabrics Act	Broadens federal authority to set safety standards for inflammable fabrics, including clothing and household products.
1967	Age Discrimination in Employment Act	Prohibits job discrimination against individuals aged 40 to 65.
1968	Consumer Credit Protection Act (Truth-in-Lending)	Requires full disclosure of terms and conditions of finance charges in credit transactions.
1968	Interstate Land Sales Full Disclosure Act	Provides safeguards against unscrupulous practices in interstate land sales.
1969	National Environmental Policy Act	Requires environmental-impact statements for federal agencies and projects.
1970	Amendments to Federal Deposit Insurance Act	Prohibits issuance of unsolicited credit cards. Limits customer's liability in case of loss or theft to $50. Regulates credit bureaus and provides consumers access to files.
1970	Securities Investor Protection Act	Provides greater protection for customers of brokers and dealers and members of national securities exchanges. Establishes a Securities Investor Protection Corporation, financed by fees on brokerage houses.

TABLE 1-1   *(Continued)*

YEAR OF ENACTMENT	NAME OF LAW	PURPOSE AND FUNCTION
1970	Poison Prevention Packaging Act	Authorizes standards for child-resistant packaging of hazardous substances.
1970	Clean Air Act Amendments	Provides for setting air quality standards.
1970	Occupational Safety and Health Act	Establishes safety and health standards that must be met by employers.
1972	Consumer Product Safety Act	Establishes a commission to set safety standards for consumer products and bans products presenting undue risk of injury.
1972	Federal Water Pollution Control Act	Declares an end to the discharge of pollutants into navigable waters by 1985 as a national goal.
1972	Noise Pollution and Control Act	Regulates noise limits of products and transportation vehicles.
1972	Equal Employment Opportunity Act	Gives EEOC the right to sue employers.
1973	Vocational Rehabilitation Act	Requires federal contracts to take affirmative action on hiring the handicapped.
1973	Highway Speed Limit Reduction	Limits vehicles to speeds of 55 miles an hour.
1973	Safe Drinking Water Act	Requires EPA to set national drinking water regulations.
1974	Campaign Finance Amendments	Restricts amounts of political contributions.
1974	Employee Retirement Income Security Act	Sets new federal standards for employee pension programs.
1974	Hazardous Materials Transportation Act	Requires standards for the transportation of hazardous materials.
1974	Magnuson-Moss Warranty Improvement Act	Establishes federal standards for written consumer-product warranties.
1975	Energy Policy and Conservation Act	Authorizes greater controls over domestic energy supplies and demands.
1976	Hart-Scott-Rodino Anti-trust Amendments	Provides for class-action suits by state attorneys general; requires large companies to notify the Department of Justice of planned mergers and acquisitions.
1976	Toxic Substances Control Act	Requires advance testing and restrictions on use of chemical substances.
1977	Department of Energy Organization Act	Establishes a permanent department to regulate energy on a continuing basis.
1977	Surface Mining Control and Reclamation Act	Regulates strip mining and reclamation of abandoned mines.
1977	Fair Labor Standards Amendments	Increases the minimum wage in three steps.

TABLE 1-1 *(Continued)*

YEAR OF ENACTMENT	NAME OF LAW	PURPOSE AND FUNCTION
1977	Export Administration Act	Imposes restrictions on complying with the Arab boycott.
1977	Business Payments Abroad Act	Provides for up to $1 million in penalties for bribes of foreign officials.
1977	Saccharin Study and Labeling Act	Requires warning labels on products containing saccharin.
1978	Fair Debt Collection Practices Act	Provides for the first nationwide control of collection agencies.
1978	Age Discrimination in Employment Act Amendments	Raises the permissible mandatory retirement age from 65 to 70 for most employees.
1980	Federal Trade Commission Improvements Act	Bars the FTC from enforcing antitrust laws against farm co-ops; prevents agency from issuing a regulation concerning funeral industry.
1980	Comprehensive Environmental Response, Compensation, and Liability Act	Creates superfund to pay for cleanup of hazardous chemical spills; taxes petroleum and chemicals.

Source: Murray L. Weidenbaum, Business, Government, and the Public, *3rd ed. (Englewood Cliffs, N.J.: Prentice Hall, 1986), pp. 24-26. Reprinted with permission.*

matters," and take actions that are "accepted as binding most of the time by most of the members so long as they act within the limits of their roles."[2]

Starting with this general definition of public policy, we can move to a more specific and functional definition that will be used in this chapter and the remainder of the book. Thus public policy may be defined as including:

1. Laws (also often referred to as statutes) enacted by the U.S. Congress and the state legislatures;
2. Rules and regulations adopted by administrative agencies;
3. Executive orders issued by the president of the United States pursuant to his constitutional authority or authority granted him by the Congress; and
4. Judicial opinions handed down by the federal and state courts, especially opinions by the U.S. Supreme Court and the various state supreme courts.

In the next chapters we will provide a detailed look at how the institutions mentioned in definitions 1 through 4 are involved in the making and implementation of public policy. For instance, as you will learn in the chapters on antitrust policy, the federal courts and administrative agencies such as the Department of Justice and the Federal Trade Commission play a major role in interpreting, refining, and in some areas expanding upon the antitrust legislation passed by Congress. In so doing, the federal courts and administrative agencies make public policy in the antitrust area.

HOW ISSUES ARISE IN THE PUBLIC-POLICY PROCESS

Before discussing the factors that influence the operation of the public-policy process, it is important to understand how the issues upon which the process operates come into being. Another way of putting this is to ask, How do issues become sufficiently recognized to be added to the *public-policy agenda*? For our purposes we can define the public-policy agenda as that set of issues which have received sufficient attention or recognition such that they are being actively considered by the policy process for adoption as the public policy of a state or the United States. Of course, for reasons discussed below, not all issues on the public-policy agenda succeed in becoming public policy. In fact, most issues (for instance, the proposal for national health care for all Americans funded by increased Social Security taxes) remain on the agenda for many years or are rejected because the factors that influence the making of public policy are never sufficiently favorable for the issue to succeed in becoming a public policy.

While the question of *how* issues arise in the public-policy process is not a simple one, most public-policy specialists agree that the factors listed in Table 1-2, which are discussed below, provide a good explanation of what occurs. While certain factors may be individually sufficient to thrust an issue onto the policy agenda, other issues may require the support of a combination of factors to achieve agenda status.

TABLE 1-2 How Issues Are Identified for the Public-Policy Agenda

Support by social, political, economic, or religious leaders/opinion makers
Media influence
Advances in science and technology
Level of education and leisure time in the population
Interest groups
Historical events: domestic and foreign
Changing economic and demographic conditions
Rational ignorance

Support by Social, Political, Economic, or Religious Leaders/Opinion Makers

Issues are often given their first important recognition and visibility before the general public when they receive the support of well-known and often charismatic leaders or opinion makers. While such support may not alone be sufficient to get the issue on the public-policy agenda, it often helps trigger additional needed backing from the media and interest groups. Examples of the importance of opinion-maker influence are numerous. The issue of automobile safety gained significant support in the mid-1960s when Ralph Nader wrote his now famous book, *Unsafe at Any Speed* (1965) about the problems of the Corvair automobile, manufactured by General Motors. Mr. Nader's crusade for automobile safety was highly publicized by the television and print media, which provided the issue with additional visibility and staying power. Once raised by Mr. Nader's book, the issue remained highly visible because of his vocal support and the influence of the media.

Rachel Carson's book, *Silent Spring*, published in 1962, is another example of a best-selling book that highlighted a vital public issue — in this case, the uncontrolled use of the insecticide DDT and the resulting pollution of the nation's streams and waterways. The book helped to raise the issue and mobilize the concern of many Americans about pesticide pollution and environmental pollution generally. It is also important to recognize that the related issues of pesticide and environmental pollution gained access to the policy agenda via a number of other factors to be discussed below; namely, media support, advances in science and technology that allowed for more accurate pollution measurement, increased levels of education and leisure time in the population that enabled many Americans to have the knowledge and time to be concerned, and a favorable economic environment that made possible the enactment of relatively costly public policies (for instance, the Clean Air and Water Acts of the 1960s and 1970s) to clean up the environment.

One last example of the importance of opinion makers in moving issues onto the policy agenda involves the charismatic leadership of Dr. Martin Luther King and the issue of civil rights. The issue of racial discrimination in employment and public accommodations (hotels, motels, restaurants, and so on) gained extraordinary visibility from his speeches, marches, and acts of civil disobedience, all of which were widely reported in the media.

Media Influence

It is difficult to overestimate the influence of the print and broadcast media as factors in determining which issues become sufficiently visible to be included on the public-policy agenda. The three major commercial television networks together with public television and the rapid growth of specialized cable television programming make national and world news instantly available to the American people. Additionally, the news divisions of the major television networks and many political leaders in Washington and around the country have long been influenced by the reporting and analysis of some of the nation's leading newspapers.[3] Thus if major elements of the media are attracted to a particular issue, perhaps because of the influence of certain key opinion makers, interest groups, or historical events, the issue acquires high visibility, and if the media interest is sustainable, the issue will be added to the policy agenda. Examples of issues where media influence has been an important factor include nuclear-power plant safety, negotiations for an end to the Vietnam War, the control of environmental pollution, the civil-rights movement, the educational-reform (in the primary and secondary schools) movement of the 1980s, catastrophic and long-term health care for seniors, and international economic competitiveness.

Advances in Science and Technology

Advances in science and technology can lead to the creation of new issues or the increased visibility and importance of existing issues. For example, rapid scientific development in the fields of genetic engineering, cellular and molecular biology, and biotechnology are causing and will continue to cause new issues to be added to the policy agenda. The widespread media coverage of developments in what has been called the "New Biology" serves to hasten the addition of these issues to the policy agenda.[4] In the area of environmental pollution control one of the factors that increased the visibility and importance of this issue in the early 1960s was the advances in measurement technology, which allowed scientists for the first time to assess and understand the extent and danger of certain pollutants in the air and water.

Advances in science and technology in the health-care field have raised a number of difficult issues that simply did not exist twenty years ago. While medical-care advances such as organ transplantation, complex surgical procedures, and diagnostic imaging devices have dramatically improved health care, they also are very expensive. One of the issues raised by this new technology is, Who should be entitled to its benefits? Only those who can pay or whose insurance companies can pay? Or should everyone who can medically benefit from the care be ensured access to the expensive procedures? In this latter case who would be required to pay for the guaranteed care? Only the further dynamics of the public-policy process will answer these questions now that the issue has been raised on the policy agenda.

Be aware here that each of the policy issues discussed above has substantial cost and regulatory implications for business. Business is involved in genetic engineering research and must be concerned about possible regulatory restrictions that may be imposed on the scope of research and development in this field. Similarly, large corporations must be concerned about the cost implications of environmental pollution issues and health-care issues.

Level of Education and Leisure Time in the Population

The number of students attending and graduating from American colleges and universities has increased dramatically over the past thirty years. Such an increase in the number of well-educated Americans is likely to affect our capacity to recognize, understand, and evaluate issues that are raised in society. Education coupled with an effective media and increased leisure time allows us to be more informed, more critical in our analysis, and perhaps most important, to have the time and resources to make our opinions known to our elected representatives. In this regard, we may act individually or as members of an interest group.

It is very likely that increased levels of education and leisure time in the population made it easier for the environmental, occupational safety and health, and consumer-protection issues to gain access to the policy agenda in the 1960s and 1970s. An educated citizenry that is not constantly concerned about losing jobs and providing food and shelter for families can better afford (both emotionally and economically) to be concerned about the environment, and health and safety in the workplace.

Interest Groups

An *interest group* can be defined as an organization of persons with shared interests who engage in lobbying activities so that their support or opposition to certain issues is communicated to legislative bodies and other political authorities who are involved in the enactment of public policy. Examples of interest groups include the Sierra Club, the U.S. Chamber of Commerce, the American Farm Bureau, labor unions, the American Association of Retired Persons (AARP), and business/trade associations.

Much will be said about interest groups later in this chapter when we discuss the factors that influence whether an issue on the policy agenda actually succeeds in becoming a public policy. At this point we should understand that they also play a role in providing visibility and recognition for issues so that they can be placed on the policy agenda and be considered for public-policy status. For example, not only are policy issues of interest to American farmers — such as agricultural trade policy, farm commodity subsidies and price supports, and water policy — supported by farm interest groups such as the American Dairymen's Association, the National Grange, and the American Farm Bureau, but often the issues are initiated by these groups.

Historical Events—Domestic and Foreign

On many occasions policy issues have been initiated or given substantially greater visibility by major historical events. Perhaps the event that led to the initiation of the greatest number of policy issues was the Great Depression. Among the issues raised by this event were proposals for an increased government role in regulating financial institutions and providing protection for investors (the Securities Acts of 1933 and 1934) and the establishment of a framework for collective bargaining (the National Labor Relations Act of 1935). Many of the issues raised by this historic event soon were transformed by the forces of the public-policy process into completed public policy. Other examples of historic events giving rise to policy issues include (1) the nuclear plant accidents at Three Mile Island and Chernobyl, which substantially increased the visibility of the issue of nuclear-plant safety; (2) the launch of the Sputnik satellite by the Soviet Union in 1957, which put the issues of an American space program and reform of the American educational system near the top of the policy agenda in the late 1950s; and (3) the South African government's policy of apartheid, which has raised the issue of whether American corporations doing business in South Africa should cease their business activities in that country.

Changing Economic and Demographic Conditions

The kinds of issues raised in American society are also influenced by the relative strength or weakness of the American economy. Issues that require large sums of government spending are unlikely to arise (or if they do arise, are unlikely to gather much visibility on the policy agenda) when the economy is in recession. On the other hand, the environment for raising issues that require substantial governmental expenditures is considerably more favorable during strong economic periods. For example, the period of the 1950s and 1960s, a time when the American economy was relatively strong, saw the rapid expansion of the interstate highway system, the enactment of a broad program providing medical care for the aged, and the initiation of a wide variety of Great Society social programs. Each of these public policies required substantial budgetary expenditures, which were financed in large part by increased taxes and a healthy, growing economy. Policy issues such as these would have been less likely to arise and considerably more difficult to enact as public policies in the 1970s and 1980s, when the economic environment was characterized by recession, inflation, a growing foreign trade debt, and a rapidly increasing national debt.

Changing demographic conditions also play a role in explaining why certain issues gain visibility and are placed on the policy agenda at a particular time. For example, the population shift from rural America to urban America was especially rapid between 1930 and 1960. This period of rapid growth for American cities raised issues of increasing and improving urban freeway systems, schools, and housing opportunities, to name but a few. Perhaps the best example of a demographic event that raised and has continued to raise policy issues is the post-World War II baby boom. The dramatic increases in the U.S. birth rate between 1946 and 1960 raised the issue of substantially increased spending for primary, secondary, and higher-education facilities and personnel. Moreover, as this large segment of the population reaches retirement age between 2006 and 2020 issues of adequate critical and extended health-care facilities and retirement security are likely to be raised. The continuing increase in the Hispanic population in certain regions of the country is another example of a demographic event currently raising education and employment issues in a number of states.

Rational Ignorance

Some economists believe that certain issues arise in the policy process as a result of rational ignorance. This theory suggests that politicians, ever mindful of the need for reelection, will sometimes raise issues in order to be able to suggest legislation to correct the perceived problems raised by the issue. Moreover, politicians need not be concerned that the public will carefully scrutinize the remedy (often in the form of legislation) proposed for addressing the issues because most voters have little time or desire to become informed on all issues. While voters are likely to be well informed on issues that affect their economic and personal livelihood, they will practice rational ignorance on most other issues. Thomas Gale Moore, a senior fellow at the Hoover Institution, explains the theory as follows:

> There are a wide variety of practices that the politician can do that increase the probability of reelection. One possible strategy is to offer new products (i.e., legislation) that appear to be addressed to perceived problems. By doing so, s/he will appear to be an activist and will be often mentioned in the press, usually favorably, as one who is attempting to deal with public grievances. In campaigning, the politician can point to a legislative record and/or bills introduced to demonstrate his/her interest in furthering the public well-being.[5]

THE IMPORTANCE OF ENVIRONMENTAL SCANNING FOR ISSUE IDENTIFICATION AND ISSUES MANAGEMENT

In the last section we analyzed some of the factors at work in American society that help initiate policy issues or provide added visibility to existing issues. Many of these policy issues can have an important impact on American business if they succeed in becoming public policy. As a result of the large number of regulatory public policies imposed on American business in the 1960s and 1970s, a growing number of corporations began to create public-affairs departments to advise top corporate management. The basic purpose of the public affairs department has been described as follows: " . . . the essential role of Public Affairs units appears to be that of a window out of the corporation through which management can perceive, monitor, and understand external change, and simultaneously, a window in through which society can influence corporate policy and practice."[6]

In their efforts to monitor the external political, social, legal, and economic environments in order to identify newly emerging issues potentially affecting the corporation, public-affairs managers use a technique called *environmental scanning.* Environmental scanners track newly emerging issues by reading the nation's major newspapers, academic journals, journals that report on trends in music, art, and literature, and research reports and publications issued by major think tanks (for example, the Brookings Institution, the Rand Corporation, the American Enterprise Institute, and the Hudson Institute). Such trends may signal cultural shifts that can affect business in the medium-to-long term. They also rely on public-opinion polling, focus groups, and discussions with experts in subject areas that are of interest to the corporation and have an impact upon it.

One of the leading exponents and practitioners of environmental scanning is Ian H. Wilson, who has written widely on the subject and served as a business-environment consultant to the General Electric Company for many years. His views on the purpose and operation of an environmental-scanning system and its relation to corporate strategic planning are set forth below.

> The primary purpose of strategic planning, as I see it, is to optimize the "fit" between the business and its current and future environment—to enable the business to operate with maximum congruence, and minimum friction, with the changing expectations and conditions of an uncertain world. By the term *environmental scanning* I mean to encompass both the monitoring of current events in the business environment and the forecasting of future trends. And by *environment* I mean the totality of the external conditions and trends in which the business lives and moves and has its being — the market and competitive situation, economic and technological trends and (increasingly) social and political developments.
>
> From the above assertion about the purpose of strategic planning, two further statements derive:
>
> 1. Environmental scanning of the total business environment becomes an essential and integral part of strategic planning. It sets up the contextual framework within which planning can then logically proceed.
> 2. A business strategy that is adequate to meet the totality of these changing conditions must, in truth, be a strategy for the total business. That is, it should encompass not merely a market strategy, but also a technology strategy, a human resources strategy, a financial strategy, a public policy/government relations strategy, and so on.
>
> If we put these two statements together, we can see the emergence of a holistic/systemic approach to planning, i.e., viewing the environment as a whole and as integral to planning, and planning for the business as a total system.
>
> To the extent that environmental scanning involves a forecasting element, it can be said to constitute an early warning system whose purpose is to buy lead time, to identify emerging issues in sufficient time for adaptive, "noncrisis" action to be taken by the corporation. So, while the system may be absorbing and analyzing current data, it should never lose its future focus...
>
> I derive the following characteristics for a successful environmental-scanning system.

1. It must be holistic in its approach to the business environment, i.e., it should view trends — social, economic, political, technological — as a piece, not piecemeal. . . .
2. It must also be continuous, iterative in its operation. In a fast-changing world, it makes little sense to rely on one-shot, or even periodic, analyses of the environment. Only constant monitoring, feedback and modification of forecasts can be truly useful. . . .
3. The system must be designed to deal with alternative futures. In an uncertain environment we can never truly know the future, no matter how much we may perfect our forecasting techniques. . . .
4. It should lay heavy stress on the need for contingency planning. This is a necessary corollary to the preceding point. In fact, there is (or should be) a strong logical connection in our thinking among uncertainty, alternatives and contingencies: the three concepts are strongly bound together. . . .
5. Most important, the environmental-scanning system should be an integral part of the decision-making system of the corporation. . . .[7]

Issues management is a necessary extension of environmental scanning. Once issues important to the corporation are identified by environmental scanning, corporate strategic planners engage in issues management by deciding how the corporation should handle the issue in order to maximize the benefits to the corporation. Issues management really deals with whether, to what extent, and how the corporation will involve itself in the public-policy process in order to support or oppose those factors that determine whether the issue eventually becomes a public policy.

The foregoing brings us to the topic of the factors involved in the making of public policy in the United States. What role does the corporation play in influencing those factors in order to ensure that it will have an input in shaping public policies that affect business? Having examined how policy issues arise in American society, the remainder of this chapter develops a model of the public-policy process.

THE PUBLIC-POLICY PROCESS — POLICY ANALYSIS

Analyzing the operation of the public-policy process is often referred to as policy analysis. *Policy analysis* may be defined as an analysis of the forces or factors that help determine whether an issue will succeed in becoming a public policy. The model set forth in Figure 1-1 describes the major factors that influence public-policy making in the United States. While no model can succeed fully in describing the complex interaction of factors that affect the making of American public policy, we believe the factors examined below provide a solid foundation for understanding the policy-making process. The model sets forth four factors that help determine whether policy issues placed on the public-policy agenda will eventually succeed in being transformed into public policy by the legislative process. Most issues debated in the public-policy process are affected by each of the factors. However, the relative weights given to each of the factors depend upon the nature of the issue being analyzed. For example, the issue of tax reform is influenced heavily by the factors of power/bargaining and the political/economic environment, whereas issues such as comprehensive national health care or reform of the antitrust laws would be affected by each of the four factors set forth in the model.

Implicit Norms and Standards

The political science and sociology literature holds that the great majority of people in any developed society carry with them certain norms and standards that influence their opinions on issues under consideration by the public-policy process. Norms and standards rise to the level of implicit norms and

FIGURE 1-1   Model of the Public-Policy Process

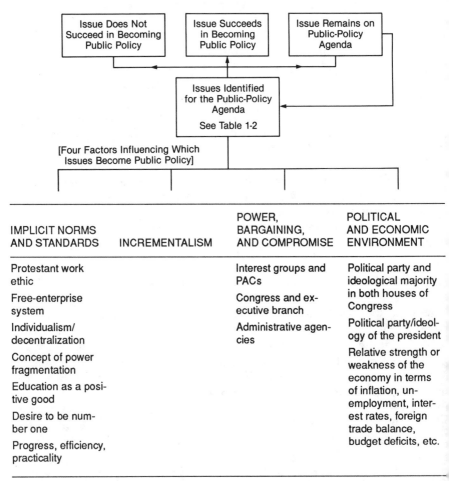

IMPLICIT NORMS AND STANDARDS	INCREMENTALISM	POWER, BARGAINING, AND COMPROMISE	POLITICAL AND ECONOMIC ENVIRONMENT
Protestant work ethic		Interest groups and PACs	Political party and ideological majority in both houses of Congress
Free-enterprise system		Congress and executive branch	
Individualism/ decentralization		Administrative agencies	Political party/ideology of the president
Concept of power fragmentation			Relative strength or weakness of the economy in terms of inflation, unemployment, interest rates, foreign trade balance, budget deficits, etc.
Education as a positive good			
Desire to be number one			
Progress, efficiency, practicality			

Source: Based partially on the work of Lee Preston and James Post. See their Private Management and Public Policy *(Englewood Cliffs, N.J.: Prentice-Hall, Inc., 1975), Ch. 5.*

standards when they are accepted by the great majority of people in a particular society. Moreover, a society's norms and standards are not static — they change over time as the society changes its values. Nevertheless, because such changes normally take place very slowly, we believe the norms and standards set forth in Figure 1-1 present a good approximation (although clearly not a complete listing) of what one well-known sociologist has identified as the "major-value orientations" in American society.[9]

(a) *The Protestant work ethic* is a standard to which most Americans have subscribed since colonial days. The work ethic was one of the principal elements of Calvinist religious philosophy and eventually found its way into the philosophies of a number of Protestant religions formed in sixteenth- and seventeenth-century Europe. The work ethic was transmitted to America in colonial times by the Puritans. Briefly stated, this ethic holds that hard work is a necessary ingredient to a good and successful life. Those who do not aspire to hard work and a moral life will not achieve success in the eyes of God.

(b) The concept of a *free-enterprise system* has long been a guiding principle of American economic life. The ideal of a competitive economy made up of privately owned businesses has always attracted strong support in America. While the role of government in the American economy has grown substantially in the last seventy-five years, often at the insistence of the American voter, most Americans still believe in the ideal of a free-enterprise economy, and this standard is one fact that influences how Americans evaluate their positions on issues in the public-policy process.

(c) *Individualism* and *decentralization* are two additional norms that have long been important in American life. The norm of individualism can be found in our literature but is perhaps most eloquently and importantly set forth in the Bill of Rights to the American Constitution, which lists many of our most important individual rights and freedoms. The importance of decentralization can be seen in our federal system. Many of the founding fathers believed in decentralization of governmental power and therefore reserved to the states all powers not expressly granted to the federal government. While the powers of the federal government have grown considerably over the past seventy-five years, the states and localities continue to be important centers of political power, reflecting the continuing importance of the norm of decentralization.

(d) The *concept of power fragmentation* is closely related to decentralization and dates back at least to the founding fathers and the American Constitution. Two major elements of the U.S. Constitution — the separation of powers among the three branches of the federal government and the provision for separating governmental powers between a federal government and the state governments — illustrate the importance of power fragmentation for the founding fathers.

Americans historically have been suspicious of too much political or economic power gathered into the hands of one sector of society or particular interest groups in society. We prefer a pluralistic society where powerful sectors or groups offset each other's power so that individual freedom for all is more likely to prevail. This preference for power fragmentation has influenced the way we evaluate issues being considered for public-policy status. Thus when the rapid growth of a number of large corporations led to monopolistic conditions in the 1880s and 1890s, Congress, reacting to pressures from the media and the electorate, responded with the enactment of the antitrust laws.[10] These laws were public policies designed to fragment the political and economic power of large corporations so that they did not become the dominant institutions in society. Likewise, in the late 1940s when the power of large national unions seemed to many to be excessive, Congress enacted the Taft-Hartley Act of 1947 (a public policy), which placed certain restraints on the power of unions and thus helped to balance or fragment the power of large unions. Today we enjoy a pluralistic society with multiple centers of political and economic power, including large corporations, large unions, the media, the federal government, the state governments, and many interest groups.

(e) *Education as a positive good* is another norm that has a long history with Americans, who have long believed in the importance of both public and private education. From colonial times to the great immigration waves of the nineteenth and twentieth centuries to the present, Americans have recognized that education is one of the principal means of moving up the economic and social ladder. As a result, education has been treated as a positive good, and to the extent that issues in the public-policy process succeed in holding themselves out as furthering or enhancing education, they have an advantage.

(f) The *desire to be number one* is arguably an implicit norm and standard of most Americans. As Vince Lombardi, the late and legendary head coach of the Green Bay Packers football team is reported to have said: "Winning isn't everything; it's the only thing." While this is something of an exaggeration, it is probably not too far off the mark for many Americans. Our attitudes toward sports, competition, the space race, and our military and economic position in the world all point to a desire to be number one. In terms of public-policy analysis, this desire to be number one is another example of an implicit norm or standard that we, as Americans, consciously and sometimes unconsciously apply in evaluating issues in the public-policy process.

(g) *Progress, efficiency, and practicality* are additional norms that apply to most Americans. Thus to the extent that supporters of an issue in the public-policy process can argue for it in terms of progress, efficiency, and/or practicality, the issue will be advantaged, everything else being equal.

Incrementalism

Incrementalism is an important and deceptively simple factor that helps to explain why some issues are more likely than others to succeed in becoming public policy. The key concept is that the average American, as well as those who are decision makers in the public-policy process (for instance, members of Congress, top officials of the administrative agencies, the president and his key advisers), are more likely to favor issues that add or subtract in small increments to existing public policy in contrast to those issues that are major departures from existing public policy. The effect of incrementalism on the making of public policy is explained by James Anderson as follows:

> Incrementalism is politically expedient because it is easier to reach agreement when the matters in dispute among various groups are only modifications of existing programs rather than policy issues of great magnitude or an "all or nothing" character. Since decision makers operate under conditions of uncertainty with regard to the future consequences of their actions, incremental decisions reduce the risks and costs of uncertainty. Incrementalism is also realistic because it recognizes that decision makers lack the time, intelligence, and other resources needed to engage in comprehensive analysis of all alternative solutions to existing problems. Moreover, people are essentially pragmatic, seeking not always the single best way to deal with a problem but,

more modestly, "something that will work." Incrementalism, in short, yields limited, practicable, acceptable decisions.[11]

An example of a public-policy issue that benefited from the workings of incrementalism involved the 1977 proposal for a new cabinet-level department of education. This proposal, which is discussed in detail later in the chapter, involved combining the education functions already carried out by many federal agencies into one unified and very visible cabinet department. The proponents of this issue argued that the new public policy being called for was little more than what already existed — indeed, the proposal for a cabinet-level department of education would result in the centralized and more efficient management of the many education programs sponsored by the federal government.

A more recent example of incrementalism involves the Medicare Catastrophic Coverage Act, which became law in 1988. This important advance in health-care policy is partly explained by the fact that many legislators saw it as a logical, incremental step beyond the Health Insurance for the Aged Act (more commonly referred to as Medical Care for the Aged or Medicare) enacted by Congress in 1965.

Power, Bargaining, and Compromise

One of the major factors influencing the making of public policy in the United States is the power and influence of interest groups and the fund-raising clout of the political action committees (PACs), which are often closely linked to *interest groups*. The leadership of the interest group represents its members in both political and nonpolitical settings. Its primary function is to further the political, economic, and social interests of the group's members by communicating and articulating those interests to the political and governmental authorities involved in the making and implementation of public policy. At the federal level such authorities include members of Congress and their staff assistants, staff members who advise and are employed by important congressional committees (the Senate Finance Committee, the House Ways and Means Committee, and the House Appropriations Committee, to name a few), key advisers in the Executive Office of the President, who help the president formulate his views on public-policy issues, and the top management people in the administrative agencies.

When interest groups involve themselves in supporting or opposing certain issues in the public-policy process by presenting their views and supplying information to political authorities, they are engaged in *lobbying* for their point of view. Thus in many ways interest groups can be seen as lobbies, which employ lobbyists to communicate and argue for an interest group's point of view before political authorities in the public-policy process. The point to keep in mind is that both interest groups and the political authorities are involved in the political give and take we have referred to as power, bargaining, and compromise. Political bargaining and compromise is an important factor that helps to influence (along with the other factors set forth in this chapter) whether an issue on the policy agenda will become public policy.

The Political Power of Interest Groups   Often an issue being considered in the policy process will be supported and opposed by a variety of interest groups. The outlook for the issue's becoming public policy may well depend on the relative political power enjoyed by the interest groups on each side of the issue. While assessing the political power of particular interest groups is not subject to a precise formula, the following criteria are helpful:

1. The number of members in the group and how they are dispersed throughout the country. As a general rule, the greater the number of members and the more widely dispersed they are in congressional districts around the country, the more powerful the group.
2. The level of education and political sophistication of the members of the group.
3. The fund-raising potential of the group or its affiliated political action committee.
4. The organizational and leadership skills of the group.
5. The degree of intensity with which members in the group support its purposes and goals. This often will vary directly with how much the group's members have to gain economically or socially from the group's lobbying activity.
6. The amount of leisure time enjoyed by members of the group. When a group's members have substantial free time and are devoted to the group's goals, the group can be quite effective in applying political pressure.
7. The cohesiveness of opinion of the group's members. For instance, the diverse backgrounds of the members of the U.S. Chamber of Commerce make it more difficult for that organization to form an opinion on an issue, in contrast to the National Education Association or the American Association of Retired Persons (AARP).

These criteria can best be illustrated by looking at two powerful interest groups that have enjoyed considerable success in influencing the public policy process: the National Education Association and the American Medical Association. As we will see, the National Education Association (NEA) played an important role in getting the Congress to enact legislation in 1979 that created the Department of Education. The NEA meets a number of the effectiveness criteria cited above:

1. It is a very large organization composed of over 1,600,000 teachers from around the country. Its members live, work, and can be politically active in every congressional district in the country.
2. The interests and objectives of the NEA's membership are relatively uniform and cohesive. The membership is bound together by a common interest in improving American public education by drawing attention to the need for quality education

and the inputs necessary to meet that objective; namely, increased federal, state, and local financial support both for the teaching profession and for the instructional, curricular, and associated program needs of the public schools.

3. The NEA's members are well educated and politically sophisticated. They are well organized and understand the importance that members of Congress place on letters, voter registration drives, and get-out-the-vote campaigns. The NEA's many members make it a very effective organization in helping or hindering a candidate in the electoral process and members of Congress and their challengers are well aware of this.

4. The NEA can raise and contribute substantial amounts of money to political incumbents or challengers running for office. An organization as large as the NEA can raise substantial sums of money even if the individual contributions are not overly large. Running for political office is an expensive proposition in the United States, and therefore a politically sophisticated interest group capable of raising large sums of money can be quite effective in influencing the making of public policy.

5. In addition to contributing money, the NEA is also able to contribute the time and organizational talent of its members. NEA members who contribute their time to a political campaign by helping to distribute a candidate's political literature, walking precincts, or taking voters to the polls are very valuable to that campaign.

Another example of an effective interest group in the power, bargaining, and compromise of the public-policy process is the American Medical Association (AMA). The effectiveness of the AMA in the policy process is explained by many of the same advantages enjoyed by the NEA. Although the AMA is not as large an organization as the NEA, its membership, which consists of approximately 260,000 physicians located in every congressional district, is still quite sizable. Its membership also is well educated and politically sophisticated. Even though the physician members of the AMA may not have much time to devote to election campaigns, their substantial incomes make it possible for the AMA's political action committee to raise and contribute considerable sums of money to many congressional political races.[12] Moreover, both the NEA and the AMA are interest groups whose attention is relatively well focused on a limited number of issues supported by a majority of the membership either because the issue is beneficial (as in the case of the NEA's all-out support for a Department of Education) or because it is harmful (as in the case of the AMA's strong opposition to the medical care for the aged proposal of the mid-1960s) to the group. The ability of a cohesive interest group to focus attention on a particular issue makes for a more politically effective interest group.

Business Interest Groups American business takes part in the process of power, bargaining, and compromise in a number of different ways. While many business people choose to participate individually in the political process by communicating with members of Congress or contributing money or time to political campaigns, our focus in this section is on the different types of business interest groups. These include the large corporation's Washington office, trade associations, the U.S. Chamber of Commerce, the National Association of Manufacturers, and the Business Roundtable. The increased visibility and activity of business interest groups in the 1970s and 1980s reflect the importance that business leaders attach to identifying and managing relevant issues in the public-policy process.

THE WASHINGTON OFFICE   Beginning in the 1960s, many large corporations opened Washington offices for the purpose of more effectively communicating their views to members of Congress, congressional staffs, and the administrative agencies. A corporation's Washington office monitors issues affecting the corporation that are raised by other interest groups (for instance, consumer or environmental interests), members of Congress, or administrative-agency staff people. The Washington office also serves as a liaison between the corporation and the political authorities in Washington whose decisions affect the corporation. In other words, it functions as an advocate or lobbyist for the corporation. In order to fulfill its public-affairs functions, the office is generally staffed by lawyers, economists, financial analysts, and public-relations experts. The staff develops working relationships with members of Congress and staff in the administrative agencies. As with all lobbyists, the quality, reliability, and accuracy of the information provided by the Washington office goes far in establishing its credibility as a corporate representative.

TRADE ASSOCIATIONS   There are approximately two thousand trade associations with offices in Washington, D.C. Their function is to represent the hundreds of thousands of small businesses around the country that are not large enough to maintain their own Washington offices. While trade associations have historically offered a number of services to their members, including development of industry standards, conducting educational programs, and industry-wide advertising, they have increasingly become involved in representing their members in the political process of power, bargaining, and compromise.[13]

Trade associations lobby members of Congress and the administrative agencies. They provide industry information necessary for informed decision making, raise money from members for political contributions to the associations' friends, and give testimony before congressional committees and administrative agencies that often consider bills or proposed regulations affecting the associations' membership. Trade associations generally communicate what is happening in Washington to their members via monthly newsletters. The newsletter and the advent of computerized membership mailing lists enable an association to inform its members quickly of important issues being debated in Washington and allow it to call on members to engage in grassroots lobbying by writing letters supporting or opposing a particular issue.

THE U.S. CHAMBER OF COMMERCE   The U.S. Chamber of Commerce is made up of business firms, trade association members, and the many city, county, and state chambers of commerce. The Chamber was formed in 1912 and has historically been one of the major voices for American business in Washington. The strength of the Chamber is its large membership, which in 1987 exceeded 220,000, and its ability to mobilize particular segments of its membership (service businesses, manufacturing corporations, companies emphasizing foreign trade, and so on) and to lobby members of Congress on particular issues through massive letter-writing campaigns, personal telephone calls, or visits to members of Congress and their staff people. Because of its large membership and the fact that its members are found in all congressional districts and are often financially successful and politically active in their local communities, the Chamber of Commerce is today an effective business lobby with the potential for even greater influence in the future. The Chamber also represents its membership by testifying at administrative agency rule-making hearings, where the agency asks for input from all interested parties to help it decide whether to enact particular regulations. As we will see in Chapter 3, these regulations can have a substantial impact on business since they are used to implement the public policies enacted by Congress. Sophisticated computer systems and communications technology make it possible for the Chamber to quickly target mailings to particular segments of its membership, alerting them to the latest developments in particular congressional committees or administrative agencies and advising them on how to best make their voices heard in Washington.

While the Chamber is a major business interest group that has been relatively effective in recent years, it also has some weaknesses. First, for many years the Chamber had a reputation for having a predictable and inflexible conservative view on most of the political and economic issues it addressed. Since politics has been described as "the art of the possible" and is almost always a process of compromise, an interest group that is perceived as inflexible and unwilling to compromise is at something of a disadvantage. In recent years, however, the Chamber has become more flexible and open to compromise in its lobbying efforts. Second, the Chamber, like any large interest group with a diverse membership, cannot always take a position on issues in the policy process because its membership may be in disagreement on the issue. This again illustrates the point that the strength of an interest group is partly determined by the cohesiveness and unity of the interests of its membership.

THE NATIONAL ASSOCIATION OF MANUFACTURERS (NAM) The NAM is a business interest group made up of a variety of manufacturing companies. The NAM was formed in 1895 as a trade association with the purpose of promoting legislation that would further the cause of trade and commerce. Its membership is less numerous and diverse than that of the U.S. Chamber of Commerce.

Like the U.S. Chamber of Commerce, the NAM also has suffered from a reputation of political inflexibility and an unwillingness to compromise on economic and regulatory issues affecting business. However, by the late

1970s the flood of regulatory legislation from the 1960s and early 1970s led the NAM to reexamine its approach to representing business interests in Washington. One observer describes the political evolution of the NAM this way:

> In the world of Washington lobbying, the National Association of Manufacturers was once viewed as a dinosaur among business trade groups. "In the past, we were generally regarded as a naysaying, foot-dragging organization," concedes Alexander Trowbridge, who became the group's president in January, 1980. Under his leadership the NAM is trying to arrest a steady decline in membership and influence by moving into a new role as a sophisticated and reasonable spokesman for business.
>
> To create a new identity, NAM is trying to shuck its obstructionist image. In the early 1970s, the association flatly opposed and refused to have anything to do with the development of government programs dealing with such issues as health, safety, the environment and pensions. They were considered "an unwarranted intrusion by the federal government." . . . But now, the NAM apparently believes it is more productive to work with government.[14]

THE BUSINESS ROUNDTABLE   The Business Roundtable has probably been the most effective interest group for large American corporations from the early 1970s to the present.[15] The Roundtable was formed in 1972 in response to the rapid increase in government regulation of business during the 1960s and early 1970s. Large corporations had not been overly successful in developing strategies to deal with the policy issues that were raised in the 1960s, many of which later became public policies. In response to the need for a more effective way of involving large corporations in the public-policy process, a number of well-known and highly regarded corporate leaders established the Roundtable. Its primary purpose is to examine public issues that affect the economy, develop positions that reflect sound economic and social principles, and make these positions known to the public and its representatives in government.

What explains the substantial success of the Business Roundtable in influencing the public-policy process through power, bargaining, and compromise? Why has the Roundtable perhaps been more effective as a business interest group than more traditional and longer established groups such as the U.S. Chamber of Commerce and the National Association of Manufacturers? Much of the answer lies in the unique organization and operating style of the Roundtable, which is outlined below:

1.   The Roundtable is a comparatively small business interest group with a membership that includes the chief executive officers (CEOs) of America's largest corporations. Rather than relying only on a staff of lobbyists, the Roundtable uses its membership of CEOs to communicate its views directly to members of Congress. The CEO of a large corporation, especially one with plants and employees in a congressional representative's district, is more likely to have access to, and be listened to by, a member of Congress than is a lower-level corporate or trade association lobbyist.

2. The Roundtable has developed a reputation for supporting its position on issues with thorough, well-researched, and accurate position papers. This reputation for accuracy and credibility is invaluable to any interest group and has certainly added to the Roundtable's influence in Washington. Members of Congress are required to take positions on literally hundreds of issues during a legislative session. They welcome information from various interest groups (both pro and con) on these issues in helping them to decide their position on an issue. An effective interest group soon learns that if it is to maintain access and credibility with a member of Congress, it must provide the member with accurate, well-researched position papers that support the interest group's position on a particular policy issue. Most of the research undertaken by the Roundtable is carried out by the corporate staffs of its member corporations at the direction of the CEO. Thus the research work winds up having high priority, and since corporate staffs are used rather than the Roundtable's own limited staff, the ability of the Roundtable to generate well-researched position papers on policy issues is practically unlimited.

3. The leadership of the Roundtable has consistently endeavored to develop an image as a business organization that is responsible and interested in developing positions on policy issues that are in the public interest as well as in the interest of large corporations. It has made a strong effort to cultivate relations with the media and to explain its positions on policy issues to the media as well as to the Washington political community. The success of the Roundtable's efforts to cast itself as a responsible, progressive, and politically effective business interest group can be seen in the generally favorable press it has received since its formation.

Administrative Agencies as Interest Groups One example of an interest group that rarely is so identified is the federal administrative agency, an institution created by Congress to implement many of the public policies enacted by Congress. Although administrative agencies will be discussed in detail in Chapter 3, here we will briefly describe their role as interest groups and how they engage in power, bargaining, and compromise in order to influence the public-policy process.

Administrative agencies are empowered by Congress to implement public policy. Congress annually appropriates money for agency budgets and may from time to time increase or decrease the functions, duties, and powers of the agencies through new legislation. As an agency becomes established, the staff and top management (the agency bureaucracy) sometimes come to believe that they have a right to continued, perpetual existence. They seek to acquire more and broader authority and more resources and prestige, thereby solidifying their power and right to existence. In addition, members of the bureaucracy often are ideologically committed to their roles, which they understand as promoting an important public interest mandated by Congress. Thus the Environmental Protection Agency sees itself as a guardian of clean air and water, and the Securities and Exchange Commission sees itself as a protector for unsophisticated investors and for the integrity of financial markets.

Administrative agencies act as interest groups to the extent that they involve themselves in attempting to persuade Congress to increase their scope of authority and their agency budgets. Some agencies have been characterized as at least partially serving or promoting the interests of their client groups (individuals or organizations that the agency was created to assist): the Department of Agriculture and farmers, the Department of Education and teachers, and the Department of Commerce and business. These client groups often work with the administrative agency to lobby Congress jointly for increased power or budget for the agency, thereby directly benefiting the agency and indirectly benefiting themselves.[16]

The Political Practices of Interest Groups   Interest groups use a variety of techniques in their efforts to influence members of Congress and, where appropriate, the general public. These techniques include direct lobbying, grassroots lobbying, advocacy advertising, and the use of political action committees.

Direct lobbying can be defined as "communication with public officials to influence their decisions in a manner that is consistent with the interests of the individual or group doing the communicating."[17]   In addition to advocating a particular point of view, direct lobbying also serves the function of providing information to members of Congress. While the information can be expected to support the interest group's position on a particular issue, it must nevertheless be accurate and factual if the group is to retain future credibility. Since members of Congress are often lobbied by interest groups supporting and opposing a particular legislative issue, they are quite likely to receive good information on both sides of the issue.

Direct lobbying is regulated by the *Regulation of Lobbying Act of 1946,* which requires lobbyists to register with Congress and provide quarterly reports on the amount of money being spent on lobbying activities. For the purposes of the act, a lobbyist is defined as an individual whose principal purpose is to influence legislation by direct contact with members of Congress. This definition is significant for those individuals *not* covered, including individuals who lobby public officials in the administrative agencies and individuals who only occasionally engage in lobbying. Individuals in this latter category include staff members in the Washington offices of large corporations and unions who do not principally engage in lobbying members of Congress. Others are attorneys in Washington law firms and members of public-relations firms who engage in lobbying for clients as one of the professional services offered by the firm.[18]   Thus the number of individuals engaged in direct lobbying of members of Congress and the administrative agencies greatly exceeds those individuals required to register as lobbyists.

Indirect or grassroots lobbying makes use of an interest group's constituencies in order to get large numbers of people to write letters, send telegrams, or make telephone calls to members of Congress in support of the interest group's position on a particular issue. Unlike direct lobbying, which makes use of individual professional lobbyists, grassroots lobbying attempts to influence members of Congress by impressing them with the large number of people, often from the member's own congressional district, who support or oppose an issue.

In order to be able to implement an effective indirect lobbying effort, the interest group must first identify a network of individuals who share its interests and then develop a means of communicating with them regularly on issues of importance to the group. A corporation like American Telephone and Telegraph, for example, might develop a grassroots lobbying effort that asks its various constituencies (employees, shareholders, retirees, suppliers, customers) to launch a massive letter-writing campaign to members of Congress supporting or opposing proposed legislation directed at the corporation.

Advocacy advertising can be defined as a "form of advertising in which a business takes a public position on controversial issues of public importance, aggressively stating and defending its viewpoint and criticizing those of opponents."[19] Some business leaders believe advocacy advertising is needed to counteract the spread of biased or uninformed business and economic reporting in the popular press. Others see this form of advertising as a means of acquainting various segments of the public with the corporation's view of issues affecting business.[20] Most advocacy advertising is placed in national newspapers and news magazines. In this way business firms attempt to reach opinion makers and those segments of the population who are interested and involved in the development of public policy.

Political Action Committees (PACs) can best be understood as the fundraising arms of interest groups. PACs are not interest groups and do not themselves engage in lobbying activity. Rather, they may be seen as a closely linked subsidiary unit responsible for raising and distributing money (principally in the form of campaign contributions) to those members of Congress who are deemed worthy of support by the interest group. Money has been described as the "mother's milk of politics."[21] Interest groups use campaign contributions raised by their political action committees in part to reward or punish members of Congress, depending on their willingness to accept the interest group's view on particular policy issues under consideration by Congress. PACs also use campaign contributions to assist their associated interest groups in gaining access to members of Congress in order to present the interest group's views on a particular issue.

Prior to the passage of the *Federal Election Campaign Act (FECA) of 1971,* which was amended in 1974 and 1976, corporations and unions were legally prohibited from spending organizational funds to influence federal elections. Many believed that unrestrained direct spending by large corporations and unions might result in these institutions gaining too much political power, which could give them an unfair advantage in the political and electoral processess. Individuals, however, were allowed to contribute any amount they chose to political campaigns. As a result, many large corporations solicited voluntary contributions from top and middle-level managers and arranged for these contributions to be forwarded to particular election campaigns with appropriate recognition for the corporation's role in the fund-raising effort. In a similar fashion, union leaders established fund-raising committees as early as the 1930s for the purpose of soliciting voluntary contributions from union members, which would then be forwarded to particular congressional campaigns. Large national unions and the AFL-CIO found this voluntary method of fund raising to be very effective.

In 1971 this informal method of corporate and union fund raising under the guise of voluntary individual contributions was formalized. The FECA of 1971, as amended, encourages corporations, unions, trade associations, and other organizations to create their own political action committees. Labor unions were major supporters of the FECA legislation. They did not foresee that business PACs would eventually greatly outnumber union PACs. The FECA sets forth the following general rules for individual and PAC contributions:

1. Individuals cannot contribute more than a total of $25,000 per year to federal election campaigns and PACs. Within this $25,000 limitation, individuals cannot contribute more than $1000 per election to any one candidate, nor more than $5000 per year to any one PAC. Individuals may also contribute up to $20,000 per calendar year to a national political party, subject, of course, to the overall limitation of $25,000 per year.

2. A PAC can contribute up to $5000 per election (a primary election is separate from the general election) to a candidate for Congress, with no limit on the number of candidates it can support.

3. There is no limit on how much an individual or PAC can spend on "independent expenditures" to support or defeat a particular candidate for Congress. An independent expenditure is defined as money spent to support or defeat a candidate which is made without consultation with or the cooperation of any candidate or campaign. As you might imagine, this is a rather wide loophole in the campaign finance laws. For instance, PACs can independently organize and finance an advertising (television, radio, newspapers, and direct mail) campaign which supports or opposes a particular candidate or candidates, ballot initiative, or referendum.

4. The FECA allows a corporation or union to sponsor more than one PAC (e.g., one PAC for each company plant location). However, all the corporation's PACs are subject as a unit to the standard PAC contribution limit of $5000 per candidate per election.

5. While corporations cannot make direct campaign contributions to their PACs, the FECA does allow them to pay for all of the PAC's administrative expenses, including salaries, legal and accounting services, rent, travel, equipment, printing, postage, consulting fees, etc.

6. Corporate PACs are allowed to solicit contributions from shareholders and management personnel and their families. They may also solicit contributions from their union members twice a year, if they use an independent third-party agent.[22]

The legal requirements for creating a PAC and the general practices followed by corporations in establishing PACs are set forth by Professor Larry Sabato of the University of Virginia, a leading authority on PACs, as follows:

> Those associations and corporations that do form PACs follow no fixed organization model. By law a PAC only has to have a treasurer and a statement

of organization filed with the Federal Election Commission at least ten days after its creation. While all PACs necessarily follow this mandate, they otherwise exhibit a variety of structures and modes of operation.
. . . Corporate PACs, for instance, are usually closely tied to the company's chief executive officer (CEO). Most often the CEO is the company official who authorizes the formation of a PAC, determines the composition of the PAC's governing board, appoints some or all of the members, specifies the scope and methods of fund raising, helps to design the criteria the PAC uses in selecting candidates for contributions, and (in a minority of cases) actually directs that donations be sent to certain candidates and officeholders.

While the CEO is crucial to the formation and sometimes the operation of a corporate PAC, in most cases the CEO then delegates much of his authority to the public-affairs (or governmental-affairs) executive in the company, and to the PAC's governing board. The public-affairs executive, normally a vice-president in the corporate structure, is the natural coordinator of PAC activity since he or she is usually responsible for the company's lobbying efforts and relations with government at all levels.[23]

In recent years there has been growing concern about the proliferation of corporate PACs and the possibility that their substantial contributions to congressional political campaigns might provide corporations with too much influence in the political process. PACs contribute much more heavily to incumbents than to challengers, thus increasing the already substantial benefits of incumbency and making it more difficult for political challengers in either party to enter Congress. Incumbents receive more PAC contributions than challengers because incumbents are likely to win reelection, and PACs want to assure themselves of access to members of Congress. These concerns take on greater significance given the rapidly increasing costs of running for political office. Additionally, there is growing evidence that PAC contributions are an important element in weakening the power and discipline that the two political parties at one time applied to their members in Congress. So long as members of Congress depended on their political parties to help them finance their reelection campaigns, the parties were able to enforce party loyalty and adherence to the party's position on major public-policy issues. PAC contributions, which are made directly to a candidate's political campaign, have made politicians less accountable to the traditional political parties and perhaps too accountable to PACs. Tables 1-3, 1-4, and 1-5 provide some recent data on the growth and behavior of PACs in the political process.

The foregoing discussion of PACs demonstrates the growing power and influence of business PACs over the past ten years. Since PACs are the fundraising arms of business interest groups, they add to business's ability to target political campaign contributions to those candidates considered to be sympathetic to the views of business on issues being debated in the public-policy process. All of this does not, however, mean that business interest groups have necessarily gotten the upper hand in the area of power, bargaining, and compromise. While the position of those groups is formidable,

TABLE 1-3 Political Action Committees—Number by Committee Type: 1974-86 (As of December 31 except 1975 as of November 24)

YEAR	TOTAL	CORPORATE	LABOR	TRADE/ MEMBERSHIP/ HEALTH	NON-CONNECTED	COOPERATIVE	CORPORATION WITHOUT STOCK
1974	608	89	201	(	318		)
1975	722	139	226	(	357		)
1976	1,146	433	224	(	489		)
1977	1,360	550	234	438	110	8	20
1978	1,653	785	217	453	162	12	24
1979	2,000	950	240	514	247	17	32
1980	2,551	1,206	297	576	374	42	56
1981	2,901	1,329	318	614	531	41	68
1982	3,371	1,469	380	649	723	47	103
1983	3,525	1,538	378	643	793	51	122
1984	4,009	1,682	394	698	1,053	52	130
1985	3,992	1,710	388	695	1,003	54	142
1986	4,157	1,744	384	745	1,077	56	151

SOURCE: U.S. Bureau of the Census, Statistical Abstract of the United States: 1988 (108th edition), Washington, D.C., 1987, Table no. 426, p. 253.

TABLE 1-4 *PAC Contributions to House of Representatives Congressional Campaigns, 1979-86 (In millions of dollars. Covers amounts given in all elections during the two-year calendar period indicated.)*

HOUSE OF REPRESENTATIVES

Type of Committee	Total	Democrats	Republicans	Incumbents	Challengers	Open Seats[1]
1979-80, total[2]	37.9	20.5	17.2	24.9	7.9	5.1
Corporate	12.2	4.8	7.5	8.1	2.6	1.5
Trade association[3]	11.7	5.1	6.6	8.0	2.2	1.5
Labor	9.4	8.9	.4	6.6	1.6	1.2
Non-connected[4]	3.1	.9	2.1	1.0	1.4	.7
1981-82, total[2]	61.1	34.2	26.8	40.8	10.9	9.4
Corporate	18.9	7.0	12.0	14.4	2.0	2.6
Trade association[3]	16.8	7.2	9.7	12.4	2.1	2.3
Labor	15.4	14.7	.7	8.5	4.3	2.6
Non-connected[4]	7.4	3.9	3.5	3.4	2.5	1.6
1983-84, total[2]	75.7	46.3	29.3	57.2	11.3	7.2
Corporate	23.4	10.4	13.1	18.8	2.6	2.0
Trade association[3]	20.4	10.5	9.9	16.5	2.1	1.7
Labor	19.8	18.8	1.0	14.3	3.5	2.0
Non-connected[4]	9.1	4.7	4.4	4.9	2.9	1.3
1985-86, total[2]	87.2	54.6	32.5	65.8	9.1	12.3
Corporate	26.8	12.8	14.0	22.8	1.0	3.0
Trade association[3]	23.4	12.2	11.1	19.3	1.3	2.8
Labor	22.6	21.0	1.6	14.7	4.3	3.6
Non-connected[4]	11.1	6.6	4.5	6.1	2.6	2.6

[1] Elections in which an incumbent did not seek reelection.
[2] Includes other types of political action committees not shown separately.
[3] Includes membership organizations and health organizations.
[4] Represents "ideological" groups as well as other issue groups not necessarily ideological in nature.

SOURCE: U.S. Bureau of the Census, Statistical Abstract of the United States: 1988 (108th edition), Washington, D.C., 1987, Table no. 427, p. 254.

TABLE 1-5 PAC Contributions to Senate Congressional Campaigns, 1979-86 (In millions of dollars. Covers amounts given in all elections during the two-year calendar period indicated.)

SENATE

Type of Committee	Total	Democrats	Republicans	Incumbents	Challengers	Open Seats[1]
1979-80, total[2]	17.3	8.4	9.0	8.6	6.6	2.1
Corporate	6.9	2.1	4.8	2.7	3.3	.9
Trade association[3]	4.1	1.9	2.2	2.2	1.4	.5
Labor	3.8	3.4	.4	2.7	.7	.4
Non-connected[4]	1.9	.5	1.4	.5	1.1	.3
1981-82, total[2]	22.6	11.2	11.4	14.3	5.2	3.9
Corporate	8.6	2.4	6.2	5.5	1.7	1.4
Trade association[3]	5.0	2.2	2.8	3.7	.8	.5
Labor	4.9	4.5	.4	3.0	1.3	.5
Non-connected[4]	3.3	1.6	1.7	1.5	1.3	.5
1983-84, total[2]	29.7	14.0	15.6	17.9	6.3	5.4
Corporate	12.0	3.2	8.8	8.8	1.1	2.2
Trade association[3]	6.3	2.7	3.7	4.5	.9	1.0
Labor	5.0	4.7	.3	1.6	2.3	1.2
Non-connected[4]	5.4	3.0	2.4	2.4	2.0	1.0
1985-86, total[2]	45.0	20.0	25.0	23.6	10.1	11.3
Corporate	19.1	4.8	14.4	11.7	2.6	4.8
Trade association[3]	9.4	3.7	5.7	5.7	1.6	2.1
Labor	7.2	6.6	.6	2.2	3.1	1.9
Non-connected[4]	7.6	4.2	3.4	3.1	2.4	2.1

[1] Elections in which an incumbent did not seek reelection.
[2] Includes other types of political action committees not shown separately.
[3] Includes membership organizations and health organizations.
[4] Represents "ideological" groups as well as other issue groups not necessarily ideological in nature.

SOURCE: U.S. Bureau of the Census, Statistical Abstract of the United States: 1988 (108th edition), Washington, D.C., 1987, Table no. 427, p. 254.

Tables 1-4 and 1-5 indicate that labor and trade/membership PACs also have substantially increased their political contributions. Moreover, business PACs tend to contribute heavily to incumbents (since these are the people who are most likely to win elections and with whom business must deal), and the Democratic party has had the greater number of congressional incumbents over the past fifty years. Thus while business PACs are more ideologically inclined to contribute to Republican candidates for Congress, to the extent they feel the need also to contribute to the campaigns of Democratic incumbents, the impact of the large sums contributed by business PACs is lessened. Finally, the dollar statistics on contributions by labor PACs understate the true political impact of these PACs for two reasons: first, while they raise less money than business PACs, the overwhelming majority of their contributions go to Democratic incumbents or challengers; and second, labor-union interest groups (not labor PACs) have provided thousands of volunteer campaign workers to assist in Democratic party political campaigns. The dollar value of these volunteers does not show up in PAC contribution statistics, but there is little doubt that they are a very substantial asset in political campaigns.

Our discussion of business interest groups and their associated political action committees has emphasized the importance of these groups in influencing whether an issue being debated in the public-policy process actually succeeds in becoming a public policy. Business has played an increasingly active and sophisticated role in the process of power, bargaining, and compromise since the late 1960s when it began to appreciate the great impact that government regulatory policies have on business freedom and profits.

The Political and Economic Environment of the Nation

Another factor that influences which issues will actually succeed in working their way through the public-policy process is the political and economic environment of the nation at the time an issue is being considered. Both the political and economic environments must be favorable for most issues to succeed in the policy process. As we shall see below, the result of a favorable political environment in the midst of an unfavorable economic environment, or vice versa, will usually be that an issue remains in a kind of public-policy limbo; that is, it neither becomes public policy nor entirely fades from the scene.

When we speak of the nation's political environment, we mean the balance of political power between the Democratic and Republican parties as measured by the party that occupies the White House, their respective voting power in the House and Senate of the U.S. Congress, and to a lesser degree the strength of the two parties at the state level as measured by the number of governorships and state legislatures (especially in the more populous and therefore politically powerful states) controlled by the two parties. The political environment must also include a measure of the ideological spectrum of the Congress, the presidency, and the country as a whole measured in terms of liberal, moderate, and conservative political philosophies. This measure is taken by reviewing the voting records and public pronouncements of members of Congress and the president and by public-opinion polls and detailed election analyses of the American electorate. In the early years of the Bush administration, for example, most political observers characterize the political environment as moderate. The president is moderate to conservative, and the House of Representatives and the Senate are controlled by the Democratic party and by an ideological majority (as opposed to a political-party majority) made up of moderates and liberals from both parties.

The economic environment of the country also has an important influence on what happens to issues in the public-policy process. By the economic environment we mean the relative strength or weakness of the economy in terms of accepted criteria of economic measurement, such as the levels of inflation, unemployment, and interest rates, the foreign-trade balance, the level of the federal budget deficit or surplus, and generally whether the economy is in a period of expansion or recession or in what economists like to call a period of economic uncertainty.

A good example of an issue in the public-policy process affected by both the political and economic environments was the proposal for medical care for the aged to be financed by an increase in Social Security taxes. This issue and a companion issue calling for a much broader program of comprehensive national health care, to be financed by a more substantial Social Security tax increase, were both considered by Congress in the early 1960s. The issue of comprehensive national health care first arose in the mid-1930s and continued on the public-policy agenda into the mid-1960s. As we know, medical care for the aged succeeded in becoming a public policy in 1965, but a comprehensive national health-care program has yet to become public policy. Why did medical care for the aged succeed in 1965 after thirty years of effort but the comprehensive plan fail? The answer, of course, goes to the heart of how the public-policy process works, and we shall study this example in detail in the next section. While many of the factors listed in the model in Figure 1-1 affected both of these issues, in this section we want to focus on the influence of the political and economic environments.

The issue of medical care for the aged became public policy in 1965 in large part because for the first time since the late 1930s, the political and economic environments were *both* favorable for the issue. In November 1964 Lyndon Johnson was elected president of the United States by a landslide majority vote. The election also continued the Democratic party's majority in both houses of Congress, but the Democratic party's landslide election victory meant that for the first time since the 1936 elections the party's majority in both houses was greater than two-thirds. This heavy majority meant that the traditional voting alliance of Republicans and conservative southern

Democrats could for the first time in many years be overcome by the large number of moderate and liberal Democrats and the smaller number of liberal Republicans. Thus the 1964 Congressional elections resulted in more than a heavy Democratic majority in Congress; it also meant that for the first time in many years there was a moderate-to-liberal ideological majority as well. Moreover, this ideological majority in the Congress was matched with a moderate-to-liberal Democratic president who was himself a creature of the Congress (President Johnson had been the Senate majority leader for the Democrats from 1955 to 1960) and therefore understood the workings of Congress very well. This favorable political environment was matched by an equally favorable economic environment. President Kennedy's demand-side tax cut in 1962 contributed to a substantial economic expansion in the 1960s. Economic growth was strong, and inflation, unemployment, and interest rates were all quite low. This was the kind of stable economic environment that could absorb a Social Security tax increase. Simply put, the country could afford medical care for the aged, and the political environment was ready to adopt this new public policy. While the political and economic environments in 1965 were probably almost equally favorable for the enactment of a public policy of comprehensive national health care, we shall see in the next section that other factors that influence the making of public policy were not yet sufficiently favorable.

APPLYING THE POLICY-PROCESS MODEL TO SELECTED ISSUES

In much of this chapter we have been developing a model of the major factors that influence the making of public policy in the United States. This model of the public-policy process argues that factors such as implicit norms and standards, incrementalism, power, bargaining, and compromise, and the political and economic environment of American society are useful for evaluating issues in the policy process and for predicting which of the many issues on the public-policy agenda are likely to be adopted as public policies.

Now we will apply the policy-process model to three different issues in order to illustrate the operation of the model. The issues to be analyzed are (a) the establishment of the cabinet-level Department of Education, (b) the establishment of medical care for the aged financed by increasing the Social Security tax, and (c) the possibility that a comprehensive national health-care plan financed by increased Social Security taxes will be approved. We know that the first two issues actually did achieve public-policy status. The model helps to explain *why* and *how* these issues succeeded in working their way through the public-policy process. The third issue has remained on the policy agenda for almost fifty years. We will analyze the factors in the policy process that have blocked this issue from becoming public policy.

The Establishment of the Department of Education

Prior to 1979 when Congress approved legislation creating a cabinet-level Department of Education, education policies at the federal level were implemented primarily by the Office of Education in the Department of Health, Education, and Welfare (HEW) and to a lesser extent by the Departments of Labor and Agriculture. In the 1970s a number of education interest groups, led by the National Education Association (NEA), decided that a separate Department of Education would provide more visibility and support for federal education policy and for new federal initiatives in education. A separate Department of Education would be a more dedicated lobbyist for education within the executive branch than would a department representing not only education but also health and welfare. Moreover, a cabinet secretary solely representing education in the president's cabinet and in high-level decision making within the executive branch would be a much more effective spokesperson than a cabinet secretary responsible for managing the large and bureaucratically complex Department of Health, Education, and Welfare. It also was argued that charging one centralized cabinet department with implementing and coordinating federal education policy would be more efficient than spreading these functions over a number of different cabinet departments.

In evaluating how the proposal for a Department of Education would fare in the public-policy process, the factor of *implicit norms and standards* argues both for and against the issue. Favoring the issue is the implicit norm accepted by most Americans that education and proposals to improve education are positive and to be desired. Public education historically has been supported by Americans. This level of support increased in the early 1960s with the space race and the challenge of the Soviet Union. It increased again in the late 1970s with the challenge of growing international economic competition, especially from Japan and other Pacific Rim nations. Opposing the issue, however, is the implicit norm of decentralized government and the long tradition of keeping education policy under the control of local school boards and state government. On balance, then, the factor of implicit norms and standards can be seen as a wash, neither strongly favoring nor strongly opposing the issue.

The factor of *incrementalism* favored the passage of legislation creating a Department of Education. Such a public policy can be seen as an incremental step beyond the education bureaucracy that existed in the 1970s; namely, the Office of Education (with thousands of employees and a multibillion-dollar budget) housed in HEW and a number of other education-related agencies housed in the Labor, Commerce, and Agriculture departments. Combining the agencies charged with implementing the federal government's education policies into one cabinet department could be described by the issue's supporters as an improvement in efficiency involving a reorganization of existing resources but requiring few, if any, additional resources.

The process of *power, bargaining, and compromise* is almost always an important factor in determining whether an issue succeeds in becoming a public policy, and the Department of Education issue was no exception. The National Education Association was the most important interest group favoring the issue. Other supportive interest groups included the AFL-CIO and the American Federation of Teachers. These interest groups, composed of millions of members, were well organized and financed and would clearly and directly benefit from the creation of a Department of Education. Thus the Department of Education had strong, focused interest-group support and only diffused opposition. In fact, no interest group mounted a vigorous, well-organized and well-financed lobbying campaign against the Department of Education. Opposition, however, did come in the form of editorials, speeches, and advocacy advertising from business and ideologically conservative interest groups. The opposition was diffused because no interest group had a sufficiently strong financial or ideological reason to coordinate forceful opposition to the issue.

A final element influencing the power and bargaining on this issue was the important role played by the Carter administration in lobbying strongly for this issue. The president and those within the executive branch moved to support the Department of Education. The NEA had been the first major interest group to endorse Jimmy Carter's candidacy for president in 1976. The endorsement was a major boost to the Carter campaign in 1976. Once elected, the president reciprocated the NEA's support by vigorously lobbying Democratic members of Congress on behalf of the Department of Education proposal. Thus in terms of power and bargaining, the interest groups supporting the Department of Education issue were more powerful and effective than its opponents, and this factor favored the issue in the public-policy process.

The *political and economic environment* of 1977-79 was marginally positive for the establishment of the Department of Education. President Carter and his administration strongly favored the issue and along with various education interest groups vigorously lobbied Congress for its approval. The Democratic party enjoyed substantial majorities in both houses of Congress, and that helped President Carter and the NEA develop support in Congress. Nevertheless, a majority of moderates and liberals from both parties was required for passage of the proposal, since conservatives from both parties opposed the proposal. Additionally, the NEA had to contend with a post-1974 political environment that was increasingly skeptical of the growth in federal regulation and the expansion of federal administrative agencies. In the end the strong personal support of President Carter, the Democratic majorities in Congress, the adroit lobbying of the education interest groups, and the preferred status of education in American society helped counteract the negative aspects of the political environment.

The economic environment of the late 1970s, characterized by high rates of inflation and unemployment (referred to by some economists as a period of stagflation), worked against any issues that required substantial government expenditures. However, the supporters of the Education Department were able to argue that their proposal calling for a reorganization of the education bureaucracy into one cabinet department would result in administrative efficiencies and little or no increase in expenditures. On balance, then, the political and economic environment of the 1970s was neutral or marginally favorable for the Department of Education issue.

While the foregoing policy analysis does not presume to suggest that there is a precise formula for predicting which issues will become public policy, it does suggest the primary factors that favored and opposed the Department of Education issue. Since the factors either favored the issue or were neutral or marginally favorable, the climate was right for the issue to become public policy.

The Establishment of Medical Care for the Aged Financed by Increasing the Social Security Tax

Government-sponsored health insurance to assist people in meeting the cost of their medical care was first placed on the public-policy agenda in 1935 as one of the proposals of President Franklin D. Roosevelt's New Deal. The issue remained on the policy agenda for the next thirty years until 1965 when the factors that influence public-policy making came together for the first time to yield the Health Insurance for the Aged Act (more commonly referred to as Medical Care for the Aged or Medicare), a public policy that provided health insurance for Americans sixty-five years of age or older. Why did this issue take so long to succeed in becoming public policy (of course, some issues never succeed), and why did success come in 1965 and not earlier? The answer is that prior to 1965 not enough factors that influence public-policy making were favorable for this issue. Simply stated, the reason Medicare succeeded in 1965 and not before was that the political and economic environment was not sufficiently favorable in earlier years. The remaining factors (implicit norms, incrementalism, and power/bargaining/compromise) remained relatively unchanged over the thirty-year period.

The *implicit-norms factor* was marginally unfavorable for Medicare given the fact that individualism and taking care of oneself are implicit norms accepted by most Americans. Countering these implicit norms is the argument that older Americans who contributed to the society during their working lives but who may not have foreseen the heavy health costs of their senior years deserve a governmental health-care program financed through Social Security taxes paid by the eventual health-care recipients as well as by current members of the labor force.

The *incrementalism factor* was also marginally unfavorable. Since Medicare was to be financed by an addition to the Social Security tax, an existing tax used to provide eligible Americans with pension benefits, it might be viewed as an incremental step in public policies. However, on net, the idea that the government should sponsor health-care insurance for retired Americans was probably more than an incremental step beyond the Social Security pension system. In terms of the *power and bargaining factor*, interest groups on both sides of the issue were focused, well organized, and well financed. Ripley and Franklin describe the opposing sides as follows:

> The intensity of views held by proponents and opponents of medical care insurance remained high throughout the thirty-year debate. Two basic positions were taken by the broad coalitions on the general questions concerning the federal government's proper role in this area. Proponents (AFL-CIO and other labor unions, a variety of public-welfare organizations, the National Medical Association (a group of black physicians), the National Council of Senior Citizens, and northern Democrats) supported full federal sponsorship of medical insurance and believed that private insurance companies could not handle the job of national medical insurance, that their high premiums would place too much burden on the elderly, and that a state charity approach was unsatisfactory because state benefits were inadequate and because only the neediest could qualify.
>
> Opponents of national medical insurance (the American Medical Association, the insurance industry, business groups like the U.S. Chamber of Commerce, Republicans, and southern Democrats) favored only a very narrow federal role, limited to encouraging private and state efforts and to providing federal health-care assistance only to the neediest (state charity) cases. . . . Opponents greatly feared government interference in private medical practice and warned against the dangers of "socialized medicine."[24]

As noted earlier in this chapter, the primary factor affecting the outcome of the Medicare issue in 1965 was the *political and economic environment* of that period. Medicare did not succeed in becoming public policy in the thirty years preceding 1965 because one or both of these environmental factors were unfavorable during that period. In the late 1930s the Roosevelt administration, while supportive of a comprehensive health-care system, concentrated its legislative efforts on other public-policy issues (policies related to the Great Depression) that had a higher priority. The late 1930s also saw the Roosevelt administration and the Congress concentrating their interests and energies on international affairs; principally, the growing threat of war in Europe. During the period of 1941-46 the American political and economic environment was almost exclusively involved with World War II. Following the war, from 1946 to 1952, the Truman administration concentrated most of its energy and concern on foreign policy by implementing the Marshall Plan, the Truman Doctrine, and other policies to contain the spread of communism. Thus while the Democratic party controlled the White House and both houses of Congress from 1935 to 1952, which suggests a positive political environment, much of this period was devoted to foreign-policy issues, with the Medicare issue relegated to the sidelines. In 1953 the Republican Eisenhower administration came into power, and for the next eight years the political environment for the Medicare issue was unfavorable. While the Congress was controlled by the Democratic party throughout most of this period, the ideological majority in the Congress was moderate to conservative. But even if the Medicare legislation had been passed by Congress, it would likely have been vetoed by President Eisenhower, whose political and economic philosophy favored private-sector solutions to most social issues. It should be noted that during much of the 1950s the economic environment in the United States was relatively strong and would have been able to sustain increased Social Security taxes to finance a Medicare program. This illustrates the importance of having both the political and economic environments work in unison to support an issue if it is to become public policy.

This brings us to the 1960s when, as we noted earlier, the political and economic environments became sufficiently positive by 1965 to be the decisive factors in causing the Medicare issue to finally succeed in becoming public policy. In 1965, just as in 1939 or 1955, the implicit norms and incrementalism factors were marginally unfavorable for the Medicare issue, and the power-and-bargaining factor was probably evenly divided. What had dramatically changed, however, was the political environment — Lyndon Johnson, the Democratic president, had been elected by a landslide in 1964, and with him the voters had also elected a Congress with a heavily Democratic majority in both the House and Senate. The economic environment of the mid-1960s also was quite favorable (characterized by low inflation, low unemployment, and moderate budget deficits) and thus able to absorb any necessary increase in Social Security taxes.

Finally, you should be aware that the rapidly increasing costs of health care in the 1980s (costs have been increasing at about twice the rate of the consumer price index) and the growing organizational sophistication and political power of senior-citizen interest groups have increased the visibility of health-care issues on the public-policy agenda. For example, the enactment in 1988 of the Medicare Catastrophic Coverage Act signaled the first substantial increase in Medicare benefits since that public policy was established in 1965. It was influenced by a number of factors operating on the public-policy process, including (1) the incremental nature of catastrophic health care, given the already existing medical care for the aged (Medicare) program; (2) the great political power of the American Association of Retired Persons (AARP), which in 1988 enjoyed a membership of twenty-four million persons; (3) the fact that 1988 was a presidential-election year that most political observers believed would involve a closely contested race for the White House by the two political parties, thereby making both parties acutely aware of the voting strength of senior citizens, and (4) a financing plan that allowed catastrophic health care to be paid for directly out of existing monthly Social Security payments to seniors, rather than by increasing the Social Security tax rate on all employees and employers.

Continuing health-care issues on the public-policy agenda include long-term health care (extended care in nursing homes, and at-home care) for seniors and a comprehensive health-care program for all Americans. It is likely that the factors influencing the establishment of catastrophic health care will also lead to legislation establishing long-term health care for seniors in the early 1990s. On the other hand, the prospect for comprehensive health care is less clear given the factors (discussed below) at work in the public-policy process. Much will depend on the political and economic environments in the 1990s and on whether health-care costs continue to increase at the rapid rate of the 1980s. What is clear, however, is that American business has a major interest in the development of national health-care policy given the large sums it currently spends on employee and retiree health plans and the likelihood that future government health-care plans will be financed by increased taxes (Social Security or otherwise), which would cut into business profitability.

Comprehensive Health Care for All Americans Financed by the Social Security Tax

While medical care for the aged succeeded in becoming public policy in 1965, a much broader program of comprehensive health care for all Americans failed to become public policy and continues to be an issue on the policy agenda. What explains the failure of this issue to become public policy while Medicare succeeded? The following analysis suggests that while the political and economic environments were favorable for a comprehensive health-care law in 1965, other factors such as implicit norms, incrementalism, and power/bargaining/compromise were sufficiently unfavorable to prevent the issue from becoming public policy.

While the *implicit norms and incrementalism factors* were marginally unfavorable for the Medicare issue, they were clearly unfavorable for comprehensive health care. A government-sponsored health-care plan for all Americans funded by the Social Security tax is contrary to the American spirit of individualism and providing for oneself. Such a plan would make the federal government the dominant force in the American health-care system, which has historically been characterized by a decentralized system of private hospitals and physicians. The step from the existing decentralized health-care system to a comprehensive government-sponsored insurance system was considerably more than an incremental one. Whereas the Medicare proposal was limited to Americans sixty-five years of age or older, who in a sense had "paid their dues" and were perhaps entitled to the assurance of adequate health care in their senior years, the comprehensive health care plan applied to all Americans, most of whom were able-bodied and capable of taking care of themselves. These comments give some flavor of the implicit norms that have to be overcome by a government-sponsored comprehensive health care plan.

The *power-and-bargaining factor* also was unfavorable for the comprehensive health care proposal in 1965 and likely is so today as well. Unlike the Medicare proposal, which was almost equally supported and opposed by well-financed, focused, and organized interest groups, the comprehensive proposal has only diffused support from interest groups, while the opposition groups are well financed and well organized with a clear, direct economic and professional interest in the outcome.

Those interest groups in support of the comprehensive proposal have not been very effective for many of the reasons listed earlier in the chapter. Most are not well organized or lack a sufficiently large number of politically sophisticated and dedicated members with a direct economic interest in the issue. The reason is that most politically organized members of American society already have health insurance. For example, union members are provided with health insurance through collective bargaining agreements with their employers; federal, state, and local government employees and most white-collar employees of medium- and large-sized corporations are also provided with health-insurance coverage by their employers; a great majority of Americans over the age of sixty-four are eligible for Medical Care for the Aged; and Americans below the poverty line are often provided with medical care by state welfare programs.

Who then are the supporters of a comprehensive publicly financed health-care plan? Liberal Democrats have long supported such a proposal as have certain interest groups such as the NAACP and some consumer groups. These groups believe that the federal government has a role in making sure that all Americans who are not covered by private health-insurance plans have access to adequate health care. This might include, for example, blue-collar employees working for small businesses, where the employee does not have sufficient economic leverage to convince the employer to provide health insurance as a fringe benefit. Such workers also are unlikely to be part of a well-organized and politically sophisticated interest group. The AFL-CIO has also been a supporter of a comprehensive health-care proposal, but its support has been more ideological than aggressive and enthusiastic. Its members, after all, are covered by employer-provided health insurance while employed and upon retirement by Medical Care for the Aged. Also its members would be required to pay the higher Social Security taxes required to finance a comprehensive national health-care plan. Thus the supporters of comprehensive health care have not yet been able to effectively marshal adequate political strength in support of this issue.

In sharp contrast, the opponents of a comprehensive health-care proposal, including the American Medical Association, the American Hospital Association, various business interest groups, and conservatives from both political parties, have been very effective in their opposition. In addition to being well organized and financed, they also have direct and clear economic, professional, or ideological reasons for their opposition. Physicians and hospitals fear that a governmentally financed health-insurance program (for instance, via the Social Security tax) would eventually interfere with their freedom to set fees and with the freedom and independence to practice medicine as the medical profession sees fit. Business interest groups and conservative political leaders are opposed to the prospect of a substantially increased level of government regulation in the health-care field as well as to the prospect of paying higher taxes to finance such a plan. In terms of the political and economic environments, it seems clear that the most favorable time for passage of a comprehensive health-care plan was in the mid-1960s when both the political and economic environments were reasonably favorable. The issue did not succeed in becoming public policy at that time because of the substantial imbalance in power and bargaining ability between the opponents and the supporters of comprehensive health care and the nonincremental nature of the issue. Since that time the political and/or economic environments have not been supportive of this issue, and the power/bargaining balance has continued to favor the opponents of a comprehensive health-care program. New support for a comprehensive health care plan may be generated in the future if rapidly rising health-care costs lead employers to require that employees become responsible for a substantial share of their health-care insurance premiums.[25] It remains to be seen whether this issue will enjoy increased support from interest groups and the political and economic environments in the 1990s.

CONCLUSION

The process of public-policy making in American society is influenced by many political, economic, and social forces and institutions. Although the process is relatively complex, it can best be understood when it is separated into its component parts and analyzed accordingly. In reviewing how issues are raised in the policy process and the four major factors that influence the making of public policy, we have examined the importance of implicit norms and standards, incrementalism, power and bargaining, and the broader forces of the political and economic environments.

Over the past twenty-five years American business has become an increasingly active participant in the public-policy process. Its level of participation is due in large part to the rapid growth of regulatory public policies costly to business. However, it also reflects the fact that business is one of the major institutions of American society and as such is directly or indirectly affected by many public policies. Business understands the importance of early identification of issues in the public-policy process and makes its presence felt in the policy process through the effective use of interest groups, trade associations, political action committees, and advocacy advertising.

Instead of merely reacting to issues in the policy process, business today recognizes that it has an interest in identifying, evaluating, and helping to shape issues in the policy process. An important question raised by this increasingly activist role for American business is whether its mission should be limited to pursuing the interests of its primary stakeholders (consumers, investors, and employees), or whether in late twentieth-century America business has the larger mission of balancing its private interest with the broader public interest. This question and related questions form the subject matter of the last chapter in this book.

NOTES

1. Rogene Buchholtz, *Business Environment/Public Policy: A Study of Teaching and Research in Schools of Business and Management* (St. Louis, Mo.: Washington University Center for the Study of American Business, 1979), working paper no. 41, pp. 109-10.

2. James E. Anderson, *Public Policy Making* (New York: Holt, Rinehart & Winston, 1979), p. 3, quoting David Easton, *A Systems Analysis of Political Life* (New York: John Wiley & Sons, 1965), p. 212.

3. Most print-media observers would include at least the following newspapers: *New York Times, Washington Post, Wall Street Journal, Los Angeles Times,* and *Christian Science Monitor.*

4. Michael Waldholz, "A Project to Identify All Human Genes Sets New Medical Horizons," *Wall Street Journal,* February 3, 1986, p. 1.

5. Thomas Gale Moore, "Rational Ignorance, Regulatory Solutions and Inefficient Outcomes," unpublished paper, Hoover Institution, Stanford, Calif.

6. Public Affairs Research Group, *Public Affairs Offices and Their Functions: Summary of Survey Responses,* participants' ed. (Boston: School of Management, Boston University, 1981), p. v.

7. Ian H. Wilson, "Environmental Scanning and Strategic Planning," *Business Environment/Public Policy: 1979 Conference Papers,* Lee E. Preston, ed. (St. Louis, Mo.: American Assembly of Collegiate Schools of Business, 1980), pp. 159-61.

8. Anderson, *Public Policy Making,* pp. 27-30.

9. Robin M. Williams, Jr., *American Society,* 2nd ed. (New York: Alfred Knopf, 1960), chap. 11.

10. The antitrust laws are discussed in chap. 4-6.

11. Anderson, *Public Policy Making,* p. 12.

12. In 1985-86 the American Medical Association Political Action Committee (AMA PAC) raised $4.9 million and contributed $2.1 million to candidates running for Congress. The AMA PAC also spent $1.5 million in *independent* expenditures for particular congressional candidates. During the same time period the National Education Association Political Action Committee (NEA PAC) raised $3.2 million and contributed $2.0 million to candidates running for Congress. Source: U.S. Federal Election Commission, *FEC Reports on Financial Activity, 1985-86, Final Report, Party and Non-Party Political Committees,* vol. III, pp. 517-22 and vol. IV, pp. 817-22.

13. "For Trade Associations, Politics Is the New Focus," *Business Week,* April 17, 1978, pp. 107-15.

14. Robert S. Greenberger, "Manufacturer's Lobby Alters Style to Combat Its Obstructionist Image," *Wall Street Journal,* May 5, 1981, p. 33.

15. For a thorough discussion of the history, operation, and effectiveness of the Business Roundtable, see John D Aram, *Managing Business and Public Policy* (Boston: Pitman Publishing 1986), pp. 680-99.

16. Randall B. Ripley and Grace A. Franklin, *Bureaucracy and Power Implementation* (Homewood, Ill.: Dorsey Press, 1982), pp. 12-16, 45-47. See also James Q. Wilson, "The Rise of the Bureaucratic State," *Public Interest* no. 41 (Fall 1975), pp. 77-103.

17. Rogene A. Buchholz, *Business Environment and Public Policy* (Englewood Cliffs, N.J.: Prentice Hall, 1982), p. 56.

18. Albert R. Hunt, "The Power Brokers: Thomas Boggs and Firm Offer Full-Service Lobbying for a Diverse Group of Clients," *Wall Street Journal*, March 23, 1982, p. 1.
19. Buchholtz, *Business Environment*, p. 178.
20. S. Prakash Sethi, *Advocacy Advertising and Large Corporations* (Lexington, Mass.: Lexington Books, 1977).
21. Attributed to the late Jesse R. Unruh, former speaker of the State Assembly of the California legislature.

22. Larry J. Sabato, *PAC Power* (New York: W. W. Norton & Co., 1985), pp. 29, 96. See also Epstein, "The PAC Phenomena: An Overview," *Arizona Law Review* 22 (1980), 358-59.
23. Ibid., p. 34.
24. Ripley and Franklin, p. 180.
25. Roger Ricklefs, "Health Insurance Becomes a Big Pain for Small Firms," *Wall Street Journal*, December 6, 1988, p. B-1.

CHAPTER TWO
The Traditional Public-Policy Institutions: The Judiciary, the Congress, and the Executive

INTRODUCTION

In the previous chapter you were exposed to the complicated interrelationships involved with the development of public policies. In particular, you learned that one focal point of the dynamic process is on the federal government institutions, since these are the ultimate places from which national public policies emanate. In this chapter and the one that follows we will pursue in more detail the mechanisms by which each of the major federal government institutions makes, affects, and changes public policies. Such an undertaking will not only enrich your understanding of the policy process but will enable you to interact more successfully and responsibly with that process.

In this chapter we will examine the three traditional branches of government: the judiciary, the Congress, and the executive. By traditional we mean that the institutions were directly established by the United States Constitution. We will explore how these branches are empowered to formulate public policies and how each branch is designed to provide input into the public-policy pronouncements of its sister institutions. In the next chapter administrative agencies will be introduced. The growth and complexity of federal public policies have necessitated the creation of a "fourth branch" to aid the traditional government institutions in their formulation and implementation. Since as a businessperson, your most direct day-to-day involvement with the federal government will be with these administrative agencies, you must have an understanding of how they operate. Again, the ultimate aim is to improve your effectiveness in dealing with the public-policy process.

THE JUDICIARY

Introduction

Article III of the Constitution provides that the federal judicial power of the United States is to be lodged in the Supreme Court and other inferior courts established by Congress. As you know, Congress has created a large array of inferior courts, such as the district courts and the courts of appeals. These courts are inferior to the Supreme Court in that their decisions are subject to the policy guidelines of the Supreme Court. Thus any time the Supreme Court develops a policy by the methods of statutory interpretation or judicial review discussed below, the inferior courts are bound to decide their cases, when relevant, on the basis of that policy. Failure to do so will subject their decisions to reversal at an appellate level or by the Supreme Court itself. However, as we shall see later, the Supreme Court can be involved in only a limited set of policy issues. Thus for a large number of policy disputes, the decisions of the inferior courts serve as the policy foundations for their respective jurisdictions. Therefore, although this section will concentrate on the operations of the Supreme Court, you should not lose sight of the importance of the inferior courts in making public policy.

According to the Constitution, judges selected for federal court posts may serve during "good behavior," which essentially means that they retain their positions for life or until they choose to relinquish their posts. The selection process for judges is a two-step undertaking requiring first that the president nominate a candidate to fill a vacant post, and then that a majority of the Senate vote to approve this candidate. As we shall see, this selection process coupled with life tenure has important political ramifications for the president and, to a lesser extent, the Congress in their abilities to shape long-lasting public policies.

Judicial Formulation of Public Policies

Statutory Interpretation   When courts settle disputes, they need to synthesize the facts and then analyze those facts in terms of the applicable law or laws. Such laws usually originate from one of three sources: (1) legislative statutes, (2) administrative agency rules, or (3) the common law as enunciated in previous court decisions. If these laws have been drafted with sufficient specificity, then the court's job is easy since the law dictates the legal consequences for the facts before it. For instance, assume that Congress passed a statute specifying that any person who discharged a liquid with a concentration of benzine exceeding six parts per million would be subject to a fine of $5000. If a corporation were sued under this statute, and the facts revealed that it had released liquid composed of nine parts per million benzine concentration, then the court simply would have to enforce the statutory penalty. However, laws very often are not designed with such clearly articulated standards. Rather, they are composed of relatively vague terms, the meanings of which are open to interpretation. The above statute, for instance, might have specified that persons who release "unreasonable" amounts of benzine would be subject to the fine. To decide the case before it, the court now would be faced with the job of interpreting whether nine parts per million was an unreasonable amount of benzine. Whatever decision it reached, the precedental value of its interpretation would set a policy for corporations contemplating a benzine discharge in the future.

The policy set by this court interpretation could subsequently be changed by various means. First and most simply, the decision of the court could be reversed on appeal based on the judgment of the reviewing court that the statute should be interpreted in another fashion. The determination of the appellate court would then control all interpretations made in the future by inferior courts. Second, the same court in a later, similar case might conclude that its own previous interpretation of the statute was incorrect and so overrule that policy decision. Its new interpretation would then take the place of the old one to serve as the policy grounds in this area. Such an outcome might occur either because the judges changed their minds or because newly appointed judges sitting on the court viewed the statute in a different light. Finally, Congress, the source of the law, could amend the statute to state more clearly how the statute should be interpreted by the courts. Here, for example, Congress could respond to the court's benzine policy by specifying that any concentration below, let's say, fifteen parts per million, is not unreasonable. This, in effect, would change the policy for future discharging operations.

Examples of how courts can make and change public policy through interpretation abound. One of the clearest examples is provided by antitrust, in which court interpretations of terms such as "in restraint of trade" and "may be to substantially lessen competition" have served as the backbone of that policy area. We will see in Chapters 4, 5, and 6 that antitrust policy has undergone a substantial change in the last twenty-five years, owing somewhat to the substitution of new judges who have held different philosophies as to the proper role of antitrust in the American competitive society.

"Insider trading" is another current example, involving court interpretations of congressional statutes dealing with securities matters and rule 10b-5, promulgated by the Securities and Exchange Commission (SEC). Rule 10b-5 specifies that any person who buys or sells a security in a fraudulent manner is subject to civil and criminal penalties. The question regarding insider trading is whether under rule 10b-5 a person who is aware of nonpublic information regarding a security but does not reveal that information to one with whom he or she trades the security commits a fraudulent act. In the 1970s most lower courts answered this question in the affirmative by interpreting rule 10b-5 as requiring disclosure of nonpublic information by anyone who trades on the basis of that information.[1] However, in the early 1980s the Supreme Court on two occasions limited the reach of the rule to situations in which the actor either breaches a fiduciary duty to another person by personally gaining on nonpublic information or misappropriates the information upon which he or she silently trades.[2] This in turn led to confusion as to the applicability of the rule to certain forms of securities-trading practices, especially when the SEC substantially increased its insider-trading enforcement actions in the mid-1980s. Members of Congress responded by introducing legislation that more clearly defined the proper application of the rule to insider trading activities. Although the SEC originally opposed these congressional efforts, it later advocated a statutory solution.[3] This attempt to clarify the law eventually failed in 1988 because members of Congress could not reach a consensus on the proper scope of insider trading. Instead, Congress enacted the Insider Trading and Enforcement Act which served only to broaden the range of persons subject to civil penalties for insider trading violations, and provided the SEC with a number of new enforcement tools. The result, we anticipate, will be even more tension and confusion regarding insider trading. Only the public-policy process will determine the future course of this important policy.

Judicial Review   Along with statutory interpretation, the courts have another important tool for formulating public policies: judicial review. Judicial review is the power assumed by the courts to judge whether rules and statutes promulgated by state and federal governmental bodies comply with the United States Constitution. Those statutes found to violate the Constitution are void and may not be enforced. That the courts should be the sole possessors of this power is nowhere stated in the Constitution, and many scholars believe that the courts have no more right to it than the elected representatives of Congress. The practical implications of the debate are moot, however, given that the courts' domain over judicial review has been firmly established since 1803 when the Supreme Court's assumption of the privilege in *Marbury* v. *Madison* was accepted by the Congress.[4] Thus we will concentrate on the policy implications that judicial review bestows on the court system.

The best means to acquaint you with the importance of judicial review is to consider just a short sample of the instances in which it has been applied. For instance, before 1937 minimum wage statutes passed by state legislatures were struck down by the Supreme Court because they violated the Fourteenth Amendment, which provides that no government shall deprive any person of life, liberty or property without due process of law. At first glance this decision might surprise you since the amendment seems intended to assure procedural fairness before a state imprisons or executes someone or before it seizes private property. However, the Supreme Court interpreted it to include protection from other government actions. Liberty of contract, it reasoned, was a "liberty" guarded by the amendment, and governments were restricted from interfering with it unless they provided substantial health and safety reasons for so doing. Minimum wage laws intruded with this freedom because they prohibited contractual wage terms at levels below the minimum designation.[5] Likewise, statutes establishing minimum working conditions or maximum hours of employment standards were sometimes voided as unconstitutional by courts using judicial review.[6] Obviously, President Roosevelt's far-reaching New Deal program would have been eviscerated by this interpretation of the Due Process Clause since many of its proposals interfered with liberty of contract. However, in 1937 one member of the Court altered his interpretation of this clause so that it would not apply so readily to economic legislation.[7] As will be seen in the next section on Supreme Court procedures, the swing of one vote often may be sufficient to alter public policy significantly. Here the shift allowed the Court to overrule its previous decisions.[8] From that instance to the present day, legislation that interferes with economic relationships need only have some rational purpose to pass muster under the Fourteenth Amendment.

This change in views by the Supreme Court had a dramatic effect on the future policy course of this country. Without it the multitude of rules passed by such agencies as the Occupational Safety and Health Administration, the Consumer Product Safety Commission, and the Department of Labor may have been unenforceable. Note again that potentially conflicting interpretations of vague terms open the door for court policy making. Here, though, the words are part of the Constitution rather than of statutes or rules. As you might suspect, if Congress or American citizens are unhappy with a Court interpretation of the Constitution, they may alter its policy by amending the Constitution with more clearly articulated standards. However, amending the Constitution is a very difficult process requiring supporting votes from two-thirds of the House of Representatives, two-thirds of the Senate, and three-fourths of the state legislatures.

The Fourteenth Amendment also provides that no government shall deny equal protection of the laws. As this amendment was added to the Constitution shortly after the Civil War, there has never been a question that it must be interpreted to compel unbiased government treatment of blacks. However, in 1896 the Supreme Court held that equal protection was satisfied even when governments required blacks to use facilities separate from those for whites as long as those facilities were physically equal to those provided to whites.[9] This decision formed the basis for the legality of a litany of "Jim Crow" laws, which established separate but equal facilities for blacks in all settings. For instance, in many states blacks had to sit in the back of busses, sit in separate courtroom sections, swear on separate Bibles, use separate restrooms, and relax in separate parks. In addition, black schoolchildren were required to attend separate schools from white children.

This policy remained intact until 1954 when the Supreme Court, in a dramatic shift in policy, reinterpreted the Equal Protection Clause in *Brown v. Board of Education of Topeka, Kansas.*[10] In this case parents of black children challenged state laws requiring their children to attend separate but allegedly equal schools. The Court determined that separate facilities, although functionally equal, are inherently unequal because of the stigma of inferiority that attends the act of racial separation. Such a practice thus violated the Fourteenth Amendment and was thereby unconstitutional. As a remedy, the Court demanded that integration efforts (through bussing and other means) be initiated "with all deliberate speed." Based on this change in interpretation and the resulting precedent set by the Supreme Court, all Jim Crow laws were soon outlawed. In addition, the Congress in 1964 passed sweeping new public-policy legislation that applied the standards of equal protection to the employment and customer practices of many private businesses.

Another important shift in constitutional interpretation opened the door for the dramatic growth in the federal government that has taken place since the 1930s. The Tenth Amendment to the Constitution instructs that the federal government can legislate only in those areas specifically listed in the Constitution as being within its domain. All other areas lie exclusively within the jurisdiction of the state governments. Such a delineation of control was a compromise between state leaders who wanted autonomy and others who desired unification. Article I, section 8 provides the domains within which the federal government may legislate if it so chooses. Simplifying somewhat, section 8 specifies that the federal Congress may make laws that are necessary and proper to carry out functions in the following areas:

1. Interstate commerce
2. Foreign affairs
3. Defense
4. Raising revenue through taxation and borrowing
5. Spending revenue for the general welfare

Suppose the federal Congress passed a law specifying standards for slaughtering chickens. Would this be a legitimate exercise of federal power? Where is such authority on the above list? Such a question came before the Supreme Court in 1935, and using judicial review, it concluded, that such legislation was unconstitutional.[11] The power of Congress over *interstate commerce*, it held, was limited to regulating activities that directly affected goods crossing state lines. Chicken slaughtering has no such direct effect. Similarly, the court perceived no relation to foreign affairs, defense, or raising or spending money. Thus the Supreme Court determined that only a state government had the power to tell its citizens under what conditions chicken could be slaughtered.

With such an understanding of Article I, section 8, many federal laws were struck down as beyond federal authority. As another example, a federal law forbidding employers to interfere with efforts by employees to organize and bargain collectively was held to be unconstitutional.[12] Again the rationale was that such legislation was not on the list. However, in 1937 in a stunning reversal the Supreme Court changed its interpretation of the words "interstate commerce," and this has provided the federal government the leeway to legislate in almost any way it chooses.[13] The center of the controversy was another comprehensive labor statute that granted protections to employees so that they could bargain collectively without intimidation by employers. When faced with the constitutionality this time, the Supreme Court said that such legislation was a valid exercise under the interstate commerce clause. Activities having a direct effect on interstate commerce, it decided, were not the only ones within federal control. In addition, activities that have an indirect effect on goods traveling across state lines are equally covered. Here the statute was aimed at reducing labor unrest. In the situation before the Court, which involved a steel company, the Court foresaw that labor strife might cause mill disruptions, which in turn would lead to a reduction in raw-material requirements. Since some of the raw materials used by the plant crossed state lines, it was proper for the federal government, in its legitimate pursuit to regulate these interstate shipments, also to monitor labor conditions that might have an indirect effect on them.

Given the interpretation that the federal government may regulate anything that indirectly affects interstate commerce, it should be easy to understand that Congress now has the power to make almost any law that does not offend another provision of the Constitution. Consider the plight of a small wheat farmer who grew more wheat than permitted under a federal law but simply ate the excess amount.[14] Could this parochial act be subject to federal control? The answer was yes! The purpose of the federal law was to raise the price of wheat crossing state lines by restricting supply. If this farmer and others similarly situated grew too much, albeit for personal consumption, then they would purchase less on the open market to feed their families. This reduction in demand would put downward pressure on the price of wheat in general and indirectly affect the price of wheat crossing state lines.

A similar argument was put forward to support the Civil Rights Act of 1964, already mentioned, which extended the principle of equal protection to the private workplace. One provision of this statute prohibited restaurants from discriminating against black patrons. An Alabama restaurant that admittedly discriminated questioned how the federal government had the authority to dictate who its customers should be when those customers were mostly Alabama citizens.[15] The Supreme Court upheld the legality of the civil-rights provision by noting that a significant amount of food sold at the restaurant traveled across state lines. Also, without the civil-rights legislation, discriminatory practices would continue in certain states, which might inhibit professionals from traveling across state lines to locate in them. Thus the legislation was aimed at activities that indirectly affected interstate commerce.

The interpretation by the Supreme Court that Congress can regulate activities that indirectly affect interstate commerce fueled the engine for federal growth. Indeed, many of the federal administrative agencies and the rules made by them owe their existence to this judicial act of policy making. You might wonder, given this interpretation, whether there remain any areas solely within the domain of state legislation. In 1985 the Supreme Court effectively responded in the negative by holding that even state government employees could be subject to federal minimum wage legislation under its commerce-clause authority.[16] Thus unless this policy is changed, either by the Supreme Court or by a constitutional amendment, the Tenth Amendment no longer provides any restraints to federal regulatory control.

You are probably aware of a number of recent public-policy controversies that are the subject of judicial review. For instance, the Supreme Court has stated that governments may not prohibit abortions before viability because this would interfere with a woman's due process right to privacy.[17] Since the Fourteenth Amendment does not specifically mention that privacy is protected (only life, liberty, and property), some constitutional scholars as well as several current Supreme Court justices believe that this interpretation is fallacious. In a similar vein the proponents of privacy rights are now looking to the courts to strike down the growing number of AIDS testing laws.

The Court has stated that many forms of affirmative action plans are legal even though the Fourteenth Amendment guarantees equal protection. Again this interpretation is subject to wide dispute. Also, the courts, using judicial review, have determined that the Equal Protection Clause provides strong protections to women and aliens but not to gays or the retarded. In the religion area the Supreme Court under its interpretation of the First Amendment has prohibited prayer in public schools as well as moments of silence. These policy actions have been fiercely debated, especially during the Reagan administration. In addition, judicial interpretations of the Fourth and Fifth Amendments, which accord rights to the criminally accused, have been the focal points of controversy. Obviously, the importance of the courts, especially the Supreme Court, in making public policy cannot be underestimated.

Supreme Court Procedures

The Supreme Court is the appellate level of last resort within the federal judicial system. However, only under a very rare set of circumstances does a party have a *right* to appellate review by this Court. Rather, the most common avenue for appeal is through a *writ of certiorari*. Essentially, a party who is dissatisfied with the judgment of a lower court, usually the court of appeals, files a petition with the Supreme Court explaining why the case should be reviewed. If four of the nine justices who sit on the Supreme Court agree that the case merits the body's attention, then a writ of certiorari will be granted, opening the avenue for the appeal. If the four votes are not obtained, certiorari will be denied, and the decision of the lower court will stand. The Supreme Court is asked to review many more cases than is physically possible for one court to hear. Thus the Court must be very selective in granting writs of certiorari. Typically, an appeal will be heard when the lower federal courts disagree on an important statutory or constitutional interpretation or when a state court has interpreted a federal law questionably. Using these criteria, the Court grants certiorari for less than 5 percent of the petitions filed.[18] Indeed, the Court reviews only about 150 cases per year, while the lower federal courts annually decide around 350,000 cases.[19] Thus the decisions of the lower courts in a wide variety of situations will establish judicial public policy.

The importance of the lower courts was not overlooked by President Reagan. During his administration, vacancies arose in almost one-half of the lower federal court bench due to either retirements or deaths. The president took extraordinary care in nominating individuals to fill those vacancies by creating the President's Committee on Federal Judicial Selection to advise him. Reagan nominated individuals who were relatively young to take advantage of the life tenure of judges. In addition, his committee painstakingly screened the nominees not only for judicial competence but to ensure that their vision of the Constitution accorded with that of the president.[20] Since the Republicans controlled the Senate for six years during the Reagan administration, most of these nominees were approved for their posts. In this way the Reagan legacy of conservativism may extend far beyond the physical departure of his administration.

When the Supreme Court grants certiorari, the parties file briefs with the Court explaining their respective positions. After the justices have reviewed the briefs, the attorneys for the parties present oral arguments to the judges, clarifying their briefs and answering the questions of the judges. The nine justices then hold a conference in which they discuss and preliminarily determine the outcome of the case.

Conference procedures typically follow this scenario: First the chief justice, currently William Rehnquist, presents his views. The other eight justices, in order of descending seniority, then discuss the case. Following the airing of views, the justices tentatively vote on the disposition of the case. If the chief justice votes to dispose of the case in a manner supported by a majority of the justices, then he decides who will draft the *opinion of the Court*. However, if he is on the minority side, the most senior justice in the majority determines which justice will write the decision.

The determination of who will write the opinion of the Court is critical. The Court currently is composed of members who are spread across the ideological spectrum. Liberal justices may give a far different interpretation to a statute or the Constitution than would a conservative justice. Thus the justice who has the opportunity to select the opinion drafter will want to choose the justice whose ideological views on that case most closely mirror his or her own. On occasion the justice may even select himself or herself. The chief justice, therefore, derives his power from his status as this selector whenever he is in the majority. This power, of course, presents to the chief justice the opportunity to vote against his convictions, if necessary, to control who will write the opinion. Former Chief Justice Warren Burger, for example, was accused on several occasions of using his position in just this way. Most notable was his vote with the majority in the key abortion case, *Roe v. Wade,* allegedly so that he could select the author of the opinion (Justice Blackmun).[21] The very liberal Justice Douglas would otherwise have been the most senior justice on the majority. Chief Justice Rehnquist, on the other hand, has been firm in voting his convictions, a policy that, early in his term, disturbed certain conservative factions because it enabled Justice Brennan, a liberal court member, to choose the author in several controversial cases.[22]

The remaining judges on the majority side have an option. They may either indicate full support for the Court's opinion by joining the opinion or write a concurrence, which indicates that they agree with the opinion's ultimate disposition but disagree with, or have something to add to, the reasoning in the opinion. Those in the minority file or may join in dissents, which explain their opposition to the Court's opinion. Although these procedures may seem technical, in actuality the process is very fluid, and the final opinions are drafted only after extensive discussions among the justices.

Given the power of the chief justice to decide which justice drafts the Court's opinion, you might believe that the justice with the most experience should be entitled to that position. However, experience is not a relevant consideration in determining the chief justice. Rather, the person selected by the president with the approval of the Senate to replace a vacating chief justice becomes the new chief justice. Thus Warren Burger became chief justice in 1969 because he was appointed to the court to replace the departing chief justice, Earl Warren. When chief justice Burger stepped down in 1986, President Reagan was given the opportunity to select his replacement. He chose the conservative William Rehnquist, who was already a member of the Court. Although there was considerable controversy in the Senate over his confirmation, especially from the minority Democrats, the Senate finally approved Rehnquist's nomination by a vote of sixty-five to thirty-three. This appointment probably will encourage a strengthening of President Reagan's conservative philosophies for as long as William Rehnquist remains on the Court. However, it should be noted that chief justice appointments backfire at times. Earl Warren, for example, was picked by President Eisenhower to support his conservative leanings. His mistake soon became evident however, as Warren became one of history's most liberal chief justices.

The ideological composition of the Court is of vital importance because its makeup will determine the majority positions of the Court. During the 1960s the Court was ideologically liberal, and through its public-policy-making powers i sanctioned an increase in federal economic regulations and strengthened personal liberties. The Court attained a more ideologically balanced position in the 1970s as a consequence of five appointments by Presidents Nixon and Ford. During the Reagan administration a conservative plurality was attained after three retiring justices were replaced with ideological conservatives. Coupled with this situation is a discrepancy in age between the conservative block, which has an average age of sixty years, and the two remaining liberals, who are both over eighty years old. Consequently, the Supreme Court may be the springboard for significant and long-lasting public-policy reversals in the near future. As will be seen, antitrust policy is in a period of substantial transition. Respect for private property and the operations of business may soon be heightened. On the other hand, protection from government interference with personal rights and individual liberties may be cut back as a result of the shift in the Court composition. Current public policies regarding affirmative action, abortion, free speech, school prayer, and criminal rights may be entering a period of flux. As always, the public-policy process discussed in Chapter 1 will be the ultimate determinant, but obviously, the Supreme Court, as well as the lower courts, will be major players.

THE CONGRESS

Introduction

The Congress derives its constitutional authority from Article 1 of the U.S. Constitution. Under the terms of this article, Congress is granted all legislative powers for the federal government. Although this article clearly establishes Congress as the preeminent lawmaker for the federal government, Congress has delegated a substantial amount of its legislative authority to administrative agencies, as we shall see in Chapter 3. This in turn puts certain lawmaking functions under the wing of the executive branch. Also, as already discussed, the enactment of generally worded statutes by Congress shifts lawmaking power to the judicial system. Thus legislative authority in practice has been diffused across the spectrum of government institutions.

In addition to its prime function as legislator, the Congress has control over other areas that serve to balance the powers of the remaining institutions. For instance, Congress is the keeper of the purse strings with the authority to fund the operations of the other branches of the federal government. As will be discussed in Chapter 3, Congress creates administrative agencies and is the ultimate source of their power and existence. Also, Congress has the authority to approve the president's nominees for a host of key federal offices and, as mentioned earlier, for federal judgeships. In addition, Congress is bestowed with controls over the judiciary by its ability to create, alter, or terminate federal courts and to initiate the difficult process of amending the Constitution.[23] Finally, Congress shares certain powers with the executive branch with respect to foreign affairs.

The Legislative and Budgetary Process

Congress is composed of two chambers, the Senate and the House of Representatives. The Senate is made up of two Senators from each of the fifty states. Every two years one-third of the Senators are elected for six-year terms. The House of Representatives has 435 members. Representatives are elected every two years for two-year terms from federal districts that house roughly the same number of voters. Based on the two-year election cycle, a Congress is said to last two years and is divided into two sessions of one year each. The first session of the first Congress met in 1789. Thus 1987 was the 100th Congress, 1st session; and 1988 represented the 100th Congress, 2nd session. We shall see that although the Senate has certain additional powers in that it is the body that confirms presidential nominations and approves treaties, for Congress's most important task, the passage of legislation, the two chambers have equal authority.

The mechanics of passing legislation are very complicated, and the intricate details are beyond the scope of this book. Nevertheless, we will review some of the salient features of the operations of Congress. As a businessperson trying to understand and influence public policies emanating from Congress, you must have some basic understanding of the power centers that shape those policies. This in turn will make you a more effective participant in the public-policy dynamic.

The long process of enacting legislation begins with the idea itself. An issue must arise through the public-policy process and must attain such a stature that an idea dealing with that issue is introduced into the Congress. Only a member of Congress may introduce an idea into his or her respective chamber, but the idea may originate from several sources. Often constituents of a member of Congress suggest that a particular idea if enacted into law would benefit them substantially. A member of Congress is usually responsive to his or her constituents' wishes both because of a genuine concern for their welfare and because of his or her own personal self-interest in being reelected. Other fertile sources of ideas are the president or other members of the executive branch. Each year the president outlines a program of ideas in his State of the Union message, and he along with the executive agencies drafts certain legislative proposals to accomplish that program. These proposals will be introduced in the chambers by the respective ranking leaders of the president's party or by chairpersons of legislative committees. Also, ideas come from senators or congressional representatives, themselves. Again, the idea may stem from an altruistic notion of bettering the condition of constituents or American society as a whole or may be devised in the hope that voters, whether well-informed or rationally ignorant, will be more favorably disposed to the member of Congress after his or her introduction of the idea.

At this stage you should be aware of some steps that might be taken if you want legislation to be considered by the Congress. One approach is to convince your senators and representative that it is worthwhile, both to them politically and to the welfare of their constituents in general, to introduce the legislation and work hard for its passage. Of course, a prerequisite to accomplishing this is communicating with those members of Congress. Often this is most easily achieved by telling them or their staffs directly what your idea is and what its benefits might be. However, you should not take this procedure lightly. Members of Congress and their staffs are extremely busy and have only limited time to apportion to the myriad of interests that wish to be heard. Thus you should consider steps that might increase your opportunities to state your position. Political contributions are most often made with this end in mind. Many people incorrectly believe that contributions to campaigns are made with the goal of "buying" candidates' allegiance. However, owing to the campaign finance restrictions, it is difficult for individuals or organizations to wield political clout through direct contributions. Why then do so many individuals and PACs contribute the maximum amount allowed by law? Put yourself in the shoes of a member of Congress. If you had thousands of persons knocking on your door, wouldn't you be more likely to entertain those who had supported your election campaign? Campaign contributions most often are made just to gain this form of potential *access*. Thus one strategy for clearing your communication channels is to support the campaigns of your senators and representative. Of course, such a strategy might backfire if the candidate you support loses his or her campaign. For this reason constituent groups with sufficient finances sometimes support the campaigns of all candidates vying in the election rather than simply that of the ideologically preferred individual.

You might contemplate other methods to increase your opportunities to communicate with a member of Congress. One effective although often expensive means to achieve this goal is to employ an ex-colleague or a friend of the member of Congress to serve as your lobbyist.[24] Usually a member of Congress is more responsive to an invitation to talk from someone he or she knows or has worked with closely than from a stranger. Another strategy is to enlarge the political visibility of your interest. This strategy can be accomplished by increasing the number of voters you purport to represent and by increasing their participation in the communication effort. The former can be achieved by enlisting supporters of the cause or by forming coalitions with established groups championing the same cause. The latter can be accomplished through a variety of grassroots techniques, as discussed in Chapter 1.

A final effective strategy is to convince the executive branch to take steps to have the idea introduced in Congress. This is rarely achieved by communicating directly with the president. Rather, certain key persons who work closely with him or are trusted by him must be persuaded to advance your cause. Depending on the issue, your approach may involve discussions with members of the White House staff, with personnel at the Office of Management and Budget (the budgetary and regulatory policy arm of the executive branch), or with other persons holding influence within the executive branch. Recognize that these individuals, possibly to a more acute degree than members of Congress, have limited time resources to apportion, thereby making access a key issue once again. Also, this route to having legislation introduced is obviously more circuitous than dealing directly with the members of Congress. Thus this avenue generally is most advantageous when the channels to one's own senators and representative have been closed.

An idea is embodied as a *bill* and may be introduced in the Senate by a senator or in the House by a representative. Except for taxing and appropriations bills, which must originate in the House, bills may be initiated in either chamber or simultaneously in both. For the forthcoming discussion we will assume that the bill is first introduced in the House. You need only be aware that when legislation originates in the Senate, the process is simply reversed.

After a representative introduces a bill in the House, the Speaker of the House usually refers the bill to the *committee* having jurisdiction over the bill's contents. A committee structure has been developed in both the House and the Senate so that sufficient in-depth consideration may be given by each body to the myriad of complex ideas that come before them annually. Currently, as depicted in Table 2-1, the House has twenty-two permanent or standing committees, and the Senate has sixteen. The composition of each committee in terms of political party affiliations roughly approximates the relative percentages of the parties within the body as a whole. Essentially, the Democrats and the Republicans have special selection committees or caucuses that determine who from their respective parties will sit on the standing committees. As members of Congress often desire to sit on particular standing committees, because of prestige, relevance to constituents, or personal preference, they may at times become beholden to the "party line" in order to achieve the preferred committee memberships. Similarly, committee chairpersons are selected by the caucus of the political party with majority membership in the body. Thus in 1989 all committee chairpersons in both the House and the Senate were Democrats by virtue of that party's majority status in each chamber. Although the caucus often selects as chairpersons the committee members from its party with the most seniority on respective standing committees, this result is not guaranteed. Thus, again the political party can command some allegiance with its positions through the selection mechanism.

The bill may receive its first consideration in the standing committee However, the usual course is for the committee chairperson to refer it to a *subcommittee* of the standing committee. Subcommittees are a further sub specialization within Congress so that it may competently deal with the ever increasing complexity of federal issues. For instance, the House Judiciary standing committee has seven subcommittees: (1) Civil and Constitutiona Rights; (2) Criminal Justice; (3) Administrative Law and Governmental Rela tions; (4) Monopolies and Commercial Law; (5) Courts, Civil Liberties, anc the Administration of Justice; (6) Crime; and (7) Immigration, Refugees anc

TABLE 2-1   Committees of the House of Representatives and Senate

HOUSE OF REPRESENTATIVES

Committee	Number of Members
Agriculture	43
Appropriations	57
Armed Services	51
Banking, Finance, and Urban Affairs	50
Budget	35
District of Columbia	11
Education and Labor	34
Energy and Commerce	42
Foreign Affairs	42
Government Operations	39
House Administration	19
Interior and Insular Affairs	37
Judiciary	35
Merchant Marine and Fisheries	42
Post Office and Civil Service	21
Public Works and Transportation	50
Rules	13
Science, Space and Technology	45
Small Business	44
Standards of Official Conduct	12
Veterans Affairs	34
Ways and Means	36

SENATE

Committee	Number of Members
Agriculture	18
Appropriations	29
Armed Services	20
Banking, Finance, and Urban Affairs	18
Budget	22
Commerce, Science, and Transportation	20
Energy and Natural Resources	19
Environment and Public Works	16
Finance	20
Foreign Relations	20
Governmental Affairs	14
Judiciary	14
Labor and Human Resources	16
Rules and Administration	16
Small Business	18
Veterans Affairs	11

SOURCE: Compiled from data reported in Congressional Quarterly (February 28, 1987 and November 8, 1987).

International Law. Thus a bill dealing with antitrust reform logically would be sent to the Monopolies and Commercial Law Subcommittee for its first consideration. Subcommittee membership composition tends to approximate that of the full chamber in terms of party loyalty. Likewise, the chairperson is selected by the majority party's appropriate caucus or selection committee.

Typically the subcommittee will hold a public *hearing* on the bill to gather information. Testimony is invited from government officials, outside experts, and special-interest groups. Also, other parties at their own request may be permitted to testify. Lobbyists often fill the subcommittee halls during the hearings because the predisposition of the members toward the bill may sometimes be determined from their questions and statements during the testimony period. After the hearing the subcommittee will meet in open session to discuss the bill and *mark up* the bill with any amendments it deems appropriate. A vote is then taken by the members on whether to recommend that the full committee approve the bill with the mark-up amendments, or to urge that it table or reject the bill.

The bill next proceeds to the full committee for its appraisal. The committee may simply ratify the actions of the subcommittee, or it can hold another set of hearings followed by its own mark-up session. If the committee members are in favor of the bill, it will be reported to the full House as amended. On the other hand, if the members are opposed to the bill, they will usually table it, although at times they will report it with an unfavorable recommendation. Accompanying a reported bill will be the *committee report*, which explains the committee's perception of the bill on a line-by-line basis. If the bill ever becomes law, this is a very important document because it often contains the most definitive statements of congressional intent behind the law. Therefore, it may be used by courts to interpret vague language in the law.

A reported bill next proceeds through the Rules Committee, which schedules the bill for chamber floor debate and sets conditions on that debate. After parliamentary discussion, including possibly the drafting of amendments, the bill is approved or disapproved by the chamber. If approved by the House, the bill, now called an act, will be sent to the Senate for similar appraisal. In this way the act will be sent to a Senate subcommittee for hearings and markup and through a committee to the full Senate chamber unless the committee decides to table it.

For congressional action on legislation to be complete, the House and the Senate must approve the terms of the act in exactly the same form. If the Senate votes in favor of the idea, it often does so on the basis of an amended act. Thus the act, as approved by the Senate, must be sent back to the House for its approval of the amendments. If this step cannot be achieved, the differences must be worked out in a *conference committee,* comprising House and Senate committee members who supported the idea. If and when the conference committee comes to an agreement about the act's terms, the act as amended by the conference committee is sent to both chambers for a vote. If both vote in favor of the act, then the act is finally ready for presidential action. If not, it's back to another conference committee, or the act may simply stagnate with no further action.

It should be clear that the passage of legislation by Congress is not a simple matter. Also, it must be recognized that because of the committee structure, blocking a bill is much easier than achieving passage. Usually, when a subcommittee gives a negative recommendation to a bill, the full committee will concur. However, the reverse cannot be so routinely expected. Also, the full chamber most often will abide by a negative report of a committee, assuming the bill is reported at all. Therefore, if you are opposed to an introduced idea, you need only convince a majority of the proper subcommittee members to perceive the issue in your light. This majority may consist of only ten or fifteen members of the full House. In the event of failure here, you can try the same strategies at the full committee level and then proceed to the proper Senate subcommittee and committee members, if necessary. The idea's advocate, on the other hand, must achieve backing at all levels of the process.

The committee structure also explains why certain members so easily can raise funds for their reelection campaigns. Given the importance of committee actions, interest groups must be very careful to ensure access to the members who sit on committees that potentially could review ideas having a large impact on the group. As discussed before, campaign contributions often are used to achieve this goal. The members who sit on committees making decisions that will have wide and significant impacts, such as the taxation committees, raise significant amounts of money from ideological proponents and opponents alike, since the need to discuss issues with these members overshadows any ideological differences that might exist. The result is that it is very difficult for challengers to unseat incumbents who sit on powerful committees.

Once legislation is approved by the House and the Senate in the same form, the road still is not completed, since presidential action is required. The president has three options regarding an act sent to him: (1) he may sign it, at which time it becomes law; (2) he may *veto* it and return it to Congress; or (3) he may take no action for ten days, after which it becomes law without his clear endorsement. In order for a vetoed act to become law, two-thirds of the members of both houses must vote in favor of the act despite the president's negative appraisal. Given how difficult approval based on majority votes often is, you can imagine how hard a veto override is to achieve. Table 2-2 vividly illustrates this fact. An override is especially difficult when one of the houses is controlled by members of the same political party as the president. Thus a final formidable avenue of attack for those that oppose an idea is through the president.

If this process were not by itself sufficiently frustrating for an issue to become policy through congressional action, one more step usually must be

TABLE 2–2   Presidential Vetoes and Veto Overrides 1923 – 88

PRESIDENT	VETOES	VETOES PER YEAR	VETOES OVERRIDDEN	% VETOES OVERRIDDEN
Coolidge	50	9	4	8%
Hoover	37	9	3	8%
Roosevelt	635	52	9	1%
Truman	250	32	12	5%
Eisenhower	181	25	2	1%
Kennedy	21	9	0	0%
Johnson	30	6	0	0%
Nixon	42	8	6	14%
Ford	72	27	12	17%
Carter	31	8	2	6%
Reagan* (as of Nov. 8, 1988)	74	9	9	12%

SOURCE: Statistical Abstract of the United States, Table no. 405, (1987)
*SOURCE: Congressional Quarterly Weekly Report, Oct. 25, 1986, p. 2685, and data accumulated by authors from Congressional Quarterly Weekly Report, Nov. 1, 1986 – Nov. 12, 1988.

achieved. Just because Congress authorizes that a program become law does not mean that the program will receive the necessary funding to achieve its objectives. Therefore, in addition, the idea must receive *appropriations* through the budget process. The budget process of Congress has been highly criticized for its haphazard approach, and numerous modifications have been proposed to remedy it.[25] In 1974 one such recommended technique was adopted in an attempt to unify the authorizing and appropriating efforts of Congress. This procedure called for the development of an initial budget resolution by Congress, relying on intensive deliberations by budget committees. The resultant budget resolution set general budget guidelines within which authorizing and appropriations committees were supposed to make specific program and capital outlay decisions. However, the budget was merely advisory and was not effective in controlling congressional action.[26] In 1985 the budget process was again altered, this time requiring more discipline on the parts of the authorizing and appropriations committees to abide by the overall budget targets established by the initial budget resolution.[27] Whether this modification will serve to streamline and rationalize the budget process is an open question. Still the fact remains that one who is against an idea can attempt to frustrate it by cutting the purse strings for it. This is most effectively accomplished, under current congressional budget practices, by persuading the members of the budget committees to reduce overall budget levels or convincing the members of the appropriations committees to provide insufficient funding for the specific program authorized to implement the idea.

Also, note that appropriations legislation, like all legislation, must be approved by the president before it may be implemented. Thus the budget once approved by Congress is subject to his veto. However, unlike governors in many states, the president does not have the *line-item veto* — the power to veto portions of an appropriations package while retaining funding levels for preferred programs. Instead, the president must either accept the budget in its entirety or veto the total package. President Reagan strongly advocated that Congress give him line-item veto power so that he could cut funding for "unnecessary" programs while allowing the rest of government to proceed. However, Congress did not acquiesce in this wish.

The political affiliations of the members of Congress, with reference to that of the president, may bear overall importance as to the prospect for new legislation. That is, if both houses are dominated by members of the same party, then one might expect that the two houses will more often agree on the terms of certain ideas for policy programs. If the president is of the same political persuasion, then it is likely that he, too, will support those programs. On the other hand, when the president represents the other party, vetoes should become more prevalent, since it is likely that the president's ideological framework will not coincide with that of the Congress. To complete the picture, one would expect that fewer pieces of legislation would be sent to the president when the two houses are dominated by different parties. These concepts are historically supported by observing that the most significant waves of federal regulation occurred when both houses were dominated by Democrats while a Democratic president was in office. This topic will be pursued further in Chapter 3.

The future strength of this observed relationship may be weakening, however. With the increasing ability of candidates to finance their campaigns independently from the political parties, their strict adherence to party lines is less predictable. The rise of PACs, in particular, has contributed to this phenomenon. Thus a Democratic president, for instance, can no longer assume that a Democratic Congress will support his policies. However, even with the rising level of individual autonomy assumed by members of Congress, Democrats and Republicans still tend to be separately bonded somewhat in that Democrats, on average, are more liberal while Republicans are more conservative. Also, political parties do have leverage to command allegiance for key issues because they continue to be important contributors to the election efforts of many candidates and also because of their input into the committee selection process.

Other Significant Congressional Policy Powers

In addition to affecting public policy by controlling domestic legislation and the purse strings for the federal government, the Congress is involved in the policy process in several other ways. One means is through the Senate's power to *confirm* the president's nominees for the federal courts, including the Supreme Court, and for the top policy-making positions in the federal administrative agencies. Usually, hearings are held by the Senate committee having jurisdiction over the nominee's policy area. For example, court nominees are scrutinized by the Senate Judiciary committee, while nominees for the Federal Reserve Board are considered by the Senate Banking, Finance, and Urban Affairs Committee. The full Senate, then, makes a decision based on the recommendations of the committee. Most nominees do receive approval by the Senate. Indeed, between 1941 and 1971 only twenty-eight nominees were actually rejected.[28] However, the specter of a public hearing, especially one to be held by a Senate with an opposing political majority, may serve to restrain the range of nominees actually considered by the president. Also, hundreds of nominees have been withdrawn by presidents when the Senate outcry has been vocal. For instance, after President Reagan's nominee for the assistant secretary of state for human rights, Ernest W. Lefever, was negatively evaluated by a thirteen-to-four margin by the Senate Foreign Relations Committee, his name was withdrawn before the vote of the full Senate. Also, as the Senate's rejection of President Reagan's Supreme Court nominee Robert Bork illustrates, this congressional body will use its ultimate authority if necessary. Therefore, the Senate approval process does serve to restrict the president's influence on public policies.

As will be discussed further in Chapter 3, the Congress serves important *oversight* functions over the operations of the federal government. Administrative agencies are required to submit to Congress periodic reports divulging the details of program implementation. Also, through informal contacts with administrative officials, members of Congress obtain a wealth of information regarding government operations. Such information can lead to congressional investigations and oversight hearings when members of Congress become concerned that the policy objectives of legislation are not being carried out faithfully. For example, a panel of the House Energy and Commerce Committee held public hearings in 1985 to question Environmental Protection Agency officials about reports that leaks at hazardous waste facilities were not being detected because of noncompliance with monitoring regulations. Given the public nature of such hearings and the attention brought to them by the media, they often are very effective in molding government activities without any formal directives from Congress.

Recently there has been controversy about the extent of Congress's jurisdiction over foreign affairs.[29] The Constitution states that the power over foreign matters is shared with the executive, but the limits for each institution are sometimes vague. The president has the power to nominate ambassadors but needs Senate approval. Also, treaties negotiated by the president must be approved by two-thirds of the Senate before becoming the supreme law of the land along with the Constitution. In addition, Congress is explicitly given the power to regulate foreign commerce. However, many activities historically considered as part of foreign affairs are not clearly defined in the Constitution. For instance, there is no reference as to which body has the power to recognize governments, to institute and break foreign relations, to regulate foreign entry, or to protect American citizens abroad.

Also, the president is the commander-in-chief of the military while only Congress can declare war and fund military operations. But what happens when the president takes a military action and informs Congress after the fact, leaving it little choice but to approve the action? Congress has passed legislation, the War Powers Act of 1973, which purports to limit the president's authority to take such actions. However, disputes between the executive and Congress over the constitutionality of the War Powers Act and the applicability of its provisions to various military endeavors have demonstrated that the act is merely a framework for executive-legislative relations, and is not a definitive solution to the problem.[30] Also, note that the Korean and Vietnam wars were never formally declared by Congress although they were funded by Congress and backed by congressional resolutions. Over the past fifty years the executive has progressively increased its authority in foreign matters with little definitive objection from Congress, primarily because of its superior information and expertise in daily foreign operations.[31] The current unresolved question is to what extent Congress may reclaim its eroded authority over foreign matters.

As explained in the previous section, Congress can exercise control over the judiciary when it disagrees with a statutory interpretation by amending the statute. However, judicial review raises more significant problems. The clearest option of Congress is to start the constitutional-amendment process. However, obtaining a two-thirds vote of both chambers is usually very difficult. Recent attempts in Congress to legalize forms of voluntary school prayer, for instance, have failed to achieve such supermajorities. Also, even if the requisite vote is obtained, three-fourths of the state legislatures still must approve the amendment. The demise of the Equal Rights Amendment attests to the difficulties posed by this process. A less frequently contemplated alternative is for Congress, through legislation signed by the president, to expand the court system or increase the number of Supreme Court justices and fill the new positions with judges who are loyal to the wishes of Congress and the president. The threat by Franklin Roosevelt to pack the Supreme Court in just this way may have contributed to the Court's policy reversals in the 1930s.[32]

THE EXECUTIVE

The Constitution provides that the executive power of the United States is to be vested in a president. In this capacity the president's most important function is to ensure that federal laws are faithfully carried out. However, the job entails other policy-making functions as well. In this section we will briefly discuss the ways the president makes and affects public policy. Do not infer from the relative brevity of this account that the president is somehow a less important policy force than the courts or the Congress. In fact, just the opposite may be true. For this reason Chapter 3 is entirely devoted to administrative agencies, the primary function of which is to execute the laws under the watchful eye of the president. The core discussion of the president's role in the public-policy process is deferred to that chapter.

Congress has created two types of administrative agencies to carry out certain functions of government: *executive* agencies and *independent* agencies. The president has a variety of techniques to influence the policy actions of these agencies. For both forms of agencies the president appoints, with the consent of the Senate, the key policy-making officials. In this way he can attempt to control the policy actions of the agencies by filling top positions with administrators whose philosophies mirror his own. For instance, when President Reagan took office he tried to change dramatically the character of the agencies by putting "deregulators" at the helms of the agencies.[33]   The appointments of James Watt to head the Interior Department, Anne Gorsuch to head the Environmental Protection Agency, and William Baxter to take charge of the antitrust division of the Justice Department were just some of the notable instances of presidential authority. A prime distinction between executive and independent agencies involves the president's capacity to fire principal administrators. For the executive agencies, the policy heads serve at the pleasure of the president. Thus executive agency administrators, once in office, remain beholden to the wishes of the president. Independent agency heads, on the other hand, serve for a predetermined term of years. The Federal Trade Commission, for instance, is led by five commissioners who each serve for five-year terms and can be removed only for "good cause." The president, therefore, has less control over the actions of FTC commissioners because after they are appointed they do not depend on his goodwill to keep their jobs. Also, unlike executive administrators, independent agency commissioners are held over from previous administrations, so a president inherits them and can replace them only when their terms expire.

The budgets for administrative agencies to carry out their duties are ultimately determined through congressional legislation. However, the executive branch is a pivotal player in the appropriations process. The annual budget requests of both forms of administrative agencies are made first to the *Office of Management and Budget* (OMB), a body under the direct control of the president. OMB then formulates the president's budget using the requests as a guide. This budget is submitted to Congress by the president, and forms the basis of its budget discussions. Although Congress is not bound by the president's budget plan, it does tend to shape the final congressional budget by serving as the foundation to which changes are adopted. And, of course, if Congress threatens to deviate far from the president's plan, he does have the veto mechanism to hold over it.

The next chapter will explain how many administrative agencies, both executive and independent, have legislative authority through their powers to promulgate rules and regulations. With regard to executive agencies, President Reagan, through executive orders, assumed significant controls over their rule-making judgments. First, any major rule proposed by an executive agency must be submitted to OMB so that a cost/benefit analysis may be undertaken by that body.[34] If OMB does not believe that the potential benefits to society outweigh the potential costs, the agency will be pressured to withdraw the rule. Second, executive agencies must submit annually to OMB an overview of their regulatory goals and information regarding their contemplated regulatory actions.[35] Based on these submissions, the administration's regulatory program for the year is developed by OMB. Thereafter any rule submitted by an executive agency to OMB that does not follow the design of the regulatory program will be sent back for reconsideration. The assumption by the president of these powers to screen executive agency rules has raised a substantial policy debate, since such policy-making authority may not have been contemplated by Congress in creating the executive agencies.[36] The basis for this controversy and its possible outcome will be considered further in Chapter 3.

Besides his influence over administrative agencies, the president affects public policy in other important ways. Many of these methods have been discussed already. For instance, the president affects judicial policies through his nomination of justices to the federal bench. Also, the president interacts with Congress in its policy determinations. A substantial portion of the legislative ideas introduced into the Congress originate from the executive office and cabinet agencies as part of the president's annual legislative package. In addition, the president can command adherence to his policy objectives through the veto. Although a veto technically is not absolute, given that it may be overriden by Congress, the fact that in the history of the country less than 5 percent of presidential vetoes have been overridden speaks to the president's substantial power.[37] Also, as previously discussed, the president shares significant policy controls with Congress in the area of foreign affairs.

One final component of executive control, which cannot be overlooked, involves the president's ability to act as a spokesperson for the American people. Especially during the Reagan years the capacity of the president to achieve his objectives by communicating through the media with U.S. citizens became evident. By virtue of his constant mention in the press and his presence on television, an effective spokesperson like Ronald Reagan may convince voters to support executive policies that are treated roughly by Congress. In this way the president may become the epitome of the grassroots campaigner. The overhaul of the tax code and aid to the Nicaraguan rebel force are only two of the many policies that were successfully assisted by President Reagan's communication skills. In conjunction with these grassroots appeals, the executive office and the cabinet agencies are staffed with lobbyists skilled in persuading Congress to adhere to the president's directives. As with any lobbyist, their success depends on the benefits that their ideas offer to the relevant members of Congress. Given all the above forces under the control of the president, such benefits are often easily recognizable.

CONCLUSION

All of the traditional public-policy institutions have an important role in the formulation of public policy. One branch alone does not have the power to dictate policy. This is the important concept of checks and balances bred into the Constitution. Thus a businessperson would be naive in attempting to influence policy by concentrating on just one branch of government. Effective interaction with government requires a unified and simultaneous approach.

The interwoven structure of the American policy institutions has become even more complex with the rise of administrative agencies. How do these organizations operate, and how might they affect your business operations? What, if anything, can you do when these agencies make policy decisions that might damage your future prospects? Has the American system of checks and balances survived in the face of the rapid growth in administrative agencies? These are some of the critical questions facing business today. The next chapter provides some insights into them.

NOTES

1. *S.E.C.* v. *Texas Gulf Sulphur Co.*, 401 F. 2d 833 (2d Cir. 1968).
2. *Chiarella* v. *U.S.*, 445 U.S. 222 (1980); *Dirks* v. *S.E.C.*, 463 U.S. 646 (1983). These principles were recently reaffirmed by the Supreme Court in *Carpenter* v. *U.S.*, 56 U.S.L.W. 4007 (Nov. 16, 1987).
3. *Wall Street Journal*, August 10, 1987, sec. 1, p. 2.
4. 5 U.S. (1 Cranch) 137 (1803).
5. *Adkins* v. *Children's Hospital*, 261 U.S. 525 (1923).
6. *Lochner* v. *New York*, 198 U.S. 45 (1905).
7. In February 1937 President Roosevelt presented Congress with a judiciary plan that would have enabled him to appoint a new federal judge for any judge over seventy years old who did not retire. This plan would have allowed him to select six new Supreme Court justices, enough to ensure approval of his New Deal programs. Almost simultaneously, Justice Owen Roberts switched his position on the applicability of the Due Process Clause to economic legislation. Paul Brest, *Processes of*

Constitutional Decisionmaking (Boston, Mass.: Little, Brown & Co., 1975), pp. 743-45.
8. *West Coast Hotel Co.* v. *Parrish*, 300 U.S. 379 (1937).
9. *Plessy* v. *Ferguson*, 163 U.S. 537 (1896).
10. 347 U.S. 483 (1954).
11. *Schechter Poultry Corp.* v. *U.S.*, 295 U.S. 495 (1935).
12. *Carter* v. *Carter Coal Co.*, 298 U.S. 238 (1936).
13. *N.L.R.B.* v. *Jones & Laughlin Steel Co.*, 301 U.S. 1 (1937).
14. *Wickard* v. *Filburn*, 317 U.S. 111 (1942).
15. *Katzenbach* v. *McClung*, 379 U.S. 294 (1964).
16. *Garcia* v. *San Antonio Metropolitan Transit Authority,*469 U.S. 528 (1985).
17. *Roe* v. *Wade*, 410 U.S. 113 (1973).
18. Brest, *Constitutional Decisionmaking*, p. 76.
19. Ibid.
20. Browning, "Reagan Molds the Federal Court in His Own Image," *ABA Journal* 71 (August 1985), pp. 60-64.
21. Bob Woodward and Scott Armstrong, *The Brethren* (New York, Simon & Schuster, 1979), pp. 170-71.

22. "The Scalia Surprise," *Washington Post National Weekly Edition*, March 23, 1987.

23. Article III, section 1 of the U.S. Constitution provides for the Supreme Court. Thus Congress's power with respect to the Supreme Court is limited to altering its structure.

24. Retired members of Congress soon may have less freedom to communicate with current members under legislation expected to be signed by President Bush.

25. *Wall Street Journal*, February 26, 1987, sec. 1, p.1.

26. Ibid.

27. The Balanced Budget and Emergency Deficit Control Act, Public Law 99-177 (December 12, 1985). For a complete discussion of the budgetary process, see Stanley E. Collender, *The Guide to the Federal Budget: Fiscal 1988* (Washington, D.C.: Urban Institute Press, 1987).

28. Charles O. Jones, *The United States Congress: People, Place, and Policy*

(Homewood, Ill.: Dorsey Press, 1982), p. 383, n.4.

29. *Wall Street Journal*, July 20, 1987, sec. 2, p.44.; *San Francisco Chronicle*, February 4, 1987, sec. A, p. 1.

30. Louis Fisher, "The War Powers Resolution of 1973," in *American Politics, Policies, and Priorities*, ed. Alan Shank (Boston: Allyn & Bacon, Inc. 1988), pp. 446-53.

31. *Wall Street Journal*, July 20, 1987, Sec. 2, p. 44.

32. Brest, *Constitutional Decisionmaking*, pp. 743-45.

33. *Wall Street Journal*, February 10, 1982, sec. 1, p.1.

34. Executive Order 12291 (February 1981).

35. Executive Order 12498 (January 1985).

36. Michael D. Reagan, *Regulation: The Politics of Policy* (Boston, Mass.: Little, Brown & Co., 1987), p. 166.

37. Rogene A. Buchholz, *Essentials of Public Policy for Management* (Englewood Cliffs, N.J.: Prentice Hall, 1985), p. 123

CHAPTER THREE
Administrative Agencies and the Regulatory Process

INTRODUCTION

In the preceding two chapters we have examined the process and institutions involved in the making of public policy in the United States. This chapter focuses on the institutions and process involved in the *implementation* of public policies articulated by Congress and the executive branch. Administrative agencies are directly linked to the public-policy process since they are the means Congress has chosen to implement many of the public policies or statutes it has enacted. The need for institutions to implement public policy arises from the fact that Congress is primarily a deliberative and policy-making body and as such has neither the time nor expertise to carry out its policies on a day-to-day basis. As a solution to the implementation problem, Congress began creating administrative agencies as early as 1789, although as we shall see, the first great wave of government regulation of business by means of administrative agencies did not come about until the late nineteenth century.

It is important that business managers be knowledgeable about administrative agencies and the regulatory process. Government regulation at the local, state, and federal levels has a very substantial impact on the operation of business firms, from small sole proprietorships to the largest corporations. Just as business firms have always paid close attention to internal factors affecting decision-making, such as accounting, financial, marketing, and production issues, today they must pay close attention to external factors affecting decision-making. Chief among these factors are the regulatory public policies affecting business that are enacted by Congress and implemented by federal administrative agencies. Many of these regulatory statutes were enacted in the 1960s and 1970s, including the Civil Rights Act of 1964, the Clean Air and Water Acts, the Consumer Product Safety Act, and the Occupational Safety and Health Act.[1] While these public policies have clearly resulted in substantial benefits to American society, they have also imposed substantial compliance costs on business, estimated in 1979 at $100 billion per year.[2] Inflation alone (assuming that the amount of regulation remained constant) suggests that an updated estimate for regulatory compliance costs in the late 1980s would exceed $200 billion per year.

The general public also is substantially affected by administrative agencies and the regulatory statutes they enforce. First, many of these statutes were enacted in response to demands from the electorate and special-interest groups that Congress do something about problems such as air and water pollution, employment discrimination, health and safety in the workplace, and improperly designed or manufactured consumer products. Second, many of the statutes enacted to address these problems have resulted in substantial compliance costs for business, which are often passed on to the consumer in the form of higher prices for products or services. Thus the consumer has a clear interest in the effectiveness and efficiency of agencies and regulation. Third, because administrative agencies are powerful institutions with functions that have important and far-reaching effects on business firms and the general public, both have an interest in understanding how agencies operate, the sources of agency power, and the effectiveness of checks or controls on agency power.

Defining Basic Terms

Before we proceed to a discussion of agencies and the regulatory process, it will be helpful to define some basic terms. One commentator has broadly defined *regulation* as follows: "a state-imposed limitation on the discretion that may be exercised by individuals or organizations, which is supported by the threat of sanction."[3] In contrast to this broad definition, regulation can be more narrowly defined as a law enacted by an administrative agency. Both definitions are useful, and you will find that the distinction between the broad and narrow definitions of regulation will usually be apparent from the context of the discussion. As we shall see later in the chapter, many agencies have been delegated legislative authority by Congress to enact rules and regulations.[4] Compare the narrow definition of regulation with the term *statute*, which is defined as a law or public policy enacted by a legislative body such as Congress. Thus government regulation of business occurs through the enactment of regulatory statutes (public policies) by Congress as well as through the enactment of rules and regulations by the administrative agencies. Moreover, as we saw in Chapter 2, both regulatory statutes and agency regulations are subject to interpretation by the courts when disputes arise as to their meaning.

Congress creates an administrative agency by passing a statute, called an *enabling act*, that sets forth the public policy (for instance, clean air and water objectives) that the agency is charged with implementing. The enabling act also specifies the agency name and general organizational structure, its internal operating rules, the powers and functions that have been delegated to it by Congress, and whether it will be an independent agency or an agency within the executive branch. Of course, in many cases Congress chooses to assign the task of implementing a new statute to an existing agency.

What then is an *administrative agency*? It has been defined as "a governmental authority, other than a court and other than a legislative body, which affects the rights of private parties through either adjudication or rulemaking."[5] In most cases it will be called a commission, board, department, agency, administration, or bureau, such as the Federal Trade Commission, the National Labor Relations Board, the Department of Justice, or the Environmental Protection Agency.

Types of Regulation

Government regulation of business can be divided into two broad categories: economic regulation and social regulation. *Economic regulation* includes those regulatory statutes and associated agencies that are primarily intended to ensure certain economic goals such as competitive market behavior, regulation of industrywide practices, and good labor-management relations. Many of these regulatory statutes were enacted at the turn of the century and during the New Deal period. They include the Sherman and Clayton Antitrust Acts (1890 and 1914), the Federal Trade Commission Act (1914), the Interstate Commerce Act (1887), the Securities Acts of 1933 and 1934, the Banking Act of 1933, and the National Labor Relations Act (1935), to name but a few.

In the mid-1960s Congress began to respond to changing societal attitudes and the growing importance and power of interest groups supporting civil rights, environmental, health and safety in the workplace, consumer protection, and senior citizens' issues by enacting regulatory statutes that addressed primarily social rather than economic concerns. These policies have been termed *social regulation*.

The regulatory statutes that make up the category of social regulation often have economywide effects. Thus unlike many economic regulations, they have effects that are not limited to one industry. Examples of such economywide regulatory statutes and their associated enforcement agencies include the Clean Air and Water Acts enforced by the Environmental Protection Agency (EPA); the Civil Rights Act of 1964, which prohibits race and sex discrimination in employment and public accommodations and is enforced by the Equal Employment Opportunity Commission (EEOC); the Consumer Product Safety Act, which protects the public from unreasonably hazardous consumer products and is enforced by the Consumer Product Safety Commission (CPSC); and the Occupational Safety and Health Act, which sets health and safety standards in the workplace and is enforced by the Occupational Safety and Health Administration (OSHA).

While most of the social regulation enacted since the mid-1960s has resulted in substantial benefits to society, a number of criticisms have also been raised. First, because most social regulation applies across industry lines, the agency charged with enforcing the regulatory statute may not be sufficiently informed or concerned about the uneven costs of compliance or the unique problems affecting a particular industry or company. Second, the broader economic costs of social regulation such as adverse effects on productivity, economic growth, employment, inflation, and increased costs to the consumer may not be objectively weighed against benefits if the agency enforcing the regulatory statute is too easily influenced by powerful interest groups that benefit from the statute. Just as agencies that enforce economic regulation affecting one particular industry run the risk of being "captured" (the theory that the industry may eventually "capture," or unduly influence, the agency charged with its regulation), so also do agencies implementing social regulation face the risk of having their objectivity compromised by interest groups that strongly support the social goals of the regulatory statute being enforced by the agency.[6] For example, the EPA's efforts to substantially reduce air- and water-pollution levels in the United States have required some corporations (for example, steel and chemical companies) to invest heavily in pollution-abatement equipment. This may result in less money available for investment in new and more productive plant and equipment. Some have argued that certain EPA air-and water-pollution regulations have not been objectively analyzed in terms of their costs and benefits owing to the political power of environmental-interest groups.

THE CONSTITUTIONAL BASIS FOR ADMINISTRATIVE AGENCIES

In the American system of government all governmental power derives from the foundation document of our republic, the United States Constitution. As we discussed in Chapter 2, the powers and authority of Congress are set forth in Article I, Section 8 of the Constitution. Particularly significant for our study of administrative agencies are the Commerce Clause and the Necessary and Proper Clause of Section 8, and the Supremacy Clause of Article VI, for they have been broadly interpreted by the United States Supreme Court as investing the Congress with extensive power to regulate both interstate commercial activity and intrastate commercial activity that affects interstate commerce. The court has also made it clear that commerce and commercial activity is synonymous with business. Thus given the Supreme Court's broad interpretation of the Commerce Clause since the mid-1930s and the fact that any properly enacted (that is, otherwise constitutional) federal statute enjoys supremacy over and voids any conflicting state statute, it is clear that Congress has ample authority to enact statutes regulating American business and labor if it chooses to do so. As we saw in Chapter 1, whether or not Congress chooses to enact a statute is often a function of the many factors and forces at work in the public-policy process.

Although Congress's constitutional authority to legislate is clearly set forth in the Constitution, administrative agencies are not mentioned. The constitutional validity of the powers granted to administrative agencies by Congress has been challenged on two separate grounds: (1) the executive, legislative, and judicial powers that Congress has granted to the agencies violate the Separation of Powers Doctrine; and (2) Congress cannot delegate its lawmaking function to the administrative agencies. The Supreme Court has concluded that neither challenge should be allowed to interfere with or diminish the powers and functions that Congress has delegated to the administrative agencies. We now examine these two constitutional challenges in more detail.

The Separation of Powers Doctrine

The problem of whether and to what extent Congress can grant to administrative agencies legislative, executive, and judicial authority while still complying with the Separation of Powers Doctrine embodied in the Constitution has been defined by two leading scholars of administrative law as follows:

> The Anglo-American separation of powers principle not only distinguishes between those who make general laws and those who implement and apply them, but also reserves a special role for the independent judiciary in the process....
> These traditional principles and practices have been threatened by the creation of administrative agencies which combine lawmaking, adjudicative, and executive functions. Agencies have been given the authority to promulgate legislative type rules and simultaneously to apply these rules in given cases. They have been invested with the power to investigate and prosecute, and with the power to decide individual controversies. Responsibility for resolving disputes between private parties has been shifted from courts to agencies....
> The basic question ... is how courts can reconcile the combination of functions characteristic of modern administrative agencies with the separation of powers principles underlying the federal Constitution. The Constitution, after all, describes and distinguishes "legislative Powers" in Article I (Congress), the "executive Power" in Article II (the President), and the "judicial Power" in Article III (the federal courts), but it contains no article authorizing administrative agencies. While the Constitution does not mandate a "watertight" system of separation but does provide in some instances for sharing of power among different branches (consider the President's power to veto legislation), the Founders certainly never contemplated an institutional beast such as the

Interstate Commerce Commission or the Federal Trade Commission. Yet, the "living" Constitution has often been interpreted by judges to accommodate the practical exigencies of an emerging nation. Defenders of the administrative process have rejected the historic principle of separation of powers as anachronistic in an urban, industrialized society, claiming, for example, that in order effectively to manage and control the complex modern economy government must emulate techniques of integrated, expert, hierarchical management practiced by business corporations.[7]

While the Separation of Powers Doctrine has raised questions about the nature and amount of power that Congress can delegate to agencies, the Supreme Court has recognized the practical importance of agencies as managerial entities in carrying out the public policies enacted by Congress. As a result, it has declared (via its power of judicial review) that Congress's delegation of executive, legislative, and judicial powers to the administrative agencies is constitutional.

The Delegation of Legislative Power to Agencies

In order to allow for the effective implementation of the public policies it enacts, Congress delegates to the administrative agencies the power to issue rules and regulations that flesh out and fill in the details of the general policies and guidelines contained in some statutes. This agency rule-making power involves the delegation of a portion of the legislative or lawmaking power that the Constitution grants to the legislative branch.

The Supreme Court has concluded that the delegation of legislative power to an administrative agency (sometimes referred to as quasi-legislative authority) is constitutional so long as two requirements are contained in the statute that delegates such power to an agency:

1. The language of delegation must be *definite* and *sufficiently clear* so that a reviewing court will be able to determine the limits or boundaries of an agency's rule-making authority. This requirement is for purposes of constitutional due process.
2. The delegation of quasi-legislative (or rule-making) authority must be *limited*. This requires that the statute contain *standards* by which a reviewing court can determine whether the limitations have been exceeded.

As is reasonably obvious, the requirements set forth above overlap considerably. Moreover, although the Supreme Court states that the language of delegation should be clear and definite, in fact the Court has repeatedly approved broad language as being sufficiently definite to meet the demands of the due process clause. Similarly, the Court has been willing to accept broadly worded standards as meeting the requirement of a limited delegation of legislative power.

Essentially, the Supreme Court has recognized that in a complex, technologically advanced society, Congress must be able to rely on agencies to issue rules and regulations to help implement the public policies Congress has enacted. The Court has accepted broadly worded standards as a sufficient limitation on the legislative power delegated to agencies. The Court has allowed Congress great discretion in economic-policy making and implementation so long as the legislation does not violate individual rights and liberties specified in the Constitution, and the opportunity for judicial review of agency rule-making and adjudication is available. A leading authority on administrative law has summed up the delegation of legislative power issue as follows:

> Congress may and does lawfully delegate legislative power to administrative agencies.... . Much of the judicial talk about requirement of standards is contrary to the action the Supreme Court takes when delegations are made without standards. The vaguest of standards are held adequate, and various delegations without standards have been upheld. ... In the absence of palpable abuse or true congressional abdication, the non delegation doctrine to which the Supreme Court has in the past often paid lip service is without practical force. ... The effective law is in accord with a 1940 statement of the Supreme Court: "Delegation by Congress has long been recognized as necessary in order that the exertion of legislative power does not become a futility."[8]

The following examples illustrate the broad standards that Congress often has used in delegating rule-making authority to administrative agencies. First, in the Consumer Product Safety Act of 1972 Congress delegated to the Consumer Product Safety Commission (CPSC) the power to make rules that may be "reasonably necessary to prevent or reduce an unreasonable risk of injury associated with" the products it is responsible for regulating.[9] Second, in the Occupational Safety and Health Act of 1970, the Occupational Safety and Health Administration (OSHA) was given the power to adopt rules that are "reasonably necessary or appropriate to provide safe or healthful employment and places of employment."[10] Finally, the Federal Trade Commission Act delegates to the Federal Trade Commission (FTC) the power to enact trade regulation rules that prohibit "unfair or deceptive practices" in or affecting interstate commerce.

REASONS FOR THE RISE OF REGULATION AND AGENCIES

The involvement of the state and federal governments in the promotion of particular segments of business and the economy dates back to the early nineteenth century. Perhaps the most famous example of early state intervention in the economy was the financing and construction of the Erie Canal by the state of New York at a cost of over $7 million. The Erie Canal, completed in 1825, was not an atypical case. In the period before the Civil War many state legislatures routinely enacted statutes either fully financing or combining with business interests to finance the construction of roads, canals, and railroads. Between 1850 and 1870 the federal government played a major role in encouraging private railroad corporations to expand the railroad system, eventually linking the eastern and midwestern sections of the country to the west coast. The federal government offered to grant railroad companies alternate sections of right-of-way land along newly constructed railroad track as an inducement to encourage construction. This assistance to the railroad companies eventually amounted to 180 million acres, an area larger in size than the states of California, Illinois, and New York.

Although the state and federal governments were involved early in encouraging the development and expansion of the American economy, substantial levels of government regulation of business did not begin until the end of the nineteenth century. We now explore the economic, historical, and political rationale for the rapid growth of government regulation of business since the 1880s. What accounts for the rapid growth of government regulation at the federal level during three "waves" of regulation: from 1887 to 1916, 1933 to 1939, and most recently, from 1964 to 1975? An appreciation of the economic, historical, and political rationale for the rise of regulation and agencies helps us to better understand why we have government regulation of business and the economy today, and to be aware of the factors that may encourage or discourage future regulation.

Economic Rationale

A rationale for regulation frequently advanced by economists is the notion of market failure. This view holds that while the free market is the preferred and most efficient method of allocating resources and enhancing consumer welfare in society, there are nevertheless imperfections in the market which occur when competitive or market forces fail to provide, as they theoretically should, the optimum allocation of goods and services. Examples of market defects that have served as a justification for government regulation of business include:

1. The need to control natural monopolies In some industries, notably utilities such as electric power, natural gas, telephone, and railroads, economies of scale are so great and capital investment so high as to make it inefficient for more than one firm to operate in a particular geographic area. In such cases one firm could increase profits by charging higher than competitive prices due to the lack of competition. Government has attempted to mitigate this market imperfection by enacting regulatory statutes that create agencies with the power to set prices (for instance, electricity or telephone rates) at levels that allow a reasonable return on investment and approximate price levels that would exist under competitive conditions.

2. The need to compensate for inadequate information One of the assumptions of a competitive free market is that consumers have adequate information upon which to evaluate competing products or services. If consumers lack adequate information because of insufficient education, inability to evaluate information, lack of access to information, or inability to afford the cost of information, they are not able to impose discipline on sellers in the way free market theory would suggest.

3. The need to correct for externalities or spillover effects Externalities are costs generated by a product's manufacture that are not included in the product's cost of production or selling price. Instead, these costs are externalized and borne by society generally rather than being directly passed on to the actual purchasers of the product or service. There are at least two unfortunate consequences: first, the product's price does not reflect its true cost of production, and second, the externalized costs are being unfairly shifted to members of society who do not benefit from the product and in many cases have no idea that they have been burdened with an unseen cost.[11]

Environmental pollution is a good example of an externalized cost. Prior to the clean-air-and-water statutes, a steel company could pollute the air and water without either the company or its customers having to include the health and environmental costs of that pollution in the price of the company's steel products. The cost was externalized and borne by the people exposed to the air and water pollution. Moreover, if one steel company decided to accept responsibility for its pollution costs and invested perhaps millions of dollars in antipollution equipment, there was nothing to guarantee that competitor steel companies would follow suit. In that event the socially aware steel company would be at a serious competitive disadvantage and might eventually be driven out of business.

This example also illustrates the market defect of inadequate information discussed above. Although a free market with good information flow and understanding should theoretically lead certain buyers of consumer products made of steel to boycott the polluting steel company, it is highly unlikely that a consumer who buys a refrigerator at a retail appliance center will have any idea of which company manufactured the steel used in the refrigerator. Further, consumers may not know they are breathing polluted air or have sufficient information to be able to evaluate the health risks, if any, flowing from the level of pollution present in the air or water.

Historical and Political Rationale

Just as economic factors have influenced the growth of regulation, so too have historical events and political forces. In fact, many believe that the historical and political rationale have been the primary determinants for the increased power and visibility of administrative agencies and regulation.[12] Three periods in the last one hundred years have been especially active in terms of regulatory growth. These include the populist and progressive era dating from 1887 to 1916, the New Deal period of 1933 to 1939, and the more recent period between 1964 and 1975. By way of introduction we focus first on the period prior to the 1880s, when little regulation existed.

Prior to the time of the American Civil War the American economy was predominantly rural, composed of small farmers and merchants operating in and around small towns. Consumers purchased from merchants and businesses in their hometowns with whom they were often personally acquainted. As a result, most disputes could be settled locally. Large factories were few in number, and the problems of industrialization and urban America, which later led to calls for government regulation, did not yet exist.

The American Civil War, the westward expansion of the country, the rapid growth of the railroad system from 1850 to 1870, and the substantial increase in inventions after the Civil War all contributed to a rapid escalation in the scale of industrial and commercial enterprise in the United States during the last three decades of the nineteenth century. By the year 1900 oligopolies and substantial monopoly power had developed in a number of major American industries including railroads, oil, chemicals, aluminum, and steel. Farmers in particular were upset at what they perceived to be anticompetitive practices by the railroads in their setting of freight rates and in determining railroad routes. Finally, as the end of the nineteenth century approached, the country was entering an important period of political and social reform, which focused on the problems generated by the rapid industrialization and urbanization of the post-Civil War period.

The Period 1887 to 1916   This was a period of social and political reaction to some of the perceived anticompetitive excesses of the railroads and other oligopolistic or monopolistic industries. The popular press and other writers helped fuel the social-reform movement by giving wide publicity to anticompetitive practices engaged in by certain large corporations and to political corruption in some of the large cities. It was in 1905, for example, that Upton Sinclair published his hard-hitting and best-selling novel, *The Jungle*, exposing the unhealthy conditions of the meat packing industry. The book helped to spur passage by Congress in 1906 of the Meat Inspection Act and the Pure Food and Drugs Act. The temper of the times during this period is described well in the following passage:

> These cross currents of concern over how best to control industrial growth were a dominant theme in national politics up to World War I. The period from 1890 to 1914 witnessed a replay—across a broader industrial panorama—of the widespread unrest over unconstrained private business activity that had existed in the Populist era. Although the sharp focus of railroad rate discrimination was absent, it was replaced by a generalized concern about bigness and the evils of monopoly that was shared by small enterprisers, civic groups, and political leaders. The muckraking journalists vividly brought this concern home to the general public in serialized articles, such as Ida Tarbell's exposé of Standard Oil, which achieved instant notoriety in the increasingly popular mass-subscription magazines. Widespread popular unrest over corporate behavior grew steadily more insistent.[13]

The first wave of regulatory statutes enacted during this period of American history and the administrative agencies charged with their implementation were the following:

1. The Interstate Commerce Act (1887) administered by the Interstate Commerce Commission (ICC)
2. The Sherman Antitrust Act (1890) administered by the Department of Justice
3. The Clayton Antitrust Act (1914) administered by the Department of Justice and the Federal Trade Commission
4. The Trade Commission Act (1914) administered by the Federal Trade Commission (FTC)
5. The Pure Food and Drugs Act (1906) administered by the Bureau of Chemistry and later by the Food and Drug Administration (FDA)
6. The Federal Reserve Act (1916) administered by the Federal Reserve Board

Although many of these statutes were not vigorously enforced by the agencies charged with implementation (an example of agency discretionary power that we shall turn to later), the regulation coming out of the 1887–1916 period was significant in that it was an early recognition of the fact that government regulation was one way of attempting to remedy defects in the free market.

The period between 1916 and 1933 saw relatively little new regulation by the federal government, for a number of reasons. First, between 1916 and 1920 the United States was involved in World War I and its immediate aftermath. The president, Congress, and the country focused primarily on the war effort and international matters rather than on domestic concerns. Second, between 1920 and 1932 the presidency and the Congress were controlled by the Republican party. Given the traditional supportive relationship between business and the Republican party, the political environment was not favorable for the enactment of public policies regulating business. Third, the 1920s were a period of strong economic growth and economic prosperity, which does not suggest an economic environment conducive to new regulatory public policies.

The New Deal Period of 1933 to 1939 The New Deal period witnessed the second wave of regulatory statutes affecting business and the economy, a wave of regulation considerably more expansive and burdensome to business than that which had occurred during the 1887–1916 period. The explanation for this period of regulation, this "New Deal" (referring to a new deal of the cards—a fresh start) for the American people, was the Great Depression.

Simply stated, the Great Depression was a deep and catastrophic economic collapse, which followed the stock market crash on October 24, 1929 (Black Thursday) and led to great social and political change in the country. For the first time in American history many people began to doubt whether the free market alone without some government intervention could guarantee a stable and prosperous economy. Confidence in business was shaken, and people were ready for political change, which came about in 1932 with the election of a Democratic Congress and Franklin D. Roosevelt as president. The economic collapse, characterized by a national unemployment rate in excess of 25 percent, hundreds of bank failures that wiped out the savings of many Americans, thousands of home and farm foreclosures, and marches on Washington by the unemployed, resulted in much social unrest and resentment.

In the short span of three years (1929 to 1932) the political and economic environment in the United States was transformed dramatically, and a major political realignment took place that still affects political and economic thinking in the 1980s. Many of the new regulatory public policies proposed by President Roosevelt and his advisers would have been almost unthinkable in earlier years, for they seemed contrary to the implicit norms and standards of free enterprise, individualism, and decentralized government, which we discussed in Chapter 1 with reference to the model for public-policy making. Moreover, these New Deal policies were unlike anything that had gone before and therefore were at odds with the notion of incrementalism, which is another important factor in successful policy making.

What then explains the success of the Roosevelt administration in enacting the regulatory public policies of the New Deal? The answer lies in the fact that the Great Depression had such an important impact on the public consciousness that implicit norms and standards were modified to allow for a substantial role for government in regulating business and the economy. The incrementalism factor, which normally is important in public-policy making, was simply overwhelmed by the great economic and social problems of the depression. Most people were looking for a way out of the economic collapse and were willing to accept major new policy initiatives that they were unlikely to have accepted in more stable times. This suggests a lesson for future public-policy development; namely, that what seems implausible from the standpoint of incrementalism or implicit norms may become quite real in the event of major economic or social disruption.

Finally, it should also be noted that President Roosevelt was a very charismatic leader with bold new ideas at a time when the country was searching for leadership. Although he and his policies did have severe critics, especially in the business community, his policies had the support of most Americans as is evidenced by the substantial electoral successes he and the Democratic party enjoyed in the congressional and presidential elections from 1932 to 1940.

The second wave of government regulation during the New Deal period resulted in many new regulatory statutes and administrative agencies including:

1. The Glass-Steagall Act (1933), which among other things, established the Federal Deposit Insurance Corporation (FDIC)
2. The Banking Act of 1935, which thoroughly revised the structure of the Federal Reserve System

3. The Agricultural Adjustment Act (1933), which introduced farm-subsidy and price-support programs and was administered by the Department of Agriculture
4. The National Labor Relations Act (1935), enforced by the National Labor Relations Board (NLRB)
5. The Securities Acts of 1933 and 1934, administered by the Securities and Exchange Commission (SEC)
6. The Fair Labor Standards Act (1938), which established minimum-wage, maximum-hour, and child-labor laws, enforced by the Department of Labor
7. The Social Security Act (1935), administered by the Social Security Administration
8. The Works Progress Administration (1935), an agency created to administer a public service jobs program
9. The Civilian Conservation Corps (1935), an agency created to administer a public-service jobs program

The impact of the New Deal period on government regulation as a supplement to free-market forces and its contrast to the more limited regulatory policies of the period between 1887 and 1916 has been described as follows:

In historical perspective, the New Deal appears as a distinct break from the past. The regulatory initiatives of the Populist and Progressive eras were largely discrete and limited measures—not dissimilar in kind from common law tort prohibitions against unfair trade practices. They were aimed largely at particularized fields of activity in which vigorous competition led to sharp market practices. Pre-New Deal regulatory initiatives rested on the common law assumption that minor government policing could ensure a smoothly functioning market. But the Depression put to rest this constrained view of national power. Even the more traditional regulatory aspects of the New Deal conceived of government activity as a permanent bulwark against deep-rooted structural shortcomings in the market economy... .

The New Deal's distributional programs further demonstrated how far the new approach to government intervention departed from the old. The public works and social insurance programs undertaken by the New Dealers put the federal government squarely in the position of employer and insurer of last resort. Instead of indirectly creating incentives for changes in private market behavior, the new government programs established a reliance principle: The public came to look upon government as its guarantor against acute economic deprivation. As a result, the spheres of public and private activity were intermingled in ways that would have a pervasive effect on succeeding waves of administrative reform.[14]

The New Deal period of regulation came to a close in 1939 as the Roosevelt administration became increasingly occupied with the outbreak of World War II in Europe. As international concerns became dominant, especially with American entry into the war in late 1941, new domestic policies were de-emphasized. Following the war, between 1946 and 1952, the Truman administration continued to be occupied with international problems and challenges such as the Cold War and the containment of communism, the implementation of the Marshall Plan and the Truman

Doctrine, and the outbreak of the Korean War. Thus while the domestic political environment was relatively favorable (although not as favorable as during the Roosevelt years) for regulation during the Truman administration, foreign policy concerns prevented the president and Congress from focusing on major domestic policy initiatives.

During the Eisenhower administration, from 1953 to 1960, the country was at peace and relatively prosperous. Little regulation occurred during this period. The 1950s were a period of relative social harmony in the country, a welcome relief from the economic hardships of the 1930s and the wartime period of the 1940s. Additionally, the political environment had turned hostile to major regulatory initiatives. The Congress remained under the control of the Democrats between 1952 and 1960, but the ideological majority in Congress was at best moderate, whereas new regulatory policies are more likely to be enacted when the ideological majority in Congress is more liberal. Also, President Eisenhower, a moderately conservative Republican, was philosophically opposed to aggressive governmental intervention in the economy and would probably have vetoed any major regulatory legislation.

The Period of Social Regulation, 1964 to 1975   A number of factors account for the fact that the 1964–75 period saw the third major wave of regulation affecting business in a hundred years. First, as we noted in Chapter 1, the political environment was especially favorable between 1964 and 1968. The ideological majority in Congress was at its most liberal since the mid-1930s, and President Johnson was a liberal and a master politician, adept at dealing with Congress. Second, public-interest groups had become better organized and were thus better able to influence public-policy making. Third, the economic prosperity of the 1950s and 1960s allowed people more leisure time and the opportunity to become more involved with and concerned about quality-of-life issues such as improved civil rights for minorities and women, improved health care for the elderly, air- and water-pollution issues, automobile safety, and health and safety in the workplace. Fourth, the nation had become better educated, owing to a large increase in the college and university student population during the 1960s and 1970s. Many of these students were idealistic and had the time and motivation to become involved with the social issues outlined above. Fifth, by the 1960s communications technology, especially television, had advanced to the point where information, analysis, and video coverage could be broadcast to the nation live or within hours of events. Once social issues had been raised, the news media were extraordinarily important in publicizing the issues, thereby assisting interest groups supporting these social issues in placing them on the public-policy agenda. Sixth, for some social issues, such as environmental pollution control, advances in science and technology were necessary to measure accurately and understand the nature and level of pollution and the degree of risk to the public health

Many of these advances took place in the 1960s. Moreover, in the case of environmental pollution, the harmful effects are often cumulative, and therefore may not have been readily apparent or easily measurable prior to the 1950s and 1960s.

All of the above factors and doubtless many others contributed to a substantial and very costly wave of regulation between 1964 and 1975. Examples of the regulatory public policies enacted by Congress during this period include:

1. The Civil Rights Act of 1964, enforced by the Equal Employment Opportunity Commission (EEOC)
2. Medical Care for the Aged (1965), administered by the Social Security Administration
3. Various environmental legislation (1969 to 1976), enforced by the Environmental Protection Agency (EPA)
4. The Occupational Safety and Health Act (1970), enforced by the Occupational Safety and Health Administration (OSHA)
5. The Employee Retirement Income Security Act (ERISA-1974), enforced by the Department of Labor
6. Various consumer protection and automobile safety legislation enforced by a number of different administrative agencies (1966 to 1974)[15]

In 1975 a backlash against the great wave of regulation of the preceding ten years began to take shape. Some economists believed the high inflation rate of the middle and late 1970s was in part caused by excessive government regulation of business, while others believed that some of the regulation was inefficient and too costly relative to the benefits received. The country needed time to adjust to the new social regulation, to see how well it was working and where improvements could be made. Also, with the election of Ronald Reagan as president in 1980 the political environment in the executive branch became unfavorable for additional social or economic regulation because of his conservative political and economic philosophy. Thus in the period since 1975 we have witnessed some selective deregulation in the areas of airline and truck transportation and financial services. On the whole, however, what has occurred is a slowdown in the rate of increase of government regulation rather than a net decrease in the level of regulation of business and the economy.

A Political Rationale for Agencies and Regulation Two political rationales for the rise of administrative agencies are suggested here. First, in an advanced society with a complex economy it is virtually impossible for Congress, which is primarily a policy-making body, to have the time, expertise, and resources to implement the regulatory policies it enacts. Therefore, if Congress is to regulate business and the economy, the only practical and efficient means of doing so is by using a public management entity like an administrative agency, which is staffed by experienced personnel who are charged with filling in the details of the broad policy announced by Congress and implementing it on a continuing basis.

Second, *the theory of bureaucratic clientelism* has been suggested as a reason for the creation of certain agencies, principally those that promote the interests of a particular client (or special-interest) group or coalition of client groups. The theory of bureaucratic clientelism has been explained as follows:

> What was striking about the period after 1861 was that government began to give formal, bureaucratic recognition to the emergence of distinctive interests in a diversifying economy. As Richard L. Schott has written, "whereas earlier federal departments had been formed around specialized governmental functions (foreign affairs, war, finance, and the like), the new departments of this period—Agriculture, Labor, and Commerce—were devoted to the interests and aspirations of particular economic groups."
>
> The original purpose behind these clientele-oriented departments was neither to subsidize nor to regulate, but to promote, chiefly by gathering and publishing statistics and (especially in the case of agriculture) by research. The formation of the Department of Agriculture in 1862 was to become a model, for better or worse, for later political campaigns for governmental recognition. ... The precedent was followed by labor groups, especially the Knights of Labor, to secure creation in 1888 of a Department of Labor.[16]

Closely associated with the theory of bureaucratic clientelism is the *self-interest theory of regulation.* James Q. Wilson writes that under the self-interest theory "regulation results when an industry successfully uses its political influence to obtain legal protection for itself or to impose legal burdens on its rivals."[17] He goes on to describe two key elements of this theory of regulation:

> (1) individuals and groups are politically more sensitive to sudden or significant decreases in their net benefits than they are to increases in net benefits, and (2) ...Any proposed policy that confers highly concentrated costs or benefits will be more likely to stimulate organized activity by a fully representative group than will a policy that confers widely distributed costs and benefits. When the benefit is entirely concentrated on a single group but the cost is diffused, an organization will quickly form to propose a regulatory arrangement to institutionalize the benefit.[18]

The formation of the Department of Education, a relatively new administrative agency created by Congress in 1979, is a good example of both bureaucratic clientelism and the self-interest theory of regulation. In terms of bureaucratic clientelism, support for the proposed cabinet department came mainly from education interest groups, especially the 1.6-million-member National Education Association and the American Federation of Teachers, which understood that the new department would promote the interests of education at the federal level by focusing federal education policy in an agency of cabinet rank. Also from the perspective of self-interest theory, education client groups stood to benefit greatly from the increased visibility accorded education issues and needs at the federal level, while any added costs of the new department did not fall on any one group but were diffused throughout the economy.

The creation of the cabinet departments of Agriculture, Labor, and Commerce also was strongly influenced by client groups from those three areas who believed that a cabinet department would help in the promotion of their economic interests. The Agriculture Department, for example, has long been active in helping farm groups to lobby Congress for agriculture research, agricultural commodity price supports and subsidies, import protection programs, and programs to expand farm exports.

The theory of bureaucratic clientelism may also help explain the creation and continued support for certain regulatory agencies such as the EPA and OSHA. While these agencies are clearly involved in regulating business, they have a promotional role as well. The EPA, for example, has the ability to promote the interests of various environmental groups (for instance, the Sierra Club and the Audubon Society) that actively lobbied for creation of the agency and continue to support the agency's regulatory efforts. Unlike the purely promotional agency, however, the EPA promotes the interests of some groups, its clients, but adversely affects the interests of many of the business firms it regulates. Thus while client groups like the Sierra Club or labor unions may offer political support in Congress for regulatory agencies such as the EPA or OSHA, this support is often countered by the special-interest groups adversely affected by the regulatory effort.

TYPES OF ADMINISTRATIVE AGENCIES

Before proceeding to a discussion of the operation and functions of administrative agencies, we should first be clear about the major types of agencies at the federal level and their similarities and differences. As Table 3-1 (p. 88) illustrates, agencies can be divided into three basic categories, which are principally distinguished by the degree of executive-branch control applicable to each agency type. The three categories include cabinet-level agencies, other executive-branch agencies, and the independent regulatory agencies. Within each agency one is likely also to find many subsidiary agencies, bureaus, or divisions. For instance, the Antitrust Division is a subpart or division of the Department of Justice, a cabinet-level administrative agency. The person in charge of the Antitrust Division, which has hundreds of employees, reports to the attorney general, who is the appointed head of the Department of Justice. Figures 3-1 and 3-2 (p. 89) provide organization charts for the Federal Trade Commission and the Environmental Protection Agency, which describe the subsidiary functional units within each agency. An agency's organization will vary depending on the functions and powers that have been granted to it by Congress. You will have occasion to refer back to these charts when we discuss the major functions of administrative agencies later in this chapter.

TABLE 3-1   Types of Administrative Agencies

ADMINISTRATIVE AGENCIES

Cabinet-Level Agencies	*Other Executive- Branch Agencies*	*Independent Regulatory Agencies*
Department of Transportation • Federal Aviation Agency • National Highway Traffic Safety Administration	Environmental Protection Agency General Services Administration Central Intelligence Agency	Federal Trade Commission National Labor Relations Board Securities and Exchange Commission
Department of Health and Human Services • Social Security Administration • Food and Drug Administration • National Institutes of Health		Equal Employment Opportunity Commission Federal Reserve Board Interstate Commerce Commission Nuclear Regulatory Commission
Department of the Treasury • Internal Revenue Service		Federal Communications Commission
Department of Justice • Antitrust Division • Criminal Division • Civil Rights Divison • Federal Bureau of Investigation		
Department of Labor • Occupational Safety and Health Administration		

Agency Differences

The major differences among administrative agencies, apart from the fact that they are created by Congress to enforce many different public policies, relate to the degree of presidential control and influence over the operations of the agency. The president has the greatest control over the operations of the cabinet level administrative agencies, often referred to as the cabinet departments of the executive branch. That is because the president not only has the authority under the Constitution to appoint the top

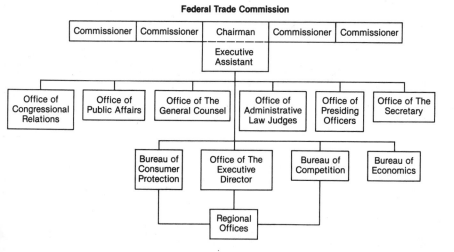

FIGURE 3-1 Organizational Chart for the Federal Trade Commission.

Source: 1986–87 U.S. Government Manual (Washington D.C.: p.869) U.S. Government Printing Office.

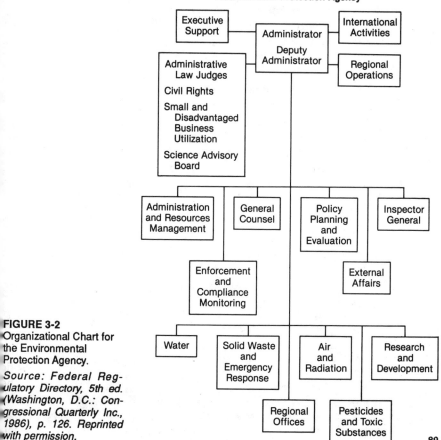

FIGURE 3-2
Organizational Chart for
the Environmental
Protection Agency.

Source: Federal Regulatory Directory, 5th ed. (Washington, D.C.: Congressional Quarterly Inc., 1986), p. 126. Reprinted with permission.

89

level administrators (the department secretary, undersecretaries, and assistant secretaries) of the cabinet-level agencies, subject to confirmation by the Senate but also, and perhaps more important, has the power to remove them from office whenever he chooses. These top-level administrators are said to serve "at the president's pleasure." Because the president appoints people who are likely to share his political and economic philosophies and who do not wish to be removed from office, the appointees will almost always promote the president's goals and philosophy within the agency.

Alternatively, the Congress may create administrative agencies outside the traditional cabinet departments but still within the executive branch, with a single head who serves at the pleasure of the president. A good example of such an executive-branch agency is the Environmental Protection Agency (EPA), which was created by Congress to administer and enforce the federal environmental statutes. The administrator of the EPA, who is the top manager and policy maker for the agency, is appointed by the president, subject to confirmation by the Senate, and thereafter serves at the president's pleasure. It is apparent from the foregoing that the president's degree of control over the top administrators in executive-branch agencies, be they cabinet agencies or other executive-branch agencies, is essentially the same.

The president has less control over the top administrators of the independent regulatory agencies. While the president has the power to appoint members to these boards or commissions, once confirmed by the Senate these appointees serve for fixed terms (usually five to seven years) and can be removed from office only by the impeachment process, which is very rarely used, or pursuant to a process provided for in the statute creating the agency. Most independent agencies have five to seven board members or commissioners, one of whom is designated by the president to chair the agency. The president also has much less control over the rule-making power of the independent regulatory agencies, in contrast to the executive branch agencies.

Agency Similarities

The three types of administrative agency outlined above have many more similarities than differences. These include the following:

1. With rare exception, all agencies are created by Congress to implement public policies enacted by Congress.
2. Congress must annually review and approve (or disapprove), all agency budgets and appropriate money for them.
3. All agencies must submit their budget requests for review to the Office of Management and Budget before they are forwarded to both houses of Congress for further review and approval.
4. The great majority of agency employees, except for high-level administrators, are selected through and protected by the Civil Service System.
5. All agencies created by Congress are subject to the Administrative Procedure Act, which specifies the procedures agencies must follow in pursuing their rule-

making and adjudicatory functions and establishes standards for judicial review of agency action.

6. Most regulatory agencies, whether independent or in the executive branch (including cabinet agencies), have similar functions including investigative, prosecutorial, advisory, rule making, and adjudicatory.

AGENCY FUNCTIONS

The substantial power of administrative agencies derives in large part from the power and functions delegated to them by Congress. The activities and functions, both formal and informal, that an agency may undertake are governed by the statute that creates the agency. Moreover, as will be discussed below, when an agency is delegated rule-making and adjudicatory functions it must also comply with the requirements of the Administrative Procedure Act. The material that follows discusses the major functions of regulatory agencies, using the Federal Trade Commission (FTC) as an example of an agency that exercises these functions. You should be aware, however, that some regulatory agencies have not been delegated all of the functions set forth below.

Investigation and Prosecution

Regulatory agencies that are charged with enforcing a statute need to determine whether violations are occurring. Section 5 of the FTC Act, for example, declares: "Unfair methods of competition, and unfair or deceptive acts or practices in or affecting commerce are unlawful." Under this section, the FTC has jurisdiction to investigate, and if necessary prosecute for antitrust violations (anticompetitive practices) as well as for false or misleading advertising and other deceptive sales practices.

In the case of business regulation an agency will often receive complaints from consumers or competitor business firms. If a consumer suspects false advertising, for example, he or she may complain by letter to one of the FTC's regional offices or to its Washington headquarters. Although a limited budget makes it necessary for the FTC to pick and choose those complaints it will investigate, the agency generally will make its decision based on the number of complaints received and its judgment concerning the severity of the allegedly deceptive practice. In pursuing an investigation the FTC will first seek the voluntary cooperation of the business against which the complaints are filed. The business may be asked to provide evidence that demonstrates the truthfulness of the allegedly deceptive advertisement. The agency has the power to subpoena documents if voluntary efforts fail.

In many cases the results of an agency investigation will fail to turn up sufficient evidence to substantiate a false advertising charge, and the case will be closed. In those cases where evidence of a violation does exist the FTC normally seeks to dispose of the case through use of a *consent order*, where the business consents to modify its advertising to avoid the allegedly deceptive content in return for the FTC's agreement not to pursue the case any further. A party who agrees to a consent order is not required to admit any violation of the law. Both the FTC and the business benefit from the consent-order procedure. The business benefits by not having to admit guilt and by avoiding the costs and adverse publicity that would result from an FTC prosecution and formal adjudicatory hearing. The FTC benefits by obtaining timely cessation of the deceptive activity at minimal cost and without having to worry about a long appeals process.

In the event the business and the FTC cannot reach agreement on a consent order, or if the FTC believes the activity complained of is especially severe, the FTC will file a formal legal complaint, which requires a formal "answer" from the business defendant. This moves the case to the prosecutorial phase which will eventually lead attorneys for the FTC and the business to an adjudicatory hearing before an FTC administrative-law judge. As the FTC organization chart in Figure 3-1 illustrates, the agency is both prosecutor and judge in the event a complaint is issued charging a violation of the FTC Act or agency regulations. Although including both of these functions within the same agency has the appearance of a conflict of interest, the courts have accepted this arrangement if two safeguards are present: first, the prosecutorial and judicial divisions within the agency must be fully separate and independent of one another, and second, there must be an opportunity for the losing party to appeal the decision of the administrative-law judge within the agency and to seek judicial review before one of the federal Circuit Courts of Appeal.

Advising

Agencies provide a valuable benefit to individuals and business by advising them on how a particular statute or regulation may affect (at least in the agency's opinion) a proposed business transaction or activity. For example, an advertising agency or the marketing department of a corporation might seek the FTC's advice on whether a particular advertising or sales-promotion campaign would be considered deceptive and therefore in violation of section 5 of the FTC Act. The request for advice may be handled informally by having a representative from the corporation's Washington office explore the matter with a staff member in the FTC's Bureau of Consumer Protection. While such informal advice may be quite useful to the corporation, it is generally not binding on the agency.

A more formal method of seeking advice from the FTC is to ask for an advisory opinion. Any individual or business may apply to the FTC for an advisory opinion applicable to a business practice or activity that is under consideration. The advisory opinion defines the limits of the FTC Act and any regulations issued by the commission in relation to the particular business practice in question. The FTC may overturn its advisory opinions at any time. However, if it does so, the commission must give the individual or business affected by the opinion a reasonable amount of time to alter its practices so as to be in compliance with the new ruling.[19] Of course, a business that seeks informal or formal advice from the FTC or any agency is not required to follow the advice. In such a case, however, the business should be prepared to legally defend its position in the event the agency decides to prosecute.

Rule Making

The rule-making function serves as a major source of power for administrative agencies. The existence, scope, and limitations of an agency's rule-making function are determined by the enabling legislation that created the agency and by the *Administrative Procedure Act (APA)*. The APA applies to all federal agencies and specifies the minimum procedural requirements (adequate notice and the opportunity to be heard by parties affected by agency rulemaking) an agency must follow when pursuing its rule-making or adjudicatory functions. Where an agency's enabling legislation provides stricter procedural standards than the APA, the stricter standards apply.

The APA defines a rule as "an agency statement of general or particular applicability and future effect designed to implement, interpret or prescribe policy." *Rule making* is defined as the "agency process for formulating, amending, or repealing a rule." Agencies can enact two types of rules: procedural and legislative (or substantive).[20] *Procedural* rules deal with the internal operating procedures an agency follows in carrying out its duties. Such rules are exempt from the rule-making requirements of the APA. *Legislative* rules are promulgated by an agency pursuant to the rule-making authority delegated to the agency by Congress. These rules are intended to "flesh out" and interpret how the broad policy statements in the statute are to be applied to particular business practices or activities (for instance, "unfair or deceptive acts or practices in or affecting commerce are illegal"). Such rules, when properly enacted pursuant to the requirements of the APA and the enabling statute, are considered by the courts to have the force and effect of law.

A noted authority on agency rule making describes its advantages in these terms:

> When more than a handful of parties are affected, creation of new law through either statutory enactment or administrative rule making is much more desirable than creation of new law through either judicial decision or administrative adjudication. ... The procedure of administrative rule making is in my opinion one of the greatest inventions of modern government. It can be, when the agency so desires, a virtual duplicate of legislative committee procedure. More often it is quicker and less expensive. The usual procedure is that prescribed by the Administrative Procedure Act, the central feature of which is publishing proposed rules and inviting interested parties to make comments. Anyone and everyone is allowed to express himself and to call atten-

tion to the impact of various possible policies on his business activity or interest. The agency's staff sifts and summarizes the presentations and prepares its own studies. The procedure is both fair and efficient.[21]

The APA describes two methods agencies can use for rule-making purposes: informal (or "notice and comment") rule making and formal (or "on the record") rule making. Often the enabling act that created the agency and gave it rule-making power will specify the method to be used.

Informal Rule Making   This method of rule making, which is used by most agencies, is characterized by the following steps as set forth in section 553 of the APA:

1. The agency must publish a *notice of proposed rule making* in the *Federal Register*.[22] The notice must contain a statement of the time, place, and nature of the rule-making proceeding; a reference to the legal authority (usually a provision of the agency's enabling act) under which the rule is proposed; and either the terms or a description of the subjects and issues involved in the proposed rule.

2. After publication of the notice of proposed rule making the agency must give interested parties an opportunity to participate in the rule-making process through the submission of written comments. An agency normally must give interested parties at least thirty days (most agencies provide several months) to comment on a proposed rule. The APA requires an agency to "consider" the written comments in its rule-making process. The agency may also hold public hearings in Washington, and possibly in other major cities as well, but it is not required to do so.

3. Once the agency has received and reviewed the written comments it can proceed in one of three ways: first, it may decide to adopt the proposed rule as originally drafted; second, it may decide to adopt the proposed rule with certain modifications, which often take into account suggestions from the written comments; or third, it may decide to withdraw the proposed rule based on what it has learned from the written comments or because of political pressure coming from Congress. With regard to the latter, such pressure often is generated by interest groups opposed to the proposed rule.

4. Once the proposed rule is adopted in final form, the agency must publish a *notice of final rule making* in the *Federal Register*. This final notice must include the language of the rule, a summary of the major written comments received, and a listing of other major sources of information relied upon by the agency in adopting the rule.

5. The rule or regulation cannot take effect any sooner than thirty days following final publication in the *Federal Register*.

6. An interested party may attempt to invalidate the final rule by appealing to the appropriate circuit court of appeals on the grounds that in the promulgation of the rule the agency's actions, findings of fact, or conclusions were arbitrary or capricious or involved an abuse of discretion.

Formal Rule Making   A few agency enabling acts require that rules or regulations be made "on the record" after an opportunity for an agency hearing. This method of formal rule making is governed by sections 556 and 557 of the APA, the major requirements of which may be summarized as follows:

1. The agency must publish a notice of proposed rule making in the *Federal Register*, which sets forth the date, time, and place for a public hearing as well as the agency's statutory authority for rule making.

2. A formal trial-type hearing is held where the agency has the burden of submitting sufficient documentary evidence or sworn testimony supporting its proposed rule. Parties opposed to the rule may also submit oral and/or documentary evidence. Both the agency and opposing parties may submit rebuttal evidence and engage in cross-examination of witnesses. The formal hearing is presided over by an administrative-law judge, who performs many of the same functions as a regular trial judge (for instance, ruling on the admissibility of evidence).

3. Upon completion of the formal hearing, the agency must make formal written findings, based on the evidence presented, which supports issuance of a final rule. The agency may alternatively decide to modify or withdraw the proposed rule.

4. The agency publishes a notice of final rule making in the *Federal Register* setting forth the language of the rule and its effective date.

5. The rule or regulation cannot take effect any sooner than thirty days following final publication in the *Federal Register*.

6. An interested party may attempt to invalidate the final rule by appealing to the appropriate circuit court of appeals on the grounds that the final rule is not supported by substantial evidence in the record as a whole.

The process of rule making, whether informal or formal, is critically important to business and other interested parties. The rule-making process provides business with its best opportunity to make a case for modification or withdrawal of a proposed rule. The agency may have overlooked important issues that affect the costs or operational effectiveness of a proposed rule. The information an agency receives from interested parties can be quite helpful in promulgating an effective rule, in terms of both cost and achievement of the desired objective.

In making their case to modify or withdraw a rule, business firms and trade associations can be much more effective while it is in the proposal stage than when it has been finalized. The legal and political strategies available to a party who seeks to modify or withdraw a proposed or final rule include:

1. A challenge in the court of appeals asserting that the agency exceeded its statutory rule-making authority in promulgating the rule

2. A challenge in the court of appeals asserting that the agency did not properly follow the APA requirements in the rule-making process

3. Presentation of sufficient evidence during or after the rule-making process to convince the agency that it should modify or revoke the rule

4. Application of political pressure on the agency to adopt alternative (3) by convincing influential members of Congress to support its position

5. Prevailing upon Congress to pass legislation that modifies or withdraws the rule, and upon the president to support the legislation

Most authorities agree that the principal advantage of informal rule making is its efficiency. The absence of required formal hearings means there is less opportunity for delay in the rule-making process. On the other hand, it can be argued that formal hearings with the right of cross-examination allow for the development of more accurate and complete information. The clear trend in agency rule making, however, has been in favor of informal rule making because of its greater efficiency and the belief that written comments allow sufficient information for agency decision making.

Adjudication

The adjudicatory function is one of a series of agency functions consisting of investigation, formal complaint, prosecution, adjudicatory hearing, and decision/order. This series of functions will usually be triggered when a party is accused of being in violation of a statute or regulation the agency is responsible for enforcing. In our earlier discussion of the investigation and prosecution functions we noted that if an agency believes a case warrants prosecution and the parties cannot agree on the provisions of a consent order, then a formal hearing before an administrative law judge (sometimes also referred to as a hearing officer) will be required. Those agencies that have not been delegated an adjudicatory function by Congress prosecute their cases in a federal district court.

A question that arises in dealing with the adjudicatory function is, Who has a right to an administrative hearing? One begins by examining the statute being implemented by the agency and the agency's own rules of internal procedure, which will ordinarily answer this question. The absence of statutory language specifying a right to a hearing in particular types of cases may not, however, be conclusive. The Supreme Court has through judicial review decided that in many cases a party has a constitutional right to a hearing before an agency can take a particular action. The constitutional basis for most of these cases are the provisions of the Fifth and Fourteenth amendments, which provide that a person may not be deprived of "life, liberty, or property, without due process of law." For example, the Supreme Court has ruled that an individual has a right to a hearing before he or she is deprived of liberty because of revocation of parole.[23] In another case the Supreme Court held that a state may not terminate public-assistance payments to a particular recipient without affording him or her the opportunity for an evidentiary hearing prior to (rather than some months after) the termination because it would be a denial of property without due process of law.[24] In each of these cases, the Supreme Court *balanced* the degree of the deprivation of a person's life, liberty, or property against the level of an agency's procedural protections for the person involved. In striking this balance the court determines whether an agency is required to provide a hearing at all, and if so, whether the hearing must be provided before or after the agency takes its action. Fortunately, in cases involving agency actions against business for violations of a statute or regulation, an adjudicatory hearing within the agency or a trial in federal court is invariably provided for either by statute or by the procedural due process protections of the Constitution.

To better understand the adjudicatory function of an agency, consider the following example. Corporation *A* complains to the Federal Trade Commission (FTC) that Corporation *B* is engaged in monopolistic business practices that are in violation of section 5 of the FTC Act, which provides that "unfair methods of competition in or affecting commerce...are declared unlawful." The FTC staff will investigate Corporation *A*'s allegations. Assuming the investigation yields sufficient evidence of illegal practices to warrant filing a legal complaint, the FTC attorneys will proceed either to settle the case via a consent order with Corporation *B* or to file a legal complaint against the corporation, which will set the stage for a formal adjudicatory hearing before an FTC administrative-law judge (ALJ).

The trial-type hearing, which is less formal than a court trial, allows both Corporation *B* and the FTC to present written and oral evidence, question and cross-examine witnesses, and submit written and oral arguments to the ALJ. A jury is not allowed in an agency hearing, and the rules of evidence are more flexible, often allowing hearsay and other types of evidence not normally admissible in a court trial. Within ninety days of completion of the hearing, which may last from a few days to several months depending on the complexity of the case, the ALJ prepares a written decision that includes findings of fact, conclusions of law, and a recommended order. The losing party, either the defendant or the FTC's Bureau of Competition, may appeal the ALJ's decision to the five-member commission, which serves as an internal appeals body. In the event of an appeal both sides submit written briefs and make oral arguments to the commission supporting their respective legal positions. The commission reviews the hearing transcript, the legal arguments of both sides, the ALJ's findings of fact, and his or her interpretation of the relevant statute and regulations. Based on this review, especially the ALJ's interpretation of the law applicable to the facts of the case, the decision of the ALJ will be affirmed or reversed by the commission.

The losing party at the commission level has a limited time (generally sixty to ninety days depending on the agency involved) to seek judicial review of the ALJ and commission decisions. *The Doctrine of Exhaustion of Administrative Remedies* established by the Supreme Court requires, however, that before a losing party may seek judicial review from the appropriate circuit court of appeals all internal appeals within the agency must first have been exhausted. The rationale for the doctrine is twofold: (1) the agency with expertise and experience in administering a regulatory statute should have the first opportunity to review and, in the appropriate case, correct the decision of the ALJ; and (2) appellate review within the agency will in some cases resolve the legal dispute, thereby reducing the workload of the courts of appeal.

AGENCY DISCRETION AND POWER

In the preceding section we surveyed the primary functions of administrative agencies. We noted that a considerable amount of the power and influence that agencies have on society generally and business in particular flows from the operation of these functions. It is important also to understand that inextricably linked to these functions is the discretionary power agencies enjoy in deciding how forcefully and completely to enforce the statutes and regulations within their jurisdiction.

One leading authority on the administrative process believes that 80 or 90 percent of the impact of administrative agencies comes from their informal discretionary actions, which are not subject to judicial review. He speaks of the discretionary power of agencies as follows:

> Informal discretionary action includes initiating, investigating, prosecuting, negotiating, settling, contracting, planning, recommending, and supervising. Often the most important informal determinations are the negative ones, such as not to initiate, not to investigate, not to prosecute, not to deal. Choices to act or not to act may involve not only the whether but also the who, the how, the when, and the how much.
>
> The big discretionary power all along the line may be the seemingly omnipresent power to do nothing. For instance, the power not to prosecute may be of greater magnitude than the power to prosecute, and it certainly is much more abused because it is so little checked. The power to do nothing, or almost nothing, or something less than might be done is a power that American administrators almost always have as a practical matter, even though no legislator at any point was ever aware of delegating any such power. For instance, every regulatory agency has a statutory assignment to carry out a program enacted by the legislative body, but the agency always can be more active or less active, more effective or less effective.[25]

Discretion in Perception of the Problem and in the Decision to Prosecute

While an agency may have the statutory authority or jurisdiction to regulate within a broad expanse of business activity and conduct, its perception of the severity of the problem and the best methods for handling it may well depend on the political and economic philosophy of the president's administration and of the top officials in the agency. The Federal Trade Commission is one agency that has exercised discretionary power within the context of broad regulatory authority and as a consequence has directly influenced and shaped public policy. As noted above, the FTC wears both an antitrust hat and a consumer protection hat, a situation that results from its statutory authority to regulate "unfair methods of competition" and "unfair and deceptive practices" affecting commerce. One of its antitrust functions is to share enforcement authority for section 7 of the Clayton Act (which deals with the legality of mergers). The agency's level of enforcement activity (that is, the number of large mergers that were challenged for being in violation of section 7) during the

Reagan administration was considerably lower than in the Johnson or Carter administrations. What explains the difference in enforcement activity during these different administrations when the regulatory authority of the FTC under section 7 was essentially unchanged? A good part of the answer lies in the more conservative economic philosophy of the Reagan administration and of the top level administrators at the FTC appointed during that administration. Their perception of the problem of anticompetitive mergers differed considerably from the earlier perceptions of FTC officials in the Johnson and Carter administrations. Essentially, they viewed the level and character of competitive forces in oligopolistic industry as being considerably more effective than did earlier FTC officials. Aside from the merits of the antitrust arguments, the point for purposes of discretionary power is that different agency administrators can in good faith perceive problems differently, and this influences the level of regulatory enforcement.

Discretion in Resources Devoted to Investigation

Because agencies have limited budgets to devote to enforcement of statutes within their jurisdiction, they must exercise discretion in determining what types of business practices to investigate, how many investigations and prosecutions to undertake, and how many agency employees and resources to devote to particular areas of regulatory enforcement. The Environmental Protection Agency (EPA), for example, is responsible for administering and enforcing fourteen major statutes covering a wide range of environmental concerns, including clean air and water, safe drinking water, pesticides, waste treatment and disposal, control of toxic substances, and the Superfund program to deal with the release of hazardous substances in spills and abandoned disposal sites. Its efforts at implementing the environmental public policies enacted by Congress have resulted in major improvements to national environmental quality and substantial regulatory costs for American business. But the agency's various statutory mandates exceed its budget, which means that top administrators at EPA have had to exercise discretion concerning which statutes to enforce most forcefully and which industries and business firms to scrutinize most carefully.

What becomes apparent from our examination of agency discretionary power is that while Congress may enact far-reaching public policies affecting the environment, antitrust, or health and safety in the workplace, the practical application of these policies in the real world depends to a considerable degree on agency discretion. In exercising this discretion, the agency is refining the public policy by determining the level and scope of enforcement. It is this combination of discretionary power and important agency functions that leads some to label administrative agencies as the fourth branch of the federal government. This also helps explain why major American corporations and trade associations spend substantial time and resources lobbying before administrative agencies and in developing informal contacts with staff people in the agencies.

CHECKS ON THE POWER OF AGENCIES

We have seen how the power of administrative agencies has grown substantially over the past one hundred years. But if they have such power, then the question that arises within our constitutional system of government is, What limits or checks exist to ensure that agency power is not unbridled and remains responsive to the will of the people? The material that follows discusses the nature and effectiveness of the judicial, executive, and legislative checks on the power of agencies.

Judicial Checks

The authority for judicial review of agency rule making or adjudication derives either from the enabling statute that creates the agency or from the Administrative Procedure Act. The Supreme Court has stated that "only upon a showing of clear and convincing evidence of a contrary legislative intent should the courts restrict access to judicial review."[26] Judicial review is one of the most important safeguards a party has against improper or arbitrary agency conduct involving either rule making or adjudication.

Two prerequisites must be met before a party may seek judicial review of an agency action. These include (1) exhausting the appeals available within the agency, which we discussed above; and (2) standing to sue. The concept of *standing* involves the question of whether a party has a sufficient interest in a case to bring an action in court. The courts want to ensure that a party appealing an agency decision is serious about the case and is willing and able to forcefully argue the legal issues involved. Over the past twenty-five years the Supreme Court has relaxed the requirements for standing, thereby increasing the opportunities for judicial review. Basically, a party must be able to show either a direct economic loss resulting from an agency action or a noneconomic, but personal, stake in the agency action. The Supreme Court has held that personal, noneconomic interests may include spiritual, aesthetic, conservational, and recreational values, among others.[27] For example, a landowner who objects to the development of a downhill ski resort near his property may have standing to sue (assuming he has a legal theory or statute upon which to base his lawsuit) because of the environmental and aesthetic harm he will allegedly suffer as a nearby landowner.

In reviewing formal agency actions, the courts generally accept the findings of fact made by the agency as long as they are supported by *substantial evidence in the record*. Such evidence exists if a review of the entire record of a *formal rule-making* or *adjudication* action would lead a reasonable person to the findings of fact reached by the agency.[28] The primary objective of judicial review is to assure that the law has been properly applied and interpreted by the agency. Thus in reviewing agency actions, the courts are primarily concerned with questions of law rather than questions of fact. Some examples of questions of law that might arise from a challenge to agency rule making or adjudication include: (1) Is the agency rule making within the statutory authority granted to it by Congress? (2) Is the agency action constitutional and not in violation of the Administrative Procedure Act? (3) Did the agency properly interpret the statute and regulations involved in the adjudicatory hearing?

Judicial review is an effective check on the power of agencies. It ensures fair procedures and adequate notice of agency actions and protects against arbitrary and capricious agency conduct. Because agencies are aware of and comply with the requirements of procedural due process and the APA, it is uncommon for a party to challenge successfully an agency action on these grounds. Likewise, it is uncommon for a party to argue successfully that Congress did not set sufficiently specific boundaries or standards within which an agency can promulgate rules, for as we have seen, the Supreme Court has been willing to allow Congress substantial latitude in broadly defining boundaries and standards.

Executive Checks

The president has two primary means for influencing the conduct of agencies. First, he has the constitutional authority to appoint the top officials of all agencies, subject to confirmation by the Senate. Since the Senate generally confirms the president's selections, he is able to staff these top management and policy-making positions with people who agree with his political and economic philosophy. This helps assure that at least the top administrators of an agency will act in a manner consistent with the president's views. Moreover, as to the executive-branch agencies, including the cabinet departments, the top administrators serve at the president's pleasure. This, too, allows the president to have some control over the actions of these agencies.

A second and more effective means for controlling agency conduct is through the *Office of Management and Budget* (OMB), which is located within the Executive Office of the president. OMB serves as the president's principal adviser on budgetary, management, and regulatory policy within the executive branch. It is a powerful agency with a highly competent staff that is directly responsible to the president.

OMB's principal responsibility is to review the budget requests of all agencies (both independent and executive branch) in order to ensure that they meet the overall federal budget spending limit that the president will recommend to Congress. In order to meet the president's budget target, which may also affect overall macroeconomic policy for the country, OMB will often cut agency budget requests. The reduced budget requests are then forwarded to Congress, which can increase, decrease, or accept the agency budget requests as modified by OMB. OMB's budgetary power serves to limit agency actions that are in conflict with the president's policies, since agencies have a strong interest in remaining on good terms with OMB. In addition to budget requests OMB also makes recommendations to Congress for or against any legislative proposals an agency may want to pursue. OMB opposition makes it very difficult for an agency to ask Congress for new legislation increasing its power or jurisdiction.

During the Reagan administration the OMB was also given extensive powers over the rule-making function of executive-branch agencies. Executive Order 12291 issued in early 1981 requires executive agencies to prepare a regulatory impact analysis for all proposed and existing regulations. Using cost-benefit analysis, agencies are required to adopt the least costly alternative in developing a proposed regulation. Regulatory analyses must be submitted for review by OMB at least sixty days prior to publication of the proposed rule in the *Federal Register*. In early 1985 President Reagan issued Executive Order 12498, which further expands OMB's authority by requiring executive branch agencies to clear their proposed regulations with OMB while they are in the early stages of development.[29] These executive orders give the president a formidable check on the rule-making ability of the executive-branch agencies. They are not, however, applicable to the independent regulatory agencies.

The Reagan administration's use of OMB to screen agency regulations that were inconsistent with its view of proper and cost-effective regulation raised serious objections in Congress. Critics claim that the executive orders allow OMB to interfere unduly with the rule-making power Congress delegated to the executive-branch agencies and not to the OMB or the president. They also argue that too much emphasis has been placed on the use of cost-benefit analysis to evaluate the effectiveness and efficiency of proposed regulations, since it is often difficult to place a precise dollar value on the benefits produced by regulation. It remains to be seen, therefore, whether OMB's regulatory check on executive-branch agencies will continue to be as effective in the post-Reagan period. For example, President Bush has the option of continuing, amending, or revoking the relevant executive orders issued by President Reagan.

Legislative Checks

The most important checks on the power of administrative agencies are in the hands of Congress. These include (1) the authority to enact legislation limiting the power of an agency or abolishing it altogether, (2) the authority to review and determine annual agency budgets, (3) legislative oversight and investigation, and (4) the credible threat by influential members of Congress (for example, committee chairs or ranking members of an agency's oversight committee or appropriations subcommittee) or a coalition of members to initiate actions (1), (2), or (3). We now analyze these checks in more detail.

Congress may choose to modify the power and behavior of an agency by enacting legislation that cuts back on the powers originally granted to the agency. The administrative agencies are often reminded that they are "creatures of the Congress." If enough members of Congress become upset at the nature or cost of rules and regulations enacted by a particular agency, they can enact legislation stripping the agency of all or part of its rule-making authority as well as invalidate certain agency rules already in effect. Congress might also "persuade" an agency to reconsider certain practices and modify or revoke certain rules by threatening to enact legislation doing so if the agency does not act.

The Federal Trade Commission (FTC) provides a good example of the kinds of restraints that can be placed on an agency when its actions alienate a powerful interest group or coalition of interest groups. Under strong pressure from certain industries regulated by the FTC Congress in 1980 passed legislation limiting the agency's authority and specifically instructed it to stop rule-making activities in certain subject areas.[30] A somewhat similar situation affected the Occupational Safety and Health Administration (OSHA) in 1977. A growing chorus of criticism from business groups charged OSHA with enacting too many regulations that were very costly to comply with and did little to improve safety and health. Business interest groups and individual corporations lobbied Congress to enact legislation limiting OSHA's rule-making power. In this case the threat of restrictive legislation coming from influential members of Congress persuaded OSHA to voluntarily abolish 1100 of its more than 10,000 rules.[31]

Another check available to limit the power of agencies involves Congress's authority to appropriate money for agency budgets. Agency budgets are first forwarded for review by the Office of Management and Budget (OMB), which is housed within the executive branch. OMB then forwards these agency budget requests along with its recommendations (which usually call for budget cuts) to the House and Senate Budget Committees. At the same time OMB also forwards the agency budget requests along with its recommendations to the particular subcommittees of the House and Senate Appropriations Committees that have jurisdiction over each government agency. The House and Senate Budget Committees place certain limits on the agency budget amounts that may be recommended for approval by the House and Senate Appropriations Committees and their various subcommittees. However, within these limits the Appropriations Subcommittees have substantial discretion in recommending increases or decreases to a particular agency's budget request.

The Appropriations Subcommittees are authorized by the full committee to scrutinize the budget requests of particular agencies. For example, one subcommittee may be charged with reviewing the budget requests of the Departments of Labor and Commerce and the FTC. Over the years subcommittee members and staff develop considerable expertise about the functions and internal operations of the agencies they review. The subcommittees report their recommendations for budget decreases or increases to the full Appropriations Committee, which in turn reports its recommendations to the full House and Senate for a vote.

Agencies soon learn that it is not in their interest to alienate members of the Appropriations Committees and particularly members of the subcommittee that reviews the agency's budget request. Thus if enough members of Congress, especially members of the Appropriations Committees, become concerned about an agency's actions or inaction, pressure can be applied on the agency via the budget-review process. Often the threat of negative action on an agency budget appropriation will be sufficient to modify agency conduct.

A final legislative check on agency power comes from the House and Senate committees that have *oversight* authority over the agency. All federal administrative agencies are subject to oversight by particular House and Senate committees. The House and Senate Banking Committees, for example, exercise *oversight* on agencies such as the Federal Reserve Board and the Federal Deposit Insurance Corporation. Similarly, the House and Senate Labor Committees exercise oversight on the Department of Labor and the National Labor Relations Board. Unlike the Appropriations Committees, which are concerned only with budgetary appropriations, the oversight committees are essentially concerned with all other operations of the agency. Of course, a reasonable amount of oversight also takes place within the Appropriations Committees as a result of their close look at agency expenditures and programs.

In a 1977 study of regulation the Senate Governmental Affairs Committee stated: "Oversight involves a wide range of congressional efforts to review and control policy implementation by regulatory agencies." The committee then listed six primary goals of congressional oversight: (1) ensuring compliance with legislative intent, (2) determining the effectiveness of regulatory policies, (3) preventing waste and dishonesty, (4) preventing abuse in the administrative process, (5) representing the public interest, and (6) preventing agency usurpation of legislative authority.[32] These broad goals of congressional oversight illustrate the high level of monitoring and control that is possible if Congress chooses to forcefully exercise its oversight authority and responsibility.

Proposed legislation to increase or decrease the powers of a particular agency must be introduced and first considered by the House and Senate committees with oversight authority over the agency. Thus if business interest groups choose to push for a decrease in the regulatory powers of OSHA or the FTC, they first must convince members of Congress sympathetic to their view to introduce an appropriate bill. The bill is then forwarded for consideration to the relevant oversight committees. If passed in committee, the bill is forwarded for approval by the full House and Senate. Since agencies want to retain as much power and authority as possible, they have a clear interest in developing and maintaining good relations with their oversight committees so that legislation harmful to the agency is not approved. Thus members of an oversight committee have a considerable amount of leverage that can be used to influence agency actions. This leverage can also be exercised by a threatened or actual investigation of agency conduct by its oversight committee. No agency wants to generate adverse publicity for itself or risk the kind of restrictive legislation that can result from an investigation of the agency.

Effectiveness of Checks

Most observers believe that the judicial and executive checks discussed above are reasonably effective in controlling agency power. Some concerns have been raised, however, about the effectiveness of legislative checks, which in theory should provide the most direct and effective controls on agency power. What follows are three commonly raised concerns.

1. Congress is a policy-making body, which at any one time is dealing with a large number of political, economic, and social issues. It is also a political body, which recognizes that there is often more political advantage to be gained from initiating new positive programs than in correcting or exercising oversight over old ones. For both these reasons it is often difficult to get a majority in Congress sufficiently concerned about questionable agency conduct so as to take effective remedial action.

2. Regarding congressional oversight, the 1977 Report of the Senate Governmental Affairs Committee noted several factors that hinder effective oversight. These include inadequate committee staff resources and the problem of developing staff expertise for effective oversight, inadequate access to agencies and delays in obtaining information from them, and the difficulty of coordination and cooperation when an agency is subject to oversight by too many committees.

3. Some observers believe that Congress's ability to check agency power is also limited by ties that may develop between industries that are regulated or promoted by an agency and the members of the agency's oversight committee. Two examples serve to illustrate the point. First, consider a business interest group, perhaps a trade association of high-technology companies, that has export interests promoted by the Department of Commerce. The trade association wishes to protect its benefactor, the Department of Commerce. One way to do so is to develop good relations with members of the congressional committee that has oversight responsibility for the Commerce Department. These relations might be developed by (a) instructing the trade association's Washington office to provide the committee with accurate and continuing information on the foreign-trade challenges and needs of the association's members and by (b) channeling campaign contributions from the association's PAC to committee members. Second, consider an industry that has developed such a close working relationship with its regulatory agency that it can be said to have "captured" the agency in the sense that the agency no longer represents the public interest but rather, represents the interests of the industry that it is supposed to regulate. Such conduct is contrary to the agency's purpose as envisioned by Congress, and we should therefore expect that the agency's oversight committees would take steps to avoid or reverse agency capture. This legislative check is weakened, however, if the industry succeeds in influencing members of the oversight committees through the use of political campaign contributions.

While these are legitimate concerns, it is important to understand that the legislative checks are reasonably effective in restraining agency power. Regulatory agencies cannot be easily captured by interest groups. They must justify their actions according to the terms and general policies of the statutes they are charged with enforcing. Moreover, most regulatory agencies affect multiple industries or multiple firms within one industry that are likely to have conflicting interests. There are very few examples of federal administrative agencies that have been captured by the industries they regulate.

The media also serve to protect against a weakening of legislative checks. Interest groups or industries that attempt to interfere with the regulatory functions of agencies or the oversight responsibilities of congressional committees run the risk of being exposed to the increased scrutiny of investigative reporting by newspapers and television. Members of Congress are subject to the same scrutiny. Finally, it is important to note that while interest-group lobbying and campaign contributions are a fact of political life, the great majority of members of Congress are men and women of integrity who have a well-developed sense of the public interest.

DEREGULATION AND REGULATORY REFORM

The Difficulties of Deregulation

The most direct method of deregulation is to enact legislation abolishing a particular statute and the agency charged with its implementation. Alternatively, Congress can abolish certain provisions of a statute and limit the authority and functions of the agency. Unfortunately for the advocates of deregulation, this straightforward approach is the most difficult to achieve politically. Agencies that have been in existence for some time often develop clients or interest groups with economic or social interests in the continued existence of the agency. Their interests are clear, substantial, and focused, whereas the forces of deregulation are often diffused since many people may be marginally benefited, but no individuals are substantially benefited. Interest groups benefited by the regulation will work hard to retain it and to dissuade the oversight committees and Congress as a whole from taking any action.

A good example of the difficulty of this direct approach to deregulation can be seen in the problems encountered by President Reagan in his efforts to abolish the Department of Education. In his 1980 election campaign President Reagan promised that the abolition of this cabinet department would be near the top of his legislative agenda. Yet during his eight years in office Congress failed to pass legislation to abolish the agency. Why? Education interest groups receive too many benefits from the Department of Education to see it abolished without putting up very strong resistance. As we discussed in Chapter 1, they are powerful and well-organized clients of the Department who are ready, willing, and able to defend it. Conversely, those who support the Department's abolition are diffused in their opposition because they individually have little tangible to gain from its abolition.

An informal or de facto method of deregulation involves cutting the budget of a regulatory agency so that it has less money to spend on its investigation and prosecution functions. In this way the executive branch may be able to lessen the pace of regulatory enforcement without having to face the political difficulties involved in getting Congress to abolish a statute or agency. The Reagan administration was relatively successful with this informal approach to deregulation during the early 1980s, although as the Congress became more heavily controlled by the Democrats following the 1984 and 1986 elections, agency budget items previously cut began to be restored.

A second approach to de facto deregulation takes advantage of the president's power to appoint the top agency administrators. A president who seeks to encourage deregulation will appoint agency heads who agree with his deregulatory philosophy. Top agency officials may, for example, exercise their discretionary authority by asking Congress for reduced budgetary funding for the agency's regulatory and investigatory functions, or they may choose to shift the agency's resources away from these functions. Alternatively, top administrators may use their discretionary authority to slow down the rate of new regulation and the pace of agency investigations. This method of deregulation was relatively successful during the early years of the Reagan presidency. For instance, his appointments to the FTC, CPSC, EPA, OSHA, EEOC, NLRB, and the Department of the Interior, among others, resulted in a slowdown in the rate of increase of new regulation as well as less vigorous enforcement of the statutes and regulations already in place.

The effectiveness of these informal approaches to deregulation began to diminish by the end of President Reagan's first term. This trend continued as his second term drew to a close in the late 1980s. The reasons are many and diverse. First, many people in the bureaucracy responsible for the day-to-day functioning and management of the agencies were opposed to deregulation both because they saw it as diminishing agency power and because they believed in the regulatory mission of the agencies. These middle and high-level managers, whose positions are protected by the Civil Service System, are responsible for "educating" the top-level administrators that the president appoints to head the agencies. Since the president's political appointees are often unfamiliar with agency operations and because they generally remain with the agency for less than four years, they depend on the bureaucracy for guidance in the administration of the agency. This state of affairs provides the opportunity for the agency bureaucracy to drag its feet in implementing the deregulatory initiatives of top agency officials and may sometimes lead to quiet efforts to sabotage these initiatives.

A second and related reason is the ability of agency personnel to leak embarrassing information about agency actions or inaction to the media and congressional oversight committees. For example, in the case of the EPA, information was leaked to the media and oversight committees concerning charges that the "EPA had been lax in enforcing toxic waste laws, made sweetheart deals with polluters, stood to profit from conflicts of interest, manipulated toxic-cleanup grants to influence elections, shredded papers subpoenaed by Congress and used political 'hit lists' to terminate the appointments of science advisers and career employees who disagreed with the Reagan environmental policies."[33] These kinds of leaks led in 1982 and 1983 to a highly publicized investigation of the EPA by its congressional oversight committees. The investigation resulted in the resignation of the agency director and more than a dozen top EPA officials and the insistence by Congress that agency regulations be more vigorously enforced. Congress also substantially increased the agency's budget to make up for cuts in the preceding two years.

Third, in a number of agencies, especially the EPA and the Department of the Interior, special interest or client groups whose social and economic interests were promoted by the agency's regulations fought against efforts at deregulation. Environmental and conservation groups helped focus media attention on the allegedly harmful effects of deregulation. In addition, they lobbied the congressional oversight and appropriations committees in support of maintaining the EPA's statutory authority and against cutting its budgetary and personnel resources.

Finally, informal methods of deregulation are inherently limited by the fact that they do not lead to a statutory or permanent form of deregulation. That is, while deregulation by means of budget cuts or sympathetic agency officials may be effective during one presidential administration, the underlying statutes and regulations remain on the books, available to be more forcefully applied by a new president with a different view of the costs and benefits of regulation.

Regulatory Reform

Before reviewing the reasons for the regulatory reform movement and suggestions for reform, we provide some perspective through the following comments by two authorities on regulatory reform. Murray L. Weidenbaum, a former chairman of President Reagan's Council of Economic Advisors, and currently director of the Center for the Study of American Business at Washington University, writes:

> There is little justification for a general attack by business or other groups on all forms of government regulation. Unless we are anarchists, we believe that government should set rules for society. ... But as in most things in life, the sensible questions are not matters of either-or but rather of more or less and how. ... Simply put there are serious questions as to what rules to set, how detailed they should be, and how they should be administered.[34]

In a similar vein Lester Thurow, a noted economist and dean of the School of Management at the Massachusetts Institute of Technology, writes:

> The real question and the real debate revolves not around the virtues of the regulated versus the unregulated economy, but around the question of what constitutes a good set of regulations. ... No one doubts that there are both sensible and senseless regulations. The problem is to maximize the proportion of regulations that fall into the sensible category.[35]

Efforts at regulatory reform are not new. In fact, a major milestone in the reform movement occurred in 1946 with the passage of the Administrative Procedure Act. Major proposals for reform also were suggested in the Hoover Commission's Reports of 1948 and 1955. The calls for regulatory reform in the late 1970s and early 1980s differed from earlier criticisms of regulation. Public consciousness of the debate concerning regulatory excess and cost was now widespread, and the debate was more intense.

A number of factors fueled the most recent period of regulatory reform. First, the argument was made that excessive and costly regulation was in part to blame for declining American competitiveness in world markets because it contributed to a decline in productivity and a reduction in innovation and capital spending on new plants and equipment. Second, some economists argued that the costs of regulation often outweighed the benefits and that these costs were often passed on to consumers in the form of higher prices, which in turn contributed to the problem of inflation in the economy. Third, some of the impetus for regulatory reform resulted from the great increase in social regulation between 1964 and 1975. Congress and the regulatory agencies alike needed time to digest the increased level of regulation and to make such adjustments in enforcement and the level of regulation as experience dictated.

A number of regulatory reforms and suggestions for reform have been made since 1975. Some of the more significant include:

1. Executive Orders 12291 and 12498, issued during the Reagan administration, which provide OMB with extensive powers over the rule-making authority of executive branch agencies. The requirements of these executive orders, which are the most substantial reforms of the regulatory apparatus of executive-branch agencies instituted during the Reagan administration, are summarized above in our discussion of executive-branch checks on agencies.

2. The *legislative veto*, a method devised by Congress to achieve additional oversight over agency rule making. Legislative veto provisions in enabling legislation provided that a rule or regulation promulgated by an agency would become effective unless either the House or the Senate passed resolutions vetoing the rule within a certain time period, usually sixty days from the date the final rule was published in the *Federal Register*. Some legislative veto provisions required that both houses of Congress pass the veto resolution. This effort at regulatory reform was declared unconstitutional by the Supreme Court in *Chadha* in 1983.[36] The Court, basing its decision on the constitutional principle of separation of powers, held that all legislative acts (including a legislative veto) must be presented to the president for his approval or veto. Prior to the *Chadha* case Congress had incorporated the legislative veto provision into nearly two hundred statutes. It remains to be seen whether Congress will be able to reform the legislative veto so that it will comply with the constitutional requirements of the *Chadha* case.

3. *Sunset legislation*, the term used for statutory provisions that automatically terminate an agency's existence after a specified number of years unless Congress votes to renew the agency's authority for a further specified length of time. Advocates of sunset legislation argue that periodic review allows Congress to evaluate the performance and effectiveness of federal programs. They believe it is an additional form of congressional oversight, which requires Congress and the agencies to reexamine the justification for the agencies' continued existence. Opponents believe that an ef-

fective program of periodic review would be expensive and severely increase the workload of congressional committees and of the full House and Senate. While this reform proposal has been the subject of considerable discussion and review, it has been applied to very few programs or agencies.

4.　Another reform would remove the adjudication function from agency control and place it exclusively in the court system. This would eliminate the potential that exists today for a conflict of interest between the prosecutorial and adjudicatory divisions of an agency. This reform proposal has not been adopted for a number of reasons, including (a) the fact that the potential for a blatant conflict of interest is remote given an agency organizational structure that separates the prosecutorial and adjudicatory divisions; (b) the availability of judicial review to a party who challenges the decision of an administrative law judge or the agency appeals body; (c) the greatly increased burden on the court system that would result from the reform proposal; and (d) the belief that agency administrative-law judges are better prepared, in terms of experience and expertise, to adjudicate disputes involving the agency's particular statutory responsibility than are trial judges in the federal court system.

5.　Legislation that would provide OMB with statutory authority to review and establish criteria for approving executive branch *and* independent agency regulations. Currently, OMB's regulatory authority is based on executive orders, which can be canceled by a new president and, perhaps more important, do not apply to the independent regulatory agencies. To date Congress has been unwilling to grant such widespread regulatory review authority to OMB, fearing that a president committed to substantial deregulation might disregard the regulatory public policies enacted by Congress by using OMB to severely limit an independent agency's rule-making function.

6.　Comprehensive changes in the enabling acts of those agencies involved in social regulation aimed at achieving greater economic efficiency by requiring the use of cost-benefit analysis where feasible. Advocates of this reform proposal also support greater use of competitive market forces and more widespread information disclosure about products and services as a substitute for some types of social and economic regulation.

While some regulatory reform and deregulation has occurred, especially in the transportation industry and the field of financial services, the general consensus is that few substantial and lasting reforms were successfully instituted in the 1980s. One analysis of regulatory reform assessed the record of the Reagan administration, a strong supporter of reform and deregulation, in this way:

> Reagan succeeded in reducing the number of regulations promulgated each year, slowing the growth of agency budgets, institutionalizing the role of OMB in the regulatory process, imposing cost-benefit analysis on executive branch rule making, and appointing regulatory and economic advisers who shared his pro-market, anti-regulatory views.
>
> Nevertheless, Reagan failed to bring about major legislative change, including the passage of a law that would (1) give OMB statutory authority to oversee the regulatory process and (2) extend that authority to the independent agencies. Nor did he succeed in changing the underlying statutes that the regulatory agencies administered, which Weidenbaum called "the major obstacles to further improvement in the regulatory process." Instead his advisers were kept busy staving off efforts to make many regulatory statutes, particularly environmental laws, more stringent.[37]

CONCLUSION

In this chapter we have discussed many of the historical, political, and economic reasons for the growth of government regulation of business. An understanding of the rationale for this growth is important for two reasons: (1) it helps us to recognize why government plays such an important role in business decision making, and (2) it provides business with some insight on how to avoid additional regulation in the future.

After analyzing the reasons for regulation, we focused on administrative agencies and the nature of the regulatory process. Congress has delegated important functions and powers to the agencies in order to create a managerial entity that can effectively implement the public policies legislated by Congress. Examining the nature and scope of these functions helps us to understand how agencies operate and why they wield a substantial amount of power. It also leads us to consider the checks that exist on agency power and the effectiveness of these checks.

In the next three chapters, you will read about public policies (the antitrust statutes) enacted by Congress in order to encourage competitive market behavior. These statutes can be implemented by individuals as well as businesses. However, as you will learn, Congress also delegated responsibility for enforcement and implementation to the Antitrust Division of the Department of Justice and to the Federal Trade Commission, both of which are administrative agencies. In studying the antitrust laws, keep in mind that they provide a good example of public policy that is at least partially implemented by administrative agencies.

NOTES

1. For a more complete listing of the regulatory public policies affecting business, see Table 1-1 in Chapter 1.
2. Murray L. Weidenbaum, *The Future of Business Regulation* (New York: AMACOM, 1979), p. 23.
3. Alan Stone, *Regulation and Its Alternatives* (Washington, D.C.: Congressional Quarterly Press, 1982), p. 10.
4. In the discussion of administrative agencies, the terms *rule* and *regulation* (narrow definition) are used interchangeably.
5. Kenneth Culp Davis, *Administrative Law Text* (St. Paul, Minn.: West Publishing Co., 1959), p. 1.
6. Murray L. Weidenbaum, *Business, Government, and the Public*, 3rd ed. (Englewood Cliffs, N.J.: Prentice Hall, 1986), pp. 30–31.
7. Stephen G. Breyer and Richard B. Stewart, *Administrative Law and Regulatory Policy* (Boston: Little, Brown & Co., 1979), pp. 38–39. The authors define *administrative law* as "those rules and principles that define the authority and structure of administrative agencies, specify the procedural formalities that agencies employ, determine the validity of particular administrative decisions, and define the role of reviewing courts and other organs of government in their relation to administrative agencies" at p. 10.
8. Davis, *Administrative Law Text*, pp. 31–32.

9. 15 *U.S.C.A.* 2056(a).
10. 29 *U.S.C.A.* 652(8).
11. Breyer and Stewart, *Administrative Law*, pp. 13–15.
12. James Q. Wilson, "The Rise of the Bureaucratic State," *Public Interest*, no. 41 (Fall 1975), pp. 77–103. See also Robert L. Rabin, "Federal Regulation in Historical Perspective," *Stanford Law Review* 38 (1986) 1189–1326.
13. Rabin, "Federal Regulation in Historical Perspective," p. 1220.
14. Ibid., pp. 1252–53.
15. For a more extensive listing, see Table 1-1 in Chapter 1.
16. Wilson, "Rise of the Bureaucratic State," p. 88.
17. Wilson, "The Politics of Regulation," in *Social Responsibility and the Business Predicament*, ed. James W. Mckie (Washington, D.C.: Brookings Institution, 1974), p. 138.
18. Ibid., pp. 139 and 141.
19. *Federal Regulatory Directory*, 5th ed. (Washington, D.C.: Congressional Quarterly Press, 1986), p. 300.
20. Interpretive rules, a third type, are often difficult to distinguish from legislative rules and are beyond the level of complexity of this chapter.
21. Kenneth Culp Davis, *Discretionary Justice* (Baton Rouge: Louisiana State University Press, 1969), p. 65.
22. The *Federal Register* is a daily publication of the federal government that provides information about proposed and final regulations, meetings, and adjudicatory hearings of administrative agencies. Final regulations published in the *Federal Register* are also listed in the *Code of Federal Regulations* (C.F.R.) The *Code of Federal Regulations* is a multivolume set of paperbound books containing all currently effective federal regulations, listed by agency. The *Federal Register* and the *Code of Federal Regulations* can be found in county law libraries and in most large general libraries.
23. *Morrissey* v. *Brewer*, 408 U.S. 471 (1972).
24. *Goldberg* v. *Kelly*, 397 U.S. 254 (1970).
25. Kenneth Culp Davis, *Administrative Law and Government* (St. Paul, Minn.: West Publishing Co., 1975), pp. 216–17.
26. *Abbot Laboratories* v. *Gardner*, 387 U.S. 136, 141 (1967).
27. *Association of Data Processing Service Organizations, Inc.* v. *Camp*, 397 U.S. 150 (1970).
28. In the case of *informal rule making* where no formal "on the record" hearings are held, a court will not exercise judicial review of the agency's findings of fact unless the complaining party can present evidence that the agency acted in an *arbitrary or capricious manner or has been involved in an abuse of discretion.*
29. *Federal Regulatory Directory*, p. 66.
30. Ibid., pp. 48, 296–98.
31. Ibid., p. 62.
32. Ibid., p. 49.
33. Ibid., p. 114.
34. Weidenbaum, *Business, Government and the Public*, p. 32.
35. Lester C. Thurow, *The Zero-Sum Society* (New York: Basic Books, Penguin Books 1980), pp. 131–32.
36. *Immigration and Naturalization Service* v. *Chadha*, 103 S. Ct. 2764 (1983).
37. *Federal Regulatory Directory*, p. 71.

CHAPTER FOUR
ANTITRUST POLICY: OVERVIEW

INTRODUCTION

One of the most pervasive concerns of any business manager is the potential impact of federal antitrust policy on the company's operations. Antitrust, unlike most other policies, potentially can affect almost any business decision and can do so with extreme repercussions. For instance, antitrust must be considered in the course of any decision regarding contractual relationships, negotiations with other parties, alterations in internal operations, pricing decisions, and mergers. Thus it is essential that managers have a basic understanding of antitrust law so that they will be attuned to the occasions when their business decisions should be reviewed by legal counsel.

On another level antitrust serves as a thorough example of the public-policy model developed in the previous chapters. Throughout the following discussion of antitrust, consider what persons, special-interest groups, and changing economic, political, and social conditions were responsible for particular aspects of antitrust policy. Note how each of the public policy institutions (the courts, the executive, the Congress, and administrative agencies) has a key role in the development of such policies. In particular, be acutely aware of how antitrust serves as a continuing compromise between competing special and public interests that engage these institutions to fulfill their specialized needs.

Also, antitrust policy must be considered when one evaluates the future interrelationships between large corporations and government, as will be done in Chapter 7. The growth of international economic competition along with rising public expectations that business meet certain social goals are placing increasing demands on business. What is the role of antitrust in the face of these new pressures? Should certain antitrust prohibitions be eliminated, as many have suggested, or should they be more strictly enforced? The answers to these questions will make a great difference to American business in the global environment of the future.

THE ANTITRUST STATUTES

The United States antitrust policy is based upon essentially three statutes: the Sherman Act, the Clayton Act, and the Federal Trade Commission Act. The discussion in this book will focus primarily on the Sherman Act and the Clayton Act, section 7, with regard to substantive antitrust law. Section 1 of the Sherman Act deals with relations between firms, while section 2 of this statute, the monopolization section, is concerned with independent behavior by an individual firm. The other provision to be substantially considered in these pages, the Clayton Act, section 7, serves as the basis for the United States merger policy. The relevant portions of these three statutory provisions are given in the box.

Do not get the idea that the Federal Trade Commission Act or the other sections of the Clayton Act are unimportant just because this book does not

---

SHERMAN ACT, Section 1

Every contract, combination in the form of trust or otherwise, or conspiracy, in restraint of trade or commerce among the several States, or with foreign nations, is declared to be illegal. Every person ... [who violates this section] shall be deemed guilty of a felony....

SHERMAN ACT, Section 2

Every person who shall monopolize, or attempt to monopolize, or combine or conspire with any other person or persons, to monopolize ... shall be deemed guilty of a felony....

CLAYTON ACT, Section 7

No corporation engaged in commerce shall acquire, ... directly or indirectly, the whole or any part of the stock ... or any part of the assets of one or more corporations engaged in commerce, where in any line of commerce in any section of the country, the effect of such acquisition, of such stock or assets ... may be substantially to lessen competition, or tend to create a monopoly.

focus its attention on them. Section 2 of the Clayton Act, for instance, prohibits various forms of price discrimination and is a substantial legal impediment to the pricing decisions of large buyers and sellers. Likewise, sections 5 and 12 of the Federal Trade Commission Act, which empower the Federal Trade Commission to prohibit unfair trade practices, unfair methods of competition, and false advertisements, are of constant concern for business people. However, the purpose of these antitrust chapters is not to make its readers become antitrust experts. Rather, their goal is to provide a basic understanding of the most important elements of antitrust while at the same time emphasizing the interplay of the public-policy process in the development of these elements. This can be accomplished only by limiting the range of the discussion of the substantive principles. Thus when reading the antitrust chapters never forget that the scope of substantive antitrust doctrine sometimes may far exceed the discussion in the text.

The Sherman Act became law in 1890, and the Clayton Act was passed in 1914. As with any statute, rule, or regulation the first questions that must be asked are: (1) Why did the issue of antitrust arise during this period? (2) Why was the issue successful in becoming a policy of the United States? and (3) Why did the statutes take the final shape in which they were passed? It is on these questions that we now focus our attention.

The turn of the century was highlighted by what is called the industrial revolution. During this period the U.S. economy was transforming rapidly from an agrarian base to a more urban status. Whereas the United States once depended substantially on small farms and locally owned businesses, during the late 1800s large businesses with operations spanning several states began to dominate many sectors of the economy. For instance, powerful firms—powerful both in terms of assets and of financial resources—arose in steel, aluminum, railroads, cotton, sugar, and oil. The reasons for the emergence of these firms are multifaceted, but the primary causes are related to a spate of industrial inventions during the period and a liberalization in corporation laws and practices that allowed firms to raise and control large sums of capital more easily. At the same time the United States experienced a massive wave of immigration. This influx was attracted to the rapidly industrializing cities and provided the industrial corporations with inexpensive labor. The urban concentration had the effect of not only increasing the profitability of the industrial corporations but also establishing the roots of urban blight in certain American cities. The result was a new stark contrast between affluence and poverty.

The rapidly changing economic conditions during this era more than anything else accounted for the emergence of the antitrust issue. The farming community, still the dominant voice in American politics, feared the possible shift in political power that might accompany the new accumulations of wealth in industrial hands. Also, the farmers in particular complained to the government about the high shipping prices allegedly charged by the new transportation "monopolists." In addition, the issue of antitrust sounded good, in a rational ignorance sense, not only to the farmers but also to the growing populations in and around the urban slums. That is to say, antitrust statutes may have appeared to address some of the perceived problems of the farmers and urban dwellers and thus gained the support of these groups. Whether the statutes actually would benefit these interests in the long run may not have been relevant to their backing of the statutes since they may not have had the time or the sophistication to analyze the actual effects of antitrust actions.

Given the advent of the antitrust issue, one next must ask whether that issue conformed to the existing norms in American society. There is little question that policies aimed at limiting the economic power of certain entities while improving the competitive posture of smaller units is squarely within prevailing American norms. Americans cherish competition, pluralism, entrepreneurship, and universal opportunity. These standards are preserved by laws designed to slash the political and economic clout of large businesses. Note also that the perceived problems associated with concentrations of assets were attacked in the United States by statutes designed to reduce these concentrations. The continued operation of these assets in private hands, albeit smaller ones, was and is the goal of antitrust policy. This fits into the American spirit of free enterprise. In other countries, such as France and England, the solution to large aggregations of assets often has been to nationalize those assets and have the government run the businesses. Resolving the issue through nationalization obviously was, and still is, untenable in the United States given the strong norm against government ownership in this country.

The antitrust statutes that evolved in Congress through the bargaining process were both unspecific as to their aims and flexible as to their operations. Such a status of ambiguity proved to be a successful compromise between those that supported antitrust (farmers, small business) and those that opposed it (the large industrialists). From the point of view of the industrialists neither the Sherman Act nor the Clayton Act definitively listed any of their operations as illegal. The meanings of the words "monopolize," "restraint of trade," and "substantially lessen competition" were ambiguous, and it certainly could be argued that they did not cover much of the industrialists' activities. The industrialists, therefore, knowing that the environment was ripe for some form of antitrust statute, may have resolved that they could most easily reckon with statutes containing no specific designations of illegal conduct.

The supporters of antitrust also could derive benefits from these general statutes. When a statute specifically lists conduct as illegal, there is a strong implication that all other conduct is legal. The Internal Revenue Code, for instance, is a forceful example of this allegation. Thus if the antitrust statutes were to point to certain arrangements and conditions as illegal (such as price fixing, boycotts, and the attainment of a certain size in terms of assets), then there would be an inference that all other structures that businesses might develop would be legal. These statutes, then, would be ones full of loopholes that the industrialists would use to their advantage in ways that the farmers and others would find disagreeable. However, with statutes phrased generally, for instance, declaring that all combinations in restraint of trade are illegal, one always could determine that any future business arrangement was just such a restraint of trade. Thus these statutes, because of their generality, could be viewed as having the most extensive future scope.

The general terms in which the antitrust laws were written opened the doors to a continuing debate about the policy objectives of antitrust. Since the statutes' objectives are not revealed clearly by their language, those attempting to interpret the purposes of the statutes have had to search the legislative history of the laws to attempt to determine the intentions of Congress. Unfortunately, the goals of Congress in passing these laws were multifaceted and not well defined.

One primary line of interpretation stresses that the antitrust laws were designed to protect the *viability of a market system composed of small businesses*. Under this line of thought, antitrust policy should strive to eliminate business actions or combinations that may establish firms of undue size, even if those combinations might result in more efficient producers and, at least in the short term, lower prices to consumers. Supporters of this idea stress that a marketplace of many small competitive businesses will achieve best the long-run American ideals of sustaining the competitive spirit (perfect competition), American ingenuity, and unlimited opportunity.[1] In association with this interpretation, many argue that antitrust should restrict the size of businesses because large firms, facing only limited competition, may not innovate as vigorously as smaller firms, which must compete for their economic survival. This in turn may have adverse long-term consequences not only on the prices and variety of future products sold in the United States but also on the ability of U.S. firms to sustain technological advantages throughout the world. In addition, supporters of this antitrust philosophy fear that large firms may possess too much political power, which might frustrate the pluralistic balance of the U.S. political system. Also, backers of this antitrust conceptualization argue that the prevalence of large, efficient firms may reduce the ability of entrepreneurs to compete successfully in an industry, thereby stultifying the American ideal that there be widespread opportunity for private business ownership.

The other major interpretive thrust about antitrust suggests that the goal of antitrust is to maximize consumer welfare by appropriately encouraging *economic efficiency*.[2] A large firm may be able to produce and/or distribute products at a lower social cost than small firms owing to its economies of scale in operations, more efficient use of management, better access to the capital markets, and other synergies it may experience through growth. These reduced costs will translate into higher consumer welfare as long as there are vigorous competitors to the large firm. That is, as long as the large firm faces competitors that will require it to keep its price at the competitive level and to keep its product quality at the competitive standard, then society will gain by the firm's ability to generate its products or services at a lower cost. Of course, if the large firm does not face sufficient competitors, then it will be able to raise its price to an oligopolistic or monopolistic profit-maximizing point, which not only will result in prices to the consumer that exceed the competitive level but also will create a net welfare loss to society. Thus the objective of antitrust is not to restrict the size of firms but to prohibit situations in which businesses produce or distribute goods or services without facing suitable competitors. This interpretation of the antitrust laws follows from the legislative history of the acts, it is argued, because the subjects of the antitrust issue were companies facing few, if any, competitors, such as the oil, steel, and aluminum corporations.

As will be demonstrated throughout these chapters, antitrust policy has shifted markedly from the 1960s to today. During the 1960s, the institutions involved in antitrust-policy making considered the role of antitrust to be the protection of a system of small and viable businesses. Thus many business arrangements that would have created definite short-term economic efficiencies were declared illegal, and many moderate-sized mergers were blocked. Today antitrust policy is grounded firmly on economic-efficiency considerations. The government institutions involved in antitrust are taking a much more permissive attitude toward various business combinations and are freely allowing companies to control relatively large pools of assets either by way of mergers or by independent growth. While reading about the specific ways in which antitrust policy can affect business, consider the flexibility of change that is possible in this field. How and why do the changes occur? What government institutions and special-interest groups are responsible for the changes? Answers to these questions are important to business people, since they may reveal if and when antitrust policy will shift once again to supporting the objective of a market system composed of small business firms.

THE INSTITUTIONS INVOLVED IN THE MAKING OF ANTITRUST POLICY

Antitrust is such a fascinating example of the public-policy process because all the government institutions and, in addition, private parties have a significant role in how the policy evolves and is carried out. This section will briefly lay out the various antitrust players and the ways they affect antitrust policy. While reading the remaining chapters on antitrust, be sure to recognize how each player was involved in specific antitrust policies and why each was effective or ineffective in framing those policies.

Congress

Since federal antitrust policy is based primarily on federal statutes rather than on the U.S. Constitution, Congress is the focal point in the antitrust arena. The basic antitrust statutes are very general in their wording, which provides the other government institutions tremendous flexibility in applying those statutes. However, Congress has several tools at its disposal to restrain the actions of the other players if the consensus of the Congress is that the proper function of antitrust is not being pursued.

The most definitive action Congress can take is to amend the antitrust statutes to enunciate more explicitly the policy Congress wants followed. This route, of course, requires either presidential approval or an override of the president's veto. For example, the Clayton Act, section 7, as originally drafted, was interpreted by the courts to apply only to mergers that were effected through securities purchases. Purchases of assets were considered outside the purview of the Clayton Act. In 1950, however, Congress passed the Celler-Kefauver Act, which amended the Clayton Act so that section 7 explicitly directed that asset purchases were subject to the Clayton Act to the same extent as securities purchases.

Similarly, Congress may pass new antitrust laws to broaden or reduce the reach of antitrust. For instance, the passage of the Federal Trade Commission Act was in part a declaration by Congress that antitrust enforcement should extend beyond the scope originally contemplated with the Sherman and Clayton Acts. One component of this statute, specifically section 5, empowers the Federal Trade Commission to investigate and prevent "unfair methods of competition." The legislative history of the act clearly indicates that this phrase was designed to supplement and bolster the Sherman Act and the Clayton Act to stop in their incipiency certain business practices that, if allowed to mature, might later violate those existing laws.[3] Under this directive the Federal Trade Commission has over the years prevented certain uncompetitive business operations that otherwise would have been permissible under the Clayton and Sherman Acts.

Congress has other methods to prevent or require specific antitrust actions. The appropriation process is one valuable tool. Congress may, as part of the appropriation package for an administrative agency, make certain directives on how the funds allocated to an agency may or may not be spent. For example, in 1984 Congress placed language in the FTC appropriation bill that prevented that agency from bringing antitrust actions against municipalities. In addition, Congress can restrain an overzealous agency by appropriating insufficient funds for the agency to proceed so broadly. Congress also can pass or threaten to pass certain antitrust legislation to bring antitrust policy into line with its wishes. In the wave of large oil mergers in 1984, for instance, several pieces of legislation were considered by Congress to prevent or delay such mergers. Although these bills never became law, they do demonstrate the power of Congress to determine policy if the members can reach the required agreement as to that policy. Likewise, as will be illustrated later, Congress at the behest of retail discounters in 1984 became involved in the Reagan administration's attempt to redefine the legality of vertical price-fixing agreements.

The final key method in which Congress can affect antitrust policy is through granting exemptions from the antitrust laws (by passing acts) to certain groups and industries. For instance, after the FTC determined in 1978 that certain soft-drink companies violated the antitrust laws when they assigned exclusive sales territories to their bottlers, Congress passed the Soft Drink Interbrand Competition Act, which partially exempted the soft-drink industry from the application of the antitrust laws with respect to assignments of exclusive territories. Similarly, fishermen and farmers have been granted exemptions from the antitrust laws, thereby permitting them to form cooperative marketing associations to sell their wares jointly. Likewise, labor unions have a broad exemption from application of the antitrust laws through sections 6 and 20 of the Clayton Act. In addition, certain industries regulated by state and federal agencies have been granted certain degrees of exemption from the antitrust laws. For instance, insurance companies that are regulated by state governments are exempted from antitrust enforcement by the McCarren-Ferguson Act, and banks that have their mergers approved by the requisite administrative agencies are exempt from application of the Clayton Act by the Bank Merger Act of 1966. In all, there may be as many as sixteen separate exemption areas covering as much as 20 percent of the nation's private economic activity.[4]

For exemptions from the antitrust laws, as with all congressional legislation, one should ask why the exemptions were granted. Question whether the exemptions were designed to promote the public interest. Some of the exemptions, such as the labor exemption, for instance, were instituted to effectuate a broader policy objective. In the labor case the exemption was a necessary component of legislation designed to strengthen the bargaining position of unions. In addition, consider what groups may have supported particular exemptions and which ones may have opposed them. In this regard investigate the resources, commitment, and cohesiveness of those supporting and opposing various exemptions. For example, during the last few years Congress has been debating the proposed Malt Beverage Interbrand Competition Act, which would grant to beer brewers the same exemption that soft-drink companies now enjoy. In support of the legislation are certain brewers and their wholesalers. Opposed to the exemption are various liquor purchasers, including liquor stores, grocery operators, and taverns. Consumers for the most part have not heard of the Malt Beverage Interbrand Competition Act, nor would they understand it completely without thoroughly studying it. Thus they likely spend their votes and money on other issues. (This is barring the doubtful occurrence that particular legislators will choose to run on the issue through relying on rational ignorance.) Therefore, the future of this exemption strictly involves special-interest politics, and its fate ultimately will rest upon the effectiveness of the lobbying campaigns on each side of the issue.

The Federal Court System

Because of the ambiguity in the antitrust statutes, the federal courts have tremendous power to shape antitrust policy through statutory interpretations. In fact, since there is so little specific direction in those statutes, it is fair to say that much of antitrust is "judge-made law." For example, as we shall see in the next chapter, horizontal price fixing, vertical price fixing, and horizontal territorial restraints are all illegal under most circumstances as violative of the Sherman Act, section 1. Determination of illegality does not come from Congress but, rather, from interpretations by the federal courts of the types of restraints that necessarily restrain trade. Likewise, the types of mergers that violate the Clayton Act, section 7, and the forms of monopolistic behavior that fall within the Sherman Act, section 2, are somewhat dependent on interpretations of these provisions issued by the courts.

As always within the federal court system, the district courts and courts of appeals shape the interpretations of the antitrust statutes, subject to the final determinations of the U.S. Supreme Court, when it chooses to make a policy statement through deciding a controversial case. The Reagan appointees to the federal courts, who constitute almost one-half of the federal bench, are somewhat consistent in their ideological backing of the "efficiency" approach to antitrust. Given that many of these new judges are relatively young, those persons who want to see the guiding philosophy of antitrust policy return to the promotion of small business units may have to look to Congress or other government players to effectuate that change in the near future. This conclusion is supported by the evolving antitrust philosophy of the Supreme Court. Beginning with its landmark opinion in *Continental T.V. v. G.T.E. Sylvania* in 1977, the Court has turned markedly toward using efficiency standards to evaluate antitrust. Given the current structure of the Court, it is unlikely that it will soon change the course of antitrust back to the days of promoting small competitors. Again, relief for those who are opposed to this form of antitrust policy will have to be gained through the other institutions involved in the making of antitrust policy.

The Administrative Agencies

Two federal administrative agencies serve as the primary public enforcers of the antitrust statutes: the *Federal Trade Commission* (FTC) and the *Antitrust Division of the Justice Department*. The FTC is an independent administrative agency. Each of its five commissioners is appointed by the president (subject to confirmation by the Senate) for a five-year term, and each can be removed from office only for malfeasance. In addition, only three commissioners of the FTC may belong to the same political party. The Antitrust Division of the Justice Department is a cabinet-level agency, and thus its head, who has the title of assistant attorney general, serves at the pleasure of the president. Therefore, the enforcement actions of the Justice Department theoretically are more subject to the wishes of the president than are those of the FTC.

The Justice Department vigorously supported President Reagan's antitrust agenda. Indeed, under the direction of William Baxter, Paul McGrath, Douglas Ginsburg, and Charles Rule, the Antitrust Division was one of the most ideologically activist agencies in antitrust history. The Division was prolific in filing "friend-of-the-court" briefs in important private antitrust actions, asking the courts to consider market-efficiency standards in their antitrust opinions. The Division also published a series of guidelines, most notably in the vertical restraint and merger areas, announcing its policy standards for enforcement. As will be seen, these guidelines are based entirely on economic efficiency grounds. In the same vein the Division was very restrained in bringing antitrust-enforcement actions. Using principles of economic welfare, the Division viewed few business arrangements as harmful in an antitrust sense except for certain instances of horizontal price fixing. Finally, the Reagan administration's Antitrust Division respectively dropped and settled two of the most significant antitrust cases ever brought by the U.S. government: the prosecutions against IBM and AT&T.

Owing to Ronald Reagan's two-term tenure in the presidency, all five commissioners of the FTC eventually were nominated by him. The chairperson, Daniel Oliver, was a fervent believer in the "hands-off" approach to government regulation, and the remaining Reagan appointees in the Commission shared this view. During this period the FTC promulgated guidelines modeled after those of the Justice Department, thereby indicating its approval of the cabinet agency's approach to antitrust. Likewise, the FTC's enforcement behavior was restrained. Thus although President Reagan had less direct control over the FTC, his antitrust philosophy nonetheless was advanced by that commission.

The enforcement duties of the administrative agencies are allocated in the following manner. The Antitrust Division has exclusive domain in bringing actions under the Sherman Act while the FTC has exclusive jurisdiction over the FTC Act. The two agencies share responsibilities or, in other words, have concurrent jurisdiction in enforcing the Clayton Act. To avoid duplication of effort the agencies informally attempt to coordinate their enforcement actions under the Clayton Act. Through this coordination the FTC has been given primary responsibility for enforcing section 2 of the Clayton Act, the price-discrimination provision, and the Antitrust Division generally does not bring actions under that section. With respect to section 7, the merger provision, the agencies concentrate on particular industries. The FTC, for instance, takes primary responsibility for reviewing the oil, auto, and retail food industries, while the Antitrust Division concentrates on steel, railroad, and communications businesses. At times, however, the agencies will negotiate certain deviations from these informal standards, especially in high-profile cases.

The administrative agencies have three *civil remedies* at their disposal to enforce the antitrust statutes: (1) injunctions, (2) orders of specific performance, and (3) damage awards for injuries to the United States. When an injunction is imposed by a court on a company, then that firm is required to discontinue a particular activity that is deemed to violate the antitrust laws. For example, an injunction in a price-fixing case may prohibit certain forms of communication between competitors. An order of specific performance requires that a company perform a particular act. For instance, in merger cases, one remedy often is to demand that the defendant divest certain assets so that competition is not restrained substantially. In addition to these court orders the Clayton Act provides, in section 4A, that the federal government can sue for damages sustained by the United States from an antitrust violation plus an amount to cover the cost of the lawsuit.

Besides pursuing civil actions the Justice Department may enforce the antitrust laws through *criminal proceedings*. By the terms of the statute a violation of the Sherman Act is a felony punishable by up to three years of imprisonment and by fines of up to $100,000 per count for an individual and up to $1 million per count for a corporation.[5] Criminal prosecutions under the antitrust laws, however, are somewhat rare, for a number of reasons. First, neither the FTC nor private parties can initiate criminal proceedings. Only the Justice Department has this option. Second, the burden of proof in a criminal case requires that the jury be certain "beyond a reasonable doubt" that an antitrust violation has occurred. It is much more difficult for a prosecutor to prove a case with this degree of certainty than it is for him or her to establish it by "a preponderance of the evidence" as is necessitated in a civil case. Third, the prosecution in a criminal action must prove that the defendant undertook the business arrangement with the conscious objective of restraining trade in an antitrust sense. In a civil action the mere fact that the defendant performed the offending act is sufficient. However, in a criminal suit the Justice Department must convince a jury that the defendant knew the action would have the probable consequence of affecting competition in an illegal manner. Depending on the type of uncompetitive conduct, this requisite criminal intent may be difficult to prove. Also, establishing criminal intent may be particularly tricky when the defendant is a corporation. What persons in the corporation knowledgeably direct the actions of that corporation to the extent that their intent may be attributed to the corporation? The answer to this issue is never clear, although the knowledge of certain chief officers and board members has been found to be sufficient.

The Justice Department is a cabinet agency that has neither rule-making capabilities nor quasi-judicial powers. Therefore, its major impact in terms of antitrust policy formulation is through its level of enforcement of antitrust statutes in the federal court system. Basically, the Antitrust Division of the Justice Department will initiate an investigation when it learns of a situation that may violate the antitrust laws as it interprets them. One primary source of information regarding these potentially violative situations is complaints made to the agency by its constituents, which in this case include customers and competitors. Another way the Division may learn of potential antitrust problems is through information that businesses are required to report to it. An example of such a report is premerger notification, which will be discussed in some detail in Chapter 6.

The basic means through which the agency investigates a situation is by issuing a form of subpoena called a *Civil Investigative Demand* (CID). A CID may be issued upon any person or business entity that reasonably may have information relevant to the investigation. The CID may compel the production of documents, or it may require that certain questions be answered. Such information then is used by the agency to validate the strength of the case, and later as evidence in the federal courts. In addition, if criminal proceedings are pursued, the information can be submitted to the grand jury.

The FTC, as discussed in Chapter 3, is an independent agency that has both rule-making and quasi-judicial functions. In the antitrust realm, the FTC most often makes policy using the case-by-case adjudicatory route. Like the Antitrust Division, the FTC generally becomes involved in antitrust matters in response to constituent complaints or information gathered from public filings. Also, the FTC has civil subpoena power similar to that enjoyed by the Antitrust Division. Where the two agencies differ is that the FTC will pursue the action, if it chooses to do so, not in the federal court system but rather before an administrative-law judge within its own quasi-judicial court system. In resolving the antitrust issue, the FTC will follow its internal procedural rules and those of the Administrative Procedure Act, as outlined in Chapter 3. Appeals of determinations by the administrative-law judge are made first to the full commission and then to the federal courts of appeals. The FTC's action against Procter & Gamble, challenging its 1957 purchase of the Clorox Chemical Company, provides a good example of these agency proceedings. This is discussed in Chapter 6 in the section on conglomerate mergers.

The FTC also has the power under various statutes to make trade regulations. For instance, the Magnuson-Moss Act authorizes the Commission to specifically define, through rule making, those practices that are unfair or deceptive under the FTC Act. The FTC employs notice-and-comment rule-making procedures, as outlined in Chapter 3, to promulgate the trade regulations, and they are subject to appeal to the federal courts of appeals. Regulations dealing with funeral parlors and used-car dealerships are just two of the several instances of rule making undertaken by the FTC under this act. As another example, section 7A of the Clayton Act authorizes the FTC to make rules regarding premerger notification using the notice-and-comment procedures. The process by which the FTC has passed such rules will be explored in Chapter 6.

Although we have been concentrating on the federal policy makers in this book, we would be remiss in overlooking the role of state government agencies in shaping antitrust policy. State attorneys general may bring civil actions under the federal antitrust statutes in two capacities: (1) representing the state, itself, when it has been damaged in its commercial transactions by companies engaging in antitrust violations; and (2) representing individual citizens of the state. Such actions currently are being brought with increasing frequency by several state attorneys general to pick up what they perceive as laxity in enforcement by the federal agencies. Indeed, the National Association of Attorneys General has adopted merger and vertical-restraint guidelines which indicate that state agencies will become more active in antitrust prosecutions to counteract the modern federal antitrust policy. In addition, most states have their own antitrust statutes under which the state agencies and private citizens may bring suits. These statutes often parallel the federal statutes, thereby empowering the state agencies to bring criminal prosecutions and private citizens to bring treble damage suits. However, unlike the federal statutes, many of these state laws provide the state agencies with the additional right to bring treble damage lawsuits. Again, state antitrust enforcement under these laws may increase in response to changes in federal antitrust policy.

The Executive

The executive branch influences antitrust policy primarily through the president's power to nominate the heads of the public enforcement agencies and the justices to the federal court system. Since the Antitrust Division is within the Justice Department, a cabinet-level administrative agency, the president can exact allegiance to his antitrust philosophy through his power to nominate heads likely to follow that philosophy and his power to fire them if they deviate from his designs. As stated before, President Reagan was very effective in shaping the Antitrust Division through his appointments of Baxter, McGrath, Ginsburg, and Rule. Also, the president has the power to fill, subject to Senate confirmation, any vacancy on the FTC when it arises, either after the end of a commissioner's five-year term or when one resigns.

The president's impact on antitrust policy through his power to nominate court justices may be even more dramatic because these appointments serve for life. President Reagan thoroughly screened judicial candidates and largely appointed relatively young persons to serve as federal justices. Those persons selected generally adhere to the efficiency concepts of antitrust and may impact future antitrust policy through their statutory interpretations for years to come. Similarly, the pendulum is swinging toward efficiency concepts in the Supreme Court, and the justices appointed by President Reagan to that body surely will push that pendulum further upon its current course.

Another avenue of influence for the president is through the executive communication to Congress by which legislation is proposed. For example, President Reagan, in conjunction with his 1987 State of the Union address, delivered legislation to the 100th Congress designed to enhance the "competitiveness" of U.S. industries. This forty-three-section package, introduced in the respective congressional houses as S. 539 and H.R. 1155, contained a number of antitrust reforms. For example, the Antitrust Remedies Improvements Act of 1987 would have amended section 4 of the Clayton Act to reduce the instances in which treble damages could be awarded and would have allowed prevailing defendants under certain circumstances to recover attorneys' fees and costs from plaintiffs. These concepts will be explored further in the next section. Also, the Merger Modernization Act of 1987 would have amended the Clayton Act, section 7, so that it would apply only when there was a significant probability that a merger would increase the ability of the firms to exercise market power rather than, as now, when a merger simply may tend to lessen competition. None of the major components of the antitrust reform measures introduced by the president in 1987 became law.

The Private Sector

Private parties who believe that they have suffered certain forms of damages from an antitrust violation are provided with huge incentives by the Clayton Act to pursue an antitrust claim against an alleged violator. Section 4 of the Clayton Act provides:

> Any person who shall be injured in his business or property by reason of anything forbidden in the antitrust laws may sue therefore ... [in the appropriate federal district court] and shall recover threefold the damages by him sustained, and the cost of suit, including a reasonable attorney's fee.

Clearly, the ability of a successful plaintiff to obtain a judgment equal to three times his proven actual damages (*treble damages*) is the most controversial portion of this provision.

One rationale for treble damages is that the opportunity for private parties to receive such a windfall stimulates them to police the antitrust laws. Typically in the United States legal system, an injured party who is considering litigation must make a cost/benefit risk analysis before bringing suit. In that calculus this party must enter, among other considerations, (1) the likelihood of convincing the judge or jury that the defendant violated the law, (2) the likelihood that the judge or jury will determine that the damages are in accordance with the party's own calculation of them, and (3) the cost of the suit and the attorney's fees this party must pay whether he wins or loses the suit. Therefore, under normal circumstances, it is not unusual for an aggrieved party to forgo a lawsuit because the result of the cost/benefit risk analysis is negative. Treble damages, however, can swing such cost/benefit calculations to the positive side by dramatically increasing the potential payoff of a successful suit. Thus the burden on the federal agencies to police the antitrust laws is reduced somewhat because most parties aggrieved by violations of the antitrust laws now find it profitable, under appropriate risk analyses, to pursue these claims themselves in court.

Besides providing potential plaintiffs a large incentive to bring antitrust actions, the specter of treble damage awards acts to inhibit businesses not only from engaging in clearly violative behavior but also from participating in activities that may be even remotely viewed as uncompetitive conduct. Thus a company considering a horizontal-price-fixing agreement will think long and hard, before actually entering the arrangement, about the treble damage consequences if it were caught. However, likewise a business contemplating a novel marketing technique may choose not to employ that technique for fear that it may be seen by a federal court as an unreasonable restraint of trade. This, of course, may or may not be socially beneficial. On the one hand, firms will stay well clear from anticompetitive actions that feasibly may have antitrust ramifications. On the other hand, businesses may refrain from socially useful and "efficient" arrangements because of just that fear of a potential treble damage lawsuit. As related above, the Reagan administration proposed that treble damages be restricted to certain practices only, because it believed that too many forms of socially efficient business arrangements were lying dormant on companies' drawing boards. This, it hypothesized, might be hurting the competitive posture of U.S. firms vis-à-vis foreign competitors.

The ability of successful antitrust plaintiffs to receive *court costs* and *attorney's fees* should not be overlooked as an added incentive for private parties to bring suits. Owing to lengthy discovery requirements antitrust actions often take years to complete. With average fees for attorneys and other experts running at $100 per hour and more, these costs can easily total in the hundreds of thousands of dollars, and in some suits may far exceed the total amount of the damages recovery. One extreme example may be found in *Greenhaw* v. *Lubbock County Beverage Association* (1983) where the attorneys' fees were $246,517, while the award to the plaintiffs, after trebling, was $17,482.[6] Thus aggrieved persons with solid antitrust claims can embark on the long and expensive course of litigation, since they know that the ultimate award will not be reduced by the necessary attorney's fees and court costs.

The liberal award provisions for private suits may also affect the number of settlements in public enforcement actions. Consider a company that is a defendant in a civil antitrust action brought by the Antitrust Division. This company realizes that if it were to litigate and lose the case, the determination of its violation could be used as prima facie evidence of that violation in subsequent court proceedings brought by private litigants complaining about the same business activity. In this event, since the violation already has been established, all the private litigants need do is prove the extent of their damage and thereby be entitled to receive three times this amount plus their attorney's fees and court costs. Thus a business that loses a public enforcement action almost necessarily will have to face a huge financial burden as well.

One way the defendant can reduce the likelihood of private suits is to enter a *consent decree* with the government agency that is prosecuting the case. In effect, a consent decree is a settlement between the government agency and the defendant under which the defendant, while not admitting its guilt, promises to do or not do what the government wishes, and the government agrees not to pursue the case further. This agreement often benefits both parties. Without spending more public funds, the government receives from the defendant a promise to perform or refrain from performing many of the acts for which it was probably suing in the first place. The defendant escapes from the settlement with only these obligations; there is no evidence that it violated the antitrust laws. Thus for a private party to collect treble damages it now will have to go through the lengthy process of proving the antitrust violation, as well as the amount of its damages. It is for these reasons that since 1973 approximately 92 percent of the antitrust actions brought by the Justice Department have ended in consent decrees.[7]

In 1974 Congress enacted the Antitrust Procedure and Penalties Act to remove certain consent decree negotiations from secrecy, and to ensure that they conform with the public interest. Under the act an antitrust consent decree is not effective until a federal court approves it as one that furthers the public interest. In reaching its determination the court reviews public comments, a competitive-impact statement furnished by the government, and possibly other forms of testimony. If the court does approve the decree, the terms of the settlement are under the court's jurisdiction, and a violation of them will be deemed an act in contempt of court.

ANTITRUST JURISDICTION

Jurisdiction within the United States

Recall that under the U.S. Constitution the federal government can regulate only in those fields expressly designated by the Constitution as being within the realm of federal authority. As illustrated earlier, the constitutional authority for a great proportion of federal statutes derives from the Commerce Clause in article I, section 8, which grants to the U.S. government the power to regulate commerce with foreign nations and among the several states. This constitutional provision is the jurisdictional basis for the antitrust statutes as well.

Under the prevailing broad interpretation of the Commerce Clause federal statutes can be applied not only to commercial activities that move directly across state lines but also to purely intrastate activities as long as those activities have some indirect effect on certain commercial flows of goods or services among the states. As we saw in Chapter 2, the Constitution even permits the federal government to regulate race-discrimination practices occurring far within a state's borders because of the possible indirect effect of that discrimination on the flow of goods and services into that state. In the same way it should be easy to see that the federal government has the clear authority not only to pass antitrust statutes but to apply them to even the most remote intrastate commercial arrangements. For instance, assume hypothetically that four competitive liquor distributors operating only in Colorado agree to divide the state into four quadrants with each agreeing to sell only in one particular quadrant. Thus in any quadrant of Colorado there will be competing three fewer distributors of liquor than there were before the agreement. Could the contract indirectly affect interstate commerce? The answer, as with practically all Commerce Clause analyses, is a resounding yes. In this situation, since there are fewer distributors selling in each quadrant of Colorado, the wholesale prices of liquor in each quadrant may increase. If the prices of liquor increase, then fewer sales of liquor in Colorado may result. If the sales of liquor in Colorado are reduced, then the quantity of liquor or ingredients to make liquor that must cross into Colorado may be diminished. The above series of links is sufficient to give the federal government the constitutional basis to apply the antitrust laws to the arrangement. Indeed, by use of similar conceptualizations the federal government has the constitutional authority to apply the federal antitrust laws to almost any conceivable intrastate arrangement. As stated by the Supreme Court in *Hospital Building Co.* v. *Trustees of the Rex Hospital* (1976), "It is settled that the [Sherman] Act encompasses far more than restraints on trade that are motivated by a desire to limit interstate commerce or have their sole impact on interstate commerce.... If it is interstate commerce that feels the pinch, it does not matter how local the operation which applies the squeeze."[8]

Although the federal antitrust laws constitutionally could be applied to virtually any commercial activity, the courts have interpreted that Congress intended the acts to cover only interstate arrangements and intrastate activities that "substantially" affect interstate commerce. Thus the courts have determined that the federal antitrust laws were not designed to regulate intrastate business arrangements that only indirectly affect a minor volume of interstate traffic. However, as already mentioned, most state governments have passed their own antitrust statutes, and these often are directly modeled on the federal antitrust laws. Therefore, even when a business may escape federal antitrust liability because its commercial arrangement has only an insubstantial effect on interstate commerce, it still must consider the state's antitrust laws, which likely will condemn the practice in a fashion equal to the federal laws.

International Jurisdiction

The extreme jurisdictional reach of the federal antitrust laws within the United States may have come as little surprise. However, the extent of their applicability to business arrangements by foreign companies in other nations not only surprises many people but greatly irritates and offends numbers of others. In the landmark case of *United States* v. *Alcoa* (1945) Judge Learned Hand determined that the Sherman Act applied to arrangements strictly between foreign companies if "they were intended to affect imports and did affect them."[9] Since this case the antitrust laws generally have been held applicable to the operations of companies in foreign countries if those operations have a substantial and reasonably foreseeable effect either on the import trade or on the domestic commerce of the United States. Two significant exceptions, based on principles of international law, may serve to limit the international reach of the antitrust laws in certain situations. First, the U.S. courts will not assume jurisdiction in cases involving suits against a foreign government. Thus if the foreign businesses in question are operated or otherwise are directed by a foreign sovereign, then the U.S. courts will not accept the antitrust claim. This is what protects OPEC from an antitrust lawsuit in the United States. Second, by following the international doctrine of comity, U.S. courts may deny jurisdiction if they consider that the policies of a foreign government that support the foreign business arrangement outweigh the United States antitrust policies.

Many foreign nationals take offense at the extraterritorial application of the U.S. antitrust laws. Conduct that may be anticompetitive by U.S. standards may be totally legal under foreign philosophies. Also, the huge liability exposure from the Clayton Act, section 4, seems unreasonable from a foreign perspective. Therefore, some foreign nations have passed retaliatory legislation to inhibit the application of the U.S. antitrust laws. For example, certain countries have passed statutes that frustrate efforts to gather evidence within those countries for U.S. antitrust suits. Other nations have passed laws limiting or denying the enforcement of U.S. antitrust judgments within those nations. Also, some countries have enacted so-called clawback statutes, which limit the impact of U.S. antitrust judgments. The most notable of these is a British statute that allows a British company that is ordered to pay a treble damage award arising from an antitrust suit to a plaintiff within the United States to sue that plaintiff in the British courts for two-thirds of that award. This, of course, has the effect of nullifying the trebling component of the U.S. damage award.

In 1988 the Justice Department released guidelines indicating that this agency perceived few international business ventures as raising antitrust concerns. For example, several types of international technology licensing practices considered to be automatically illegal by previous Department staffs will be analyzed more liberally under a case-by-case approach. Since these guidelines were released at the end of the Reagan administration, their longevity obviously is somewhat dependent on the antitrust philosophies of subsequent presidents and of those persons placed in charge of the Justice Department and the Antitrust Division. However, one should expect that the Justice Department will be less active in the international arena for at least the near future.

CONCLUSION

The antitrust laws are of vital concern to business people because of their broad applicability and potentially severe consequences. These laws also serve as a splendid example of the public-policy process discussed in detail in the previous chapters. All of the major governmental institutions have a role in defining the policies underlying antitrust, and numerous business and consumer interests constantly lobby these institutions to promote the policy that best supports them.

In the next two chapters, some specific antitrust policies will be discussed in detail. In Chapter 5, various forms of concerted arrangements that might restrain trade will be investigated. In particular, the current state of the law and the policy objectives behind the Sherman Act, section 1, will be reviewed. In Chapter 6 the antitrust concerns relevant to large industrial organizations will be highlighted. Here the public-policy controversies involved with monopolization and mergers will be considered.

NOTES

1. Robert Pitofsky, "The Political Content of Antitrust," 121 *Univ. of Penn. Law Review* 1051 (1979); Kenneth Elzinga, "The Goals of Antitrust: Other than Competition and Efficiency, What Else Counts?" 125 *Univ. of Penn. Law Review* 1191 (1977).

2. Conference Board, "Antitrust and New Views of Microeconomics: Antitrust Forum 1985," *Conference Board Research Bulletin*, no. 195 (1985).

3. *Federal Trade Commission v. Brown Shoe Co., Inc.*, 384 U.S. 316 (1965).

4. Thomas W. Dunfee and Frank F. Gibson, *Antitrust and Trade Regulation*, 2d ed. (New York: John Wiley & Sons, 1985), p. 239.

5. Under the Comprehensive Crimes Control Act an individual may be fined up to $250,000 per count.

6. 721 F. 2d 1019 (5th Cir. 1983).

7. McDavid, Sankbeil, Schmidt, and Brett, "Antitrust Consent: Ten Years of Experience under the Tunney Act," *Antitrust Law Journal* 52 (1983), 883.

8. 425 U.S. 738, 743 (1976).

CHAPTER FIVE
Antitrust Policy: Concerted Activities in Restraint of Trade

INTRODUCTION

In this chapter we will analyze in more specificity some of the business arrangements condemned by the Sherman Act, section 1. Recall that section 1 of the Sherman Act prohibits contracts, combinations, and conspiracies in restraint of trade. The discussion here will begin with an exploration of the meanings of the phrases "contract, combination, and conspiracy" and "in restraint of trade." Then we will turn to various business practices that the public-policy institutions have determined may restrain trade, and the conditions under which they will most likely be deemed illegal under this antitrust act. In this regard we will review:

- Horizontal price fixing
- Horizontal market divisions
- Vertical nonprice restraints
- Vertical price fixing

Note that this is not an exhaustive list of those types of business arrangements that may restrain trade. Boycotts, tying arrangements, and joint ventures, for example, are just a few of the many other forms of concerted business activities that draw antitrust scrutiny under the Sherman Act, section 1.

However, we have selected topics that will give you a flavor for the ways the policy institutions interact to shape the components of antitrust policy. As a result you should have an understanding of how other business arrangements may be approached within the antitrust policy dynamic.

THE REQUIREMENT OF A CONTRACT, COMBINATION, OR CONSPIRACY

Two conditions must be met in order for a person to violate section 1 of the Sherman Act:

1. There must be a contract, combination, or conspiracy.
2. There must be a restraint of trade.

Therefore, a prerequisite to a finding of liability under section 1 is that there be a contract, combination, or conspiracy. Unilateral behavior (that is, behavior undertaken by one firm without any collusive or joint aspects), no matter how much it might restrain trade, cannot come under section 1. Antitrust relief from such unilateral actions must be found, if anywhere, within the terms of other antitrust provisions. The Sherman Act, section 2, for instance, is specifically aimed at unilateral efforts to monopolize.

Assume that a lawsuit is initiated in which it is alleged that the defendant engaged in conduct that violated section 1 of the Sherman Act. The first task for the court is to determine if there is sufficient evidence to prove that two or more persons (or firms) reached some form of agreement. If the persons put the terms of their agreement into writing, then the court's job is easy, since production of the written document fulfills the first prerequisite. However, if the parties did not express their agreement in writing, then the court's task is significantly more difficult. Oral testimony confirming that an agreement was made may be sufficient evidence to meet the first requirement of the Sherman Act. However, since all the parties to the agreement may have violated the antitrust laws, there may be no one willing to testify to the existence of that agreement. In this case the court must rely on *circumstantial evidence* to prove that a contract, combination, or conspiracy took place.

Circumstantial evidence consists of facts that strongly imply that a certain event or sequence of events occurred. For instance, if we walked into a room with locked windows and saw two individuals, one writhing on the floor and the other holding a smoking gun, then we might infer that the individual holding the gun shot the dying person on the floor. This type of evidence is circumstantial, since the conclusion is obtained only through a logical analysis of indirect facts. Of course, from these events one cannot be certain that the gun holder actually shot the victim. Someone else may have fired the shots, thrust the gun into the hands of the person seen holding the weapon, leaped out of the window, closed that window sufficiently hard to engage its lock, and dashed out of sight. However, this possibility is so slim that one readily dismisses it. Therefore, the supposition with circumstantial evidence is derived because all other possible conclusions are so unlikely that they logically can be ignored.

Circumstantial evidence is used in the same way to prove the existence of an agreement for lawsuits under the Sherman Act, section 1. In these cases there must be facts that strongly imply an agreement because other possibilities are so remote. As the Supreme Court announced in *Monsanto Co. v. Spray-Rite Service Corp.* (1984), "There must be evidence that tends to exclude the possibility that the . . . [alleged agreeing parties] were acting independently."[1] In other words, an agreement may be inferred from circumstantial evidence only if the facts presented most likely could not have evolved from independent decision making by individual firms.

Possibly the most puzzling events in this area involve firms that are behaving in a parallel fashion. Can one infer from the fact that firms are doing the same thing that they agreed to perform similarly? The answer depends on whether there exist sensible commercial reasons that would induce each firm to take the same actions without the existence of an agreement. In this regard consider the following case.

THEATRE ENTERPRISES, INC.
v.
PARAMOUNT FILM DISTRIBUTING CORP.
United States Supreme Court
346 U.S. 537 (1954)

Background

Theatre Enterprises, the petitioner, brought suit in federal district court alleging that Paramount and other motion picture distributors had violated the antitrust laws by conspiring to restrict first-run films to downtown Baltimore theaters, thereby limiting Theatre Enterprises' suburban Baltimore theater, the Crest, to subsequent-run films. The district court returned a verdict for the defendant distributors, and the court of appeals affirmed. The Supreme Court granted certiorari.

Opinion

Justice Clark

. . . (P)etitioner owns and operates the Crest Theatre, located in a neighborhood shopping district some six miles from the downtown shopping center in Baltimore, Maryland. The Crest, possessing the most modern improvements and appointments, opened on February 26, 1949. Before and after the opening, petitioner, through its president, repeatedly sought to obtain first-run features for the theatre. Petitioner approached each respondent separately, initially requesting exclusive first-runs, later asking for first-runs on a "day and date" basis. But respondents uniformly rebuffed petitioner's efforts and adhered to an established policy of restricting first-runs in Baltimore to eight downtown theatres. Admittedly there is no direct evidence of illegal agreement between the respondents and no conspiracy is charged as to the independent exhibitors in Baltimore, who account for 63 percent of first-run exhibitions. The various respondents advance much the same reasons for denying petitioner's offers. Among other reasons, they asserted that day and date first-runs are normally granted only to noncompeting theatres. Since the Crest is in "substantial competition" with the downtown theatres, a day and date arrangement would be economically unfeasible. And even if respondents wished to grant petitioner such a license, no downtown exhibitor would waive his clearance rights over the Crest and agree to a simultaneous showing. As a result, if petitioner were to receive first-runs, the license would have to be an exclusive one. However, an exclusive license would be economically unsound because the Crest is a suburban theatre, located in a small shopping center, and served by limited public transportation facilities; and, with a drawing area of less than one-tenth that of a downtown theatre, it cannot compare with those easily accessible theatres in the power to draw patrons. Hence, the downtown theatres offer far greater opportunities for the widespread advertisement and exploitation of newly released features, which is thought necessary to maximize the over-all return from subsequent runs as well as first-runs. . . .

The crucial question is whether respondents' conduct toward petitioner stemmed from independent decision or from an agreement, tacit or express. To be sure, business behavior is admissible circumstantial evidence from which the fact finder may infer agreement. . . . But this Court has never held that proof of parallel business behavior conclusively establishes agreement or, phrased differently, that such behavior itself constitutes a Sherman Act offense. Circumstantial evidence of consciously parallel behavior may have made heavy inroads into the traditional judicial attitude toward conspiracy; but "conscious parallelism" has not yet read conspiracy out of the Sherman Act entirely. . . .

Affirmed.

A particularly vexing problem associated with businesses behaving in a parallel fashion revolves around oligopolistic *price leadership*. This is a situation in which one firm, called the price leader, raises its price, and soon thereafter its competitors raise their prices to the same level. For instance, consider the following hypothetical example:

> There are three tunafish canners: Turkey-of-the-Sea, Moonkiss, and Honeybee. Each is selling six-ounce cans of chunk light tuna for 99¢ per can. Then Honeybee raises its price to $1.19 per can. Soon thereafter, Moonkiss begins selling chunk light tuna for $1.19 per can, and finally Turkey-of-the-Sea starts selling its chunk light for $1.19 per can.

From these facts can one infer an agreement between the three firms to follow Honeybee's lead in raising its price? As with all inferences derived solely from parallel actions, the answer depends on whether these facts may sensibly have evolved through independent decision making by the three firms. Generally, price leadership evidence as presented is insufficient to prove an agreement. That is because each firm, by making its own independent cost/benefit risk analysis, may have independently arrived at the decision to charge $1.19 per can. The reasoning accords with these considerations:

> Honeybee evaluates the market demand characteristics of tuna and determines that if all three competitors charge $1.19 per can, they all will make more profits. It also realizes that if it alone were to raise its price to $1.19 and the other companies did not follow suit, it would lose a great portion of its sales and consequently would suffer a reduction in profits.
>
> Honeybee raises its price to $1.19 under a cost/benefit risk plan. It decides to leave the price at $1.19 for a certain period of time, say thirty days. If its competitors have not raised their prices to $1.19 within that period, it will lower its price to the lowest charged by any competitor. It thus has decided to forgo some sales for at most a thirty-day period as an investment in possibly gaining greater long-term profits.
>
> Moonkiss perceives the price hike by Honeybee and independently considers its options. It, too, understands that all three companies can earn higher profits if they all charge $1.19. It also recognizes that Honeybee will not sell at $1.19 for very long if its competitors continue selling at 99¢ per can. Thus Moonkiss decides to raise its price to $1.19 for a period of time, say forty days. If Turkey-of-the-Sea does not raise its price during that period, then Moonkiss will drop its price to the lowest charged by any competitor. Like Honeybee, Moonkiss has decided to forgo sales for at most a forty-day period as an investment in higher long-term profitability.
>
> Turkey-of-the-Sea perceives that its lower price will attract many new customers. However, this will continue only as long as the other companies charge $1.19 per can. Turkey-of-the-Sea knows that its competitors will not forgo sales for long. So it must decide to compete at 99¢ per can or $1.19 per can or anything in between. It logically and independently opts for $1.19 because it realizes that given the number of total market sales that will be made at that price, the companies will make the most money if they charge it. Since its proportion of sales will remain constant, its profits will be highest at $1.19 per can. It therefore raises its price to $1.19.

The above illustration involves solely evidence of parallel-pricing behavior. What if there were in addition to the similar pricing pattern other evidence that tended to indicate an agreement? For instance, consider whether there might be a different conclusion regarding an inference of agreement if the facts indicated that Honeybee had called a meeting with its two competitors, and following the meeting, all three companies had charged the higher price. In this situation an agreement logically could be inferred since it is difficult to understand the purpose for the meeting except for it to serve as a vehicle for an agreement.

THE MEANING OF "IN RESTRAINT OF TRADE"

The Rule of Reason

Section 1 of the Sherman Act prohibits all contracts, combinations and conspiracies "in restraint of trade." Taken literally, this prohibition would serve as a condemnation of every form of contract. For instance, a contract between a homeowner and a house painter must in a sense restrain trade because, under the contract, the painter cannot paint another person's home during the time that he is bound to paint that of this homeowner. However, to apply the Sherman Act to contracts such as this would be to destroy the free-market system, since it depends so strongly on the legality and enforceability of just these forms of contracts. Thus from the beginning the Supreme Court has refused to apply the statute to all contracts that restrain trade. Instead, it has interpreted the Sherman Act to prohibit only *unreasonable* restraints of trade. This conceptualization stems from the case brought by the Justice Department against the Standard Oil Company in which the Supreme Court stated in 1911 that "it was intended that the standard of reason be the measure used for the purpose of determining whether in a given case a particular act had or had not brought about the wrong against which the statute provided."[2] The meaning of the "standard (or rule) of reason" was clarified in *Chicago Board of Trade* v. *U.S.* (1938), wherein the Court announced:

> Every agreement concerning trade, every regulation of trade, restrains. To bind, to restrain, is of their very essence. The true test of legality is whether the restraint imposed is such as merely regulates and perhaps thereby promotes competition or whether it is such as may suppress or even destroy competition. . . . To determine that question the Court must ordinarily consider the facts peculiar to the business to which the restraint is applied; its conditions before and after the restraint was imposed; the nature of the restraint and its effect, actual or probable. The history of the restraint, the evil believed to exist, the reason for adopting the particular remedy, the purpose or end sought to be attained, are all relevant factors.[3]

Analysis under the Sherman Act of joint action thus requires a balancing of many factors to determine if the net effect of that particular action is either a reasonable or an unreasonable restraint on the competitive system. In other words, in determining the legality under the Sherman Act of joint business arrangements, one must first consider all the possible benefits to the ideal competitive system which that arrangement might establish. Then one must analyze all the ways in which the arrangement might harm the competitive market. The final task is to *balance* those benefits against the harms and to arrive at a judgment of whether the possible benefits derived from the restraint outweigh the possible harms associated with it. This balancing approach to section 1 is called the *rule of reason*, and its application can be visualized as in the diagram below:

RULE OF REASON

| Possible harms to | ∧ | Possible benefits to |
| "competition" | | "competition" |

If the see-saw we have described tips to the left (toward the harms), then under the rule of reason, the particular restraint is unreasonable and thus illegal under the Sherman Act. However, if the see-saw tips to the right (toward the benefits), then the restraint is probably legal. This must be qualified because one also must consider whether those benefits derived from the arrangement could be achieved through an alternative venture that would involve fewer harms to competition and thus, in the balance, would cause the see-saw to tip even further to the right.

Be aware that the rule-of-reason analysis is highly dependent on how the term *competition* is defined by the person holding the scale. Recall that one set of antitrust proponents believes that the market system is competitive only if it is composed of numerous small businesses. Thus when these persons are in charge of the weighing process, arrangements that interfere with the objective of protecting the viability of small business concerns will likely tilt the scale toward the unreasonable side. On the other hand, if the objective of antitrust is efficiency, and *competition* is defined in its terms, then the factors influencing the balancing analysis may be very different. For instance, the effect that coordinated arrangements may have on the size of viable firms may be less important than the ability of the remaining firms to raise prices.

Contrast how the rule of reason might lead to different conclusions as to the antitrust legality of the following two hypotheticals. Also, while reviewing the examples, consider whether the final determinations would be affected by one's conception of competition.

Forestbark is a new paper-products company. It faces many large established competitors such as Potlach, Crown Zellerbach, and Burlington Northern. Forestbark enters a contract with Prentice-Hall, Inc. under which Prentice-Hall agrees to buy all its paper-product requirements for one year from Forestbark.

Firestone is one of the largest manufacturers of tires in the United States. Its competitors include, among others, Dunlop, Goodyear, Goodrich, Michelin, and Continental. Firestone enters a contract with General Motors, Ford and Toyota under which each company agrees to purchase only Firestone tires for its automobiles for five years.

These two contracts are called *requirements contracts*, which are just one of the many types of *exclusive-dealing* arrangements. In exclusive-dealing situations, one party agrees to transact business, either in a purchasing or selling role, exclusively with another party for a certain period of time. From another perspective one could say that there is a pledge by the promisor not to transact business with the promisee's competitors. Above, for instance, Prentice-Hall promises not to buy from Forestbark's competitors for one year. Output contracts, in which one party agrees to sell all that it makes to another party, and exclusive licenses, also fall within the purview of exclusive-dealing arrangements.

In the first scenario Forestbark is a new entrant in the paper-production market. If Forestbark succeeds in establishing its business, then the competitive market in paper production should be benefited since there will be one more company serving as a competitor. The requirements contract may aid Forestbark in this goal. For Forestbark to make the necessary investments in paper mills, land, equipment, materials, and other industrial needs, it might require certain assurances that its operations will generate sufficient revenue to cover these expenditures. The requirements contract with Prentice-Hall serves this purpose by providing one definite source for Forestbark's production.

This contract also may have a harmful effect on competition. Since Prentice-Hall has promised to buy all its paper needs from Forestbark for one year, all of Forestbark's competitors are foreclosed from selling to Prentice-Hall for that period. With Forestbark's usurpation of this large paper-products purchaser, certain paper companies may have to cut back production severely or even go out of business. The rule-of-reason scale must balance these conflicting considerations.

RULE OF REASON

Possible Harms	Possible Benefits
Some Forestbark competitors fail because of lack of available paper purchaser	Forestbark is a new competitor in the paper-products industry

In employing the rule of reason the likelihood of each occurrence must be considered. In this case what is the probability that Forestbark's competitors will be endangered by the contract? A thorough analysis of the industry would reveal that the odds are extremely low. After this contract Forestbark's competitors still will have available to them for sales all the remaining book publishing houses, of which there are a great number with huge paper needs, and also companies in all the other types of industries that use paper (paper products for dining, tissues, paper towel, newspapers, magazines, and so on). On the other side of the scale the probabilities are high that this contract will contribute in getting this new venture established. Therefore, in the balance the likely benefits outweigh the possible harms, and thus this requirements contract is reasonable.

For the second hypothetical the same considerations apply in the rule-of-reason balance. Here, though, the possible benefits are greatly reduced because Firestone is a powerful existing firm. No new competitors are being created, nor does the survival of Firestone depend on the contract. On the other side of the scale, the harms may be substantial. Owing to the contract, three significant tire purchasers are foreclosed from Firestone's competitors for five years. With Firestone tying up such a large percentage of the tire purchasers for such a long period of time, it becomes quite likely that some of its competitors will fail to find sufficient customers to remain profitable. On balance, then, this contract probably will reduce competition in the tire-manufacturing market and therefore is an unreasonable restraint of trade.

As one can envision, the rule of reason can be very complex, requiring laborious analyses of industry statistics, economic reports, market surveys, and the like. Also, determinations often must be founded on expert testimony from economists, management consultants, and industry technicians. Therefore, because of the large amount of data that must be synthesized, the rule of reason often leads to very long trials in which the outcomes are somewhat unpredictable.

Per Se Illegality

Through experience with various types of business arrangements the Supreme Court has determined that certain joint relationships have the potential for being so harmful to the goals of competition that no argument as to their possible benefits ever could establish their legality under the rule of reason. Thus, using the see-saw diagram, the Court considers certain situations to be so heavy on the left side of harms that no benefits ever could be suggested that might tip it back to the right. These arrangements are deemed *illegal per se*.

When a plaintiff brings a section 1 suit, its task is greatly simplified if it can establish that the defendant engaged in an illegal per se arrangement because a court will presume that the arrangement unreasonably restrains trade. No experts or industry statistics are required to prove to the court that the harms outweigh the benefits. Thus in per se situations the plaintiff need only prove that the defendants participated in the scheme. Alternatively, when a per se arrangement is not at issue, the plaintiff must establish not only that the defendant participated in the scheme but also that the combination was unreasonable in the balance. Therefore, cases involving per se arrangements are relatively brief and predictable, whereas those not considering per se combinations are more laborious and unpredictable.

Policy makers who support a populist approach to antitrust, wherein a premium is placed on the viability of small business units, tend also to advocate per se designations for business transactions. That is, their philosophy conforms to an antitrust approach that automatically prohibits combinations that might increase the scope or power of firms. On the other hand, backers of the efficiency approach to antitrust tend to look disfavorably upon the use of per se designations. They often believe that the per se judgments ignore significant benefits to competition that the combinations may produce. To these individuals, the per se approach is simplistic and many times results in a reduction of net economic welfare to society.

It is not surprising that a large number of arrangements were included in the per se category during the earlier years of antitrust, when the populist philosophy predominated. The list of business dealings ruled to be illegal per se once included, among others, the following:

- Horizontal price fixing
- Horizontal territorial restraints
- Vertical nonprice restraints
- Vertical price fixing
- Group boycotts
- Tying arrangements

Since the mid-1970s and especially in the 1980s the philosophy behind antitrust policy shifted toward the efficiency approach. For this reason certain arrangements, such as vertical nonprice restraints, are no longer on the per se list, and other arrangements are subject to a qualified per se approach. In addition, there are strong indications that in the near future, several other arrangements will be removed from the per se list or even further qualified.

HORIZONTAL PRICE FIXING

Basically, horizontal price fixing refers to an agreement between competitors to charge specified prices for their products. From the beginning the Supreme Court has looked with disdain upon such arrangements and has held them to be illegal per se, at least until recently, with no hesitation. The Supreme Court set the stage for horizontal price fixing's illegal per se status in the landmark case of *United States* v. *Trenton Potteries Co.* (1926) wherein it made the following evaluation of them:

> That only those restraints upon interstate commerce which are unreasonable are prohibited by the Sherman Law was the rule laid down by the opinions of this Court in the *Standard Oil* and *Tobacco* cases. But it does not follow that agreements to fix or maintain prices are reasonable restraints and therefore permitted by the statute merely because the prices themselves are reasonable.... The aim and result of every price-fixing agreement, if effective, is the elimination of one form of competition. The power to fix prices, whether reasonably exercised or not, involves power to control the market and to fix arbitrary and unreasonable prices. The reasonable price fixed today may through economic and business changes become the unreasonable price of tomorrow.... [I]n the absence of express legislation requiring it, we should hesitate to adopt a construction making the difference between legal and illegal conduct in the field of business relations depend on so uncertain a test as whether prices are reasonable.[4]

Soon after this case the courts made it clear that any act of horizontal price fixing would be held illegal without any inquiry into the possible benefits that might be a product of the situation. Also, the scope of activities included in horizontal price fixing was widened. In this regard almost any agreements that might affect price, including those that specify credit terms, discount policies, and trade-in conditions, have been ruled as within the illegal per se status. Likewise, agreements between competitors regarding their future sales quantities have been viewed as illegal per se price fixing arrangements because under supply and demand analyses output restrictions will ultimately affect price. In fact, the illegal per se rule has been extended even to situations in which competitors have agreed not to charge *above* a certain price.

The applicability of the per se rule to horizontal price fixing is one of the firmest doctrines in antitrust law. Even the "efficiency" policy makers of antitrust consider the per se rule to be most justifiable in this context. However, horizontal price fixing has not been immune from the changes in antitrust philosophy sweeping the public-policy forum. For instance, in *Broadcast Music, Inc.* v. *Columbia Broadcasting System, Inc.* (1979), the Supreme Court ruled that a blanket license price agreement between separate music composers should be judged under the rule of reason and should not be condemned by a per se determination without a balancing analysis.[5] Here the Supreme Court was impressed that the blanket license could be offered only by a price agreement and not by composers individually and thus was, in essence, a new product established by the combination. Also, the license substantially lowered costs, was efficient, and was preferred by consumers. Following this case some lower courts have shown some flexibility in relaxing the per se rule where the price agreements might be needed to allow the parties to market their products effectively or where they might have redeeming competitive virtues. These cases, however, are still the minor exception to the overriding rule that price fixing between competitors is always to be condemned. The most recent Supreme Court case dealing with horizontal price fixing, *National Collegiate Athletic Association* v. *Board of Regents of the University of Oklahoma*, clearly explains the general applicability of the per se rule in this context and evaluates the limited situations for which the rule of reason should be utilized.

NATIONAL COLLEGIATE ATHLETIC ASSOCIATION
v.
BOARD OF REGENTS OF THE UNIVERSITY OF OKLAHOMA
United States Supreme Court
104 S. Ct. 2948 (1984)

BACKGROUND

The National Collegiate Athletic Association (NCAA) is an association of approximately 850 colleges designed to regulate amateur collegiate sports. Since 1951 the NCAA has adopted various plans to control the adverse effects that live television has upon college football attendance. The plan involved in this action established, among other things, the following criteria for television contracts between the NCAA member schools and television networks:

1. Only certain networks under specified conditions are permitted to televise live NCAA football games.
2. The NCAA, in effect, sets fees for television rights that the networks can pay to member schools, depending on the type of telecast (national, regional) and the division of the school.
3. The networks must schedule appearances for at least 82 different institutions during each two-year period, and no NCAA member is eligible to appear on television more than a total of six times.

A number of members of the NCAA with major football programs, including the Universities of Oklahoma and Georgia, formed a separate association, called the College Football Association (CFA). The CFA developed an independent television-rights plan and signed a separate contract with a television network allowing a more liberal number of appearances for its members on the network. In response, the NCAA threatened disciplinary action against any school complying with the CFA contract. This lawsuit was commenced to enjoin the NCAA from carrying out its threats.

The District Court concluded that the NCAA controls over college football were those of a classic cartel, illegal under the Sherman Act, and the Court of Appeals affirmed, declaring that the NCAA plan constituted illegal per se price fixing.

OPINION

Justice Stevens

... There can be no doubt that the challenged practices of the NCAA constitute a "restraint of trade" in the sense that they limit members' freedom to negotiate and enter into their own television contracts. In that sense, however, every contract is a restraint of trade, and as we have repeatedly recognized, the Sherman Act was intended to prohibit only unreasonable restraints of trade. ...

By participating in an association which prevents member institutions from competing against each other on the basis of price or kind of television rights that can be offered to broadcasters, the NCAA member institutions have created a horizontal restraint—an agreement among competitors on the way in which they will compete with one another. A restraint of this type has often been held to be unreasonable as a matter of law. Because it places a ceiling on the number of games member institutions may televise, the horizontal agreement places an artificial limit on the quantity of televised football that is available to broadcasters and consumers. ... Moreover, the district court found that the minimum aggregate price in fact operates to preclude any price negotiation between broadcasters and institutions, thereby constituting horizontal price fixing, perhaps the paradigm of an unreasonable restraint of trade.

Horizontal price fixing and output limitations are ordinarily condemned as a matter of law under an "illegal per se" approach because the probability that these practices are anticompetitive is so high; a per se rule is applied when "the practice facially appears to be one that would always or almost always tend to restrict competition and decrease output." . . . In such circumstances a restraint is presumed unreasonable without inquiry into the particular market context in which it is found. Nevertheless, we have decided that it would be inappropriate to apply a per se rule to this case. . . . Rather, what is critical is that this case involves an industry in which horizontal restraints on competition are essential if the product is to be available at all. . . .

What the NCAA and its member institutions market in this case is competition itself—contests between competing institutions. Of course, this would be completely ineffective if there were no rules on which the competitors agreed to create and define the competition to be marketed. . . . Moreover, the NCAA seeks to market a particular brand of football —college football. . . . In order to preserve the character and quality of the "product," athletes must not be paid, must be required to attend class, and the like. And the integrity of the "product" cannot be preserved except by mutual agreement; if an institution adopted such restrictions unilaterally, its effectiveness as a competitor on the playing field might soon be destroyed. . . .

Broadcast Music squarely holds that a joint selling arrangement may be so efficient that it will increase sellers' aggregate output and thus be procompetitive. . . . Similarly, as we indicated in *Continental T.V., Inc. v. GTE Sylvania Inc* . . . . a restraint in a limited aspect of a market may actually enhance marketwide competition. Respondents concede that the great majority of the NCAA's regulations enhance competition among member institutions. Thus, despite the fact that this case involves restraints on the ability of member institutions to compete in terms of price and output, a fair evaluation of their competitive character requires consideration of the NCAA's justifications for the restraints. . . .

Because it restrains price and output, the NCAA's television plan has a significant potential for anticompetitive effects. The findings of the District Court indicate that this potential has been realized. The District Court found that if member institutions were free to sell television rights, many more games would be shown on television, and that the NCAA's output restriction has the effect of raising the price the networks pay for television rights. Moreover, the court found that by fixing a price for television rights to all games, the NCAA creates a price structure that is unresponsive to viewer demand and unresponsive to the prices that would prevail in a competitive market. . . .

The District Court did not find that the NCAA's television plan produced any procompetitive efficiencies which enhanced the competitiveness of college football television rights; to the contrary it concluded that NCAA football could be marketed just as effectively without the television plan. . . .

Affirmed.

HORIZONTAL DIVISION OF MARKET AREAS

Agreements by competitors designating in which territorial areas each may sell have long been held to be illegal per se. Therefore, when competitors arrange between themselves where each is permitted to sell, they are violating the Sherman Act, section 1, no matter what evidence of possible procompetitive results they might proffer. Considering the stereotypical situation of horizontal market divisions, this makes sense. For instance, assume that Chrysler, Ford, and General Motors agree that, among themselves, Chrysler and only Chrysler will sell in the western third of the United States, Ford and only Ford will sell in the midsection of the nation, and GM and only GM will sell in the East. Now automobile shoppers, say in California, will face less variety in American automobiles and higher prices. When they search for American cars, they will find that only Chrysler offers what they want. Also, since Chrysler does not have to consider the competitive responses of GM and Ford, it can raise its prices and reduce its services without fear of losing sales to these companies. Therefore, the agreement obviously reduces competition among the agreeing parties. Can the agreement produce benefits that are worth weighing against the definite economic harms? Considering this form of case, the courts could envision few countervailing benefits and thus articulated the per se rule to apply to all horizontal market divisions.

Unfortunately, not all situations of horizontal market divisions are as clear as the above hypothetical in terms of possible competitive effects. Consider the case of Topco Associates, Inc. (Topco). In the 1930s large supermarket chains, such as Kroger and Safeway, established "private-label" brand merchandise, which often was sold at prices below the name brands. Customers naturally were attracted to the lower prices, and thus the competitive posture of the national chains improved. Smaller regional supermarkets were unable to offer their own private labels because individually they could not handle a sufficient amount of merchandise to achieve the economies of scale or volume discounts that made the national programs successful. Facing a declining competitive position, certain regional grocery chains formed the cooperative Topco to establish a new private label. Under the Topco arrangement the regionals jointly purchased and distributed merchandise for the Topco brand label, thereby achieving economies of scale and volume discounts. In addition, each member of Topco was assigned an exclusive territory in which only that member could sell the Topco-label merchandise. Thus as with all horizontal market divisions, competition among the parties to the agreement decreased in each territory. In this case one might say that competition among those selling the Topco brand, or in other words *intrabrand competition*, was lessened by the exclusive territories.

Unlike the automobile example, there may be countervailing benefits to the exclusive territories assigned in the Topco arrangement. Since the Topco label was newly established, it had little or no public acceptance. Thus heavy promotion might have been required to draw patronage from the private labels of the national chains. By assigning exclusive territories, the Topco members increased the likelihood that each member would promote the Topco label.

When a merchant is the only seller of an item in an area, he may be confident that if he advertises that item and thereby interests a consumer in it, he will be rewarded by the patronage of that customer. However, if this merchant has competing sellers of that item in the area, he may for a variety of reasons forgo the advertising of that item. First, he has a reduced incentive to advertise that item since the result of his advertising investment may be that consumers will frequent his competitors to obtain it. In other words, he may fear that competitors will *free-ride* off of his advertising investment and thereby sell the item without corresponding costs. Second, he may hope that his competitors will advertise the item, thereby allowing him to free-ride off of their investments. Thus if the Topco Association did not assign exclusive territories to its competing members, the label might not have been promoted and so might have failed in its task to attract customers to the regional grocery stores.

A horizontal market division, such as in the Topco case, is ripe for a rule-of-reason balancing analysis. On the harm side is the reduction of competition among stores selling the Topco brand. However, on the benefit side is the possibility that a new viable brand would emerge to compete effectively with the dominant private-label brands of the national chains. In this way competition among the brands, sometimes called *interbrand competition*, may have increased. Under the rule of reason, this possibility would be analyzed and weighed against the possible economic harms. However, since horizontal market divisions are governed by the per se rule, the courts would not consider the possible benefits.

The Justice Department filed suit against Topco in the 1960s, alleging a violation of section 1 of the Sherman Act, and the Supreme Court rendered its decision about the arrangement in 1972. Pay special attention to the concurring opinions of Justices Brennan and Blackmun, and note their conceptualization of the respective roles of Congress and the Supreme Court in making antitrust policy. Also, consider the dissent of Chief Justice Burger, for his opinion may parallel closely the current thinking of the Supreme Court.[6]

UNITED STATES
v.
TOPCO ASSOCIATES
United States Supreme Court
405 U.S. 596 (1972)

BACKGROUND

Topco is a cooperative association of approximately twenty-five small and medium sized regional supermarket chains that operate stores in thirty-three states. Its basic function is to serve as a purchasing agent for its members. In this capacity it procures and distributes to the members more than one thousand different food and related nonfood items, most of which are distributed under private label brand names owned by Topco.

The bylaws of Topco provide members with exclusive territories in which they are permitted to sell Topco private-label products. The bylaws also prohibit members from selling Topco-supplied products at wholesale without permission from the association.

The government brought an action for injunctive relief, contending that the restrictions violated the Sherman Act. The District Court entered a judgment for Topco, and the United States appealed directly to the Supreme Court.

OPINION

Justice Marshall

. . . The Government maintains that this scheme of dividing markets violates the Sherman Act because it operates to prohibit competition in Topco-brand products among grocery chains engaged in retail operations. . . .

Topco essentially maintains that it needs territorial divisions to compete with larger chains; that the association could not exist if the territorial divisions were anything but exclusive; and that by restricting competition in the sale of Topco-brand goods, the association actually increases competition by enabling its members to compete successfully with larger regional and national chains.

The District Court, considering all these things relevant to its decision, agreed with Topco. It recognized that the panoply of restraints that Topco imposed on its members worked to prevent competition in Topco-brand products, but concluded that "[w]hatever anti-competitive effect these practices may have on competition in the sale of Topco private label brands is far outweighed by the increased ability of Topco members to compete both with the national chains and other supermarkets operating in their respective territories." . . . The court held that Topco's practices were procompetitive and, therefore, consistent with the purposes of the antitrust laws. . . .

While the Court has utilized the "rule of reason" in evaluating the legality of most restraints alleged to be violative of the Sherman Act, it has also developed the doctrine that certain business relationships are per se violations of the Act without regard to a consideration of their reasonableness. . . . It is only after considerable experience with certain business relationships that courts classify them as per se violations of the Sherman Act. . . . One of the classic examples of a per se violation of §1 is an agreement between competitors at the same level of the market structure to allocate territories in order to minimize competition. . . . This Court has reiterated time and time again that "[h]orizontal territorial limitations. . . . are naked restraints of trade with no purpose except stifling of competition. . . . We think that it is clear that the restraint in this case is a horizontal one, and, therefore, a per se violation of §1. . . .

Whether or not we would decide this case the same way under the rule of reason used by the District Court is irrelevant to the issue before us. The fact is that courts are of limited utility in examining difficult economic problems. Our inability to weigh, in any meaningful sense, destruction of competition in one sector of the economy against promotion of competition in another sector is one important reason we have formulated *per se* rules. . . .

Antitrust laws in general, and the Sherman Act in particular, are the Magna Carta of free enterprise. . . . And the freedom guaranteed each and every business, no matter how small, is the freedom to compete—to assert with vigor, imagination, devotion, and ingenuity whatever economic muscle it can muster. . . .

The District Court determined that by limiting the freedom of its individual members to compete with each other, Topco was doing a greater good by fostering competition between members and other large supermarket chains. But, the fallacy in this is that Topco has no authority under the Sherman Act to determine the respective values of competition in various sectors of the economy. On the contrary, the Sherman Act gives to each Topco member and to each prospective member the right to ascertain for itself whether or not competition with other supermarket chains is more desirable than competition in the sale of Topco-brand products. Without territorial restrictions, Topco members may indeed "[cut] each other's throats." . . . But, we have never found this possibility sufficient to warrant condoning horizontal restraints of trade. . . .

We reverse the judgment of the District Court and remand the case for entry of an appropriate decree.

(Justice Brennan, concurring)

There have been tremendous departures from the notion of a free-enterprise system as it was originally conceived in this country. These departures have been the product of congressional action and the will of the people. If a decision is to be made to sacrifice competition in one portion of the economy for greater competition in another portion, this too is a decision that must be made by Congress and not by private forces or by the courts. Private forces are too keenly aware of their own interests in making such decisions and courts are ill-equipped and ill-situated for such decision making. To analyze, interpret, and evaluate the myriad of competing interests and the endless data that would surely be brought to bear on such decisions, and to make the delicate judgment on the relative values to society of competitive areas of the economy, the judgment of the elected representatives of the people is required.

(Justice Blackmun, concurring)

The conclusion the Court reaches has its anomalous aspects, for surely, as the District Court's findings make clear, today's decision in the Government's favor will tend to stultify Topco members' competition with the great and larger chains. The bigs, therefore, should find it easier to get bigger and, as a consequence, reality seems at odds with the public interest. The per se rule, however, now appears to be so firmly established by the Court that, at this late date, I could not oppose it. Relief, if any is to be forthcoming, apparently must be by way of legislation.

(Chief Justice Burger, dissenting)

This case does not involve restraints on interbrand competition or an allocation of markets by an association with monopoly or near-monopoly control of the sources of supply of one or more varieties of staple goods. Rather, we have here an agreement among several small grocery chains to join in a cooperative endeavor that, in my view, has an unquestionably lawful principal purpose. . . .

In joining in this cooperative endeavor, these small chains did not agree to the restraints here at issue in order to make it possible for them to exploit an already established line of products through noncompetitive pricing. There was no such thing as a Topco line of products until this cooperative was formed. The restraints to which the cooperative's members have agreed deal only with the marketing of the products in the Topco line, and the only function of those restraints is to permit each member chain to establish, within its own geographical area and through its own local advertising and marketing efforts, a local consumer awareness of the trademarked family of products as that member's "private-label" line. The goal sought was the enhancement of the individual members' abilities to compete, albeit to a modest degree, with the large national chains which had been successfully marketing private-label lines for several years. . . .

The issues presented by the antitrust cases reaching this Court are rarely simple to resolve under the rule of reason; they do indeed frequently require us to make difficult economic determinations. We should not for that reason alone, however, be overly zealous in formulating new per se rules, for an excess of zeal in that regard is both contrary to the policy of the Sherman Act and detrimental to the welfare of consumers generally. . . .

VERTICAL NONPRICE RESTRAINTS

So far, we have discussed certain business arrangements in a horizontal context; that is, between competitors. Here, we will begin to look at transactions that are vertical in nature. The term *vertical* refers to the fact that the agreement is between firms that are on different levels of the distribution chain. For clarity refer to the diagram below.

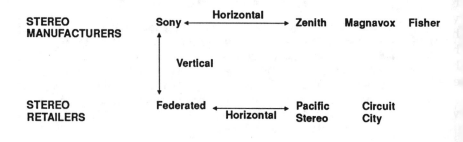

In this example an agreement between Sony and Zenith would be horizontal, since the two stereo manufacturers are competitors. Likewise, an arrangement between Federated and Pacific Stereo would amount to a horizontal combination of competing stereo retailers. An agreement between Sony and Federated is somewhat different, however, because in this case a manufacturer is dealing with a retailer. Since the association is between businesses on different levels of the stereo distribution chain, it is a vertical relationship.

Vertical nonprice restraints generally refer to situations in which a supplier (often a manufacturer) of a product or service agrees with a buyer (often a distributor or retailer) about where or to whom the buyer may resell the product or service. The following are the most prevalent forms of these restraints:

1. Exclusive geographic territories — The distributor obtains the right to be the sole seller of the manufacturer's product in an area.
2. Customer sales restrictions — The distributor may sell the manufacturer's product only to particular kinds of buyers.
3. Location clauses — The distributor may sell the manufacturer's product only from a particular physical site.
4. Areas of primary responsibility — The distributor must market the manufacturer's product satisfactorily in a defined geographical area, and as long as it does so, it may also sell the product outside that area.
5. Profit passovers — If a distributor sells outside its area of primary responsibility and in another distributor's area, then it will have to "pass over" a percentage of its profits on the sales to the other distributor.

All vertical nonprice restraints will reduce intrabrand competition to some degree, but they also may have the capacity to increase interbrand competition as well. Consider the possible competitive effects of the following hypothetical usage of an exclusive geographical territory restraint.

Leesky is a new competitor in the stereo electronics industry. Leesky makes an excellent product but faces stiff competition from such established stereo giants as Sony, Onkyo, Fisher, Marantz, Kenwood, Magnavox, and Technics. Leesky recognizes that in this industry it cannot sell merchandise without name recognition. Thus it wants to ensure that the advertising of its products has wide reach. Also, Leesky would like to be certain that its retailers have experienced salespersons who can competently explain the advantages of the Leesky products. In addition, Leesky wants these retailers to have listening rooms so that customers unfamiliar with the Leesky name will have the opportunity to hear its quality. Finally, Leesky finds it desirable to have its retailers invest in servicing capabilities so that Leesky customers who experience difficulties may get them solved in a satisfactory manner.

One effective way to give a retailer the incentive to provide these various services is to grant it an exclusive sales territory. For instance, assume that Leesky agrees that Audio Fantasy will be its exclusive retailer on the central California coast. Since Audio Fantasy is the only Leesky seller in the area, it is willing to invest in advertising depicting the high quality of the Leesky products. That is because any success it may have in heightening the interest of consumers in Leesky products will translate into greater patronage of its stores. If there were competitor sellers of Leesky products in the area, Audio Fantasy might not advertise Leesky products because of its fear that "free-riding" competitors might reap the benefits of its advertising or because it might hope to free-ride itself on the Leesky advertising of its competitors. Instead, when Audio Fantasy advertised, it would try to persuade consumers of the superiority of its store over those of its competitors rather than of the superiority of the Leesky products.

For similar reasons Audio Fantasy is more willing to invest in showrooms and expert personnel when it has an exclusive on the central California coast. Again, any consumers who are excited about Leeskys after hearing them in the showroom and after considering the salesperson's advice will buy them at Audio Fantasy. Without the exclusive, of course, over-the-counter outlets that provide no service or advice might free-ride on Audio Fantasy's investments and thereby sell Leeskys at discount prices that reflect their lower overhead. As with advertising in this competitive environment, Audio Fantasy may choose not to invest in these services at all. Likewise, Audio Fantasy may be less willing to invest in repair facilities when it might have to repair Leeskys that were sold at competitor establishments.

One should see from this example that vertical nonprice restraints potentially may increase competition in the marketplace in some respects while simultaneously reducing it in others. Here competition among retail establishments selling Leesky products is lessened since there can be only one Leesky retailer in a given area. In other words, intrabrand competition definitely is reduced. However, the restrictions may increase the competitive viability of Leesky against the other established stereo brands such as Sony. In this regard, there is a possibility that interbrand competition will improve.

If the primary goal of antitrust policy is to further economic efficiency, then in each case of a vertical nonprice restraint, the rule of reason should be used to balance the restraint's effects on interbrand and intrabrand competition. As illustrated by *Continental T.V., Inc.* v. *GTE Sylvania*, the next case we present, this is the current antitrust policy. However, it was not always the policy. In 1963 the Court, for the first time, reviewed a vertical nonprice restraint case and, owing to its inexperience with the form of restraint, used the rule of reason to analyze its impact. Nonetheless, in 1967 the Supreme Court announced in *U.S.* v. *Arnold, Schwinn & Co.* that such vertical restraints were illegal per se.[7] Thus by 1967 the antitrust philosophy of the Supreme Court led it to prohibit all instances of vertical nonprice restraints, even in those situations where there might be clear short-term consumer economic benefits. Other concerns, such as the potential size and power of business organizations, therefore must have been behind this policy.

The decision by the Supreme Court in *Continental T.V., Inc.* v. *GTE Sylvania* to overrule its opinion in *Schwinn* may be the most significant pronouncement on antitrust policy in the Court's history. The fact that it is the only instance when the Court has overruled itself overtly in antitrust is important by itself. However, the clear statement by the Court that the Sherman Act must be analyzed in terms of economic effects definitively marked the beginning of the modern Supreme Court philosophy of antitrust policy. The ramifications of this case are broad, and it should be read several times. Be sure to consider how this case might influence the future legality of certain horizontal territorial restraints. In addition, when vertical price restraints are discussed in the next section, think about how this case might have a bearing on future Supreme Court policy with respect to such restraints.

CONTINENTAL T.V., INC.
v.
GTE SYLVANIA INCORPORATED
United States Supreme Court
433 U.S. 36 (1977)

BACKGROUND

In 1962 Sylvania, a manufacturer of television sets, instituted a revised marketing strategy to combat its decline in market share, which had fallen to 1 to 2 percent of national TV sales. As a component of the plan, Sylvania limited its franchisee-retailers to selling only from specified locations. Franchisees were not given exclusive territories, and Sylvania retained sole discretion to increase the number of franchisees in a given area. The marketing strategy apparently was successful since Sylvania's market share rose to 5 percent by 1965.

In the spring of 1965, to boost sales in San Francisco, Sylvania franchised a new retail outlet in the city to sell Sylvania products. This outlet was one mile from an existing retail outlet run by Continental T.V., and Continental protested the action.

At the same time Continental asked Sylvania for a Sacramento outlet, but its request was denied. In spite of the denial, Continental advised Sylvania that it was moving Sylvania merchandise from its San Jose warehouse to a retail location in Sacramento.

Soon thereafter Sylvania reduced Continental's credit line from $300,000 to $50,000. In response Continental withheld all payments owed to the finance company that handled credit arrangements between Sylvania and its retailers. Sylvania then terminated Continental's franchises and along with the finance company sued for the money owed. Continental counterclaimed, arguing that Sylvania's enforcement of the location clause violated section 1 of the Sherman Act.

The trial judge instructed the jury that if Sylvania had entered an agreement to restrict the store outlets from which its franchisees could resell merchandise after title to that merchandise passed to the franchisees, then Sylvania had violated section 1 of the Sherman Act regardless of the reasonableness of the restrictions. The jury found for Continental. The Ninth Circuit Court of Appeals reversed, and the Supreme Court granted certiorari.

OPINION

Justice Powell

Franchise agreements between manufacturers and retailers frequently include provisions barring the retailers from selling franchised products from locations other than those specified in the agreements. This case presents important questions concerning the appropriate antitrust analysis of these restrictions under §1 of the Sherman Act. . . .

We turn first to Continental's contention that Sylvania's restriction on retail locations is a per se violation of §1 of the Sherman Act as interpreted in *Schwinn*. The restrictions at issue in *Schwinn* were part of a three-tier distribution system comprising, in addition to Arnold Schwinn & Co (Schwinn), twenty-two intermediate distributors and a network of franchised retailers. Each distributor had a defined geographic area in which it had the exclusive right to supply franchised retailers. Sales to the public were made only through franchised retailers, who were authorized to sell Schwinn bicycles only from specified locations. In support of this limitation, Schwinn prohibited both distributors and retailers from selling Schwinn bicycles to nonfranchised retailers. At the retail level, therefore, Schwinn was able to control the number of retailers of its bicycles in any given area according to its view of the needs of that market. . . .

[T]he Court proceeded to articulate the following "bright line" per se rule of illegality for vertical restrictions: "Under the Sherman Act, it is unreasonable without more for a manufacturer to seek to restrict and confine areas or persons with whom an article may be traded after the manufacturer has parted with dominion over it." . . . But the Court expressly stated that the rule of reason governs when "the manufacturer retains title, dominion, and risk with respect to the product and the position and function of the dealer in question are, in fact, indistinguishable from those of an agent or salesman of the manufacturer." . . .

In the present case, it is undisputed that title to the televisions passed from Sylvania to Continental. Thus, the Schwinn per se rule applies unless Sylvania's restriction on locations falls outside Schwinn's prohibition against a manufacturer's attempting to restrict a "retailer's freedom as to where and to whom it will resell the products." . . . Unlike the Court of Appeals . . . we are unable to find a principled basis for distinguishing *Schwinn* from the case now before us. . . .

Sylvania argues that if *Schwinn* cannot be distinguished, it should be reconsidered. . . . *Schwinn* itself was an abrupt and largely unexplained departure from *White Motor Co. v. United States* . . . where only four years earlier the Court had refused to endorse a per se rule for vertical restrictions. Since its announcement, *Schwinn* has been the subject of continuing controversy and confusion, both in the scholarly journals and in the federal courts. The great weight of scholarly opinion has been critical of the decision, and a number of the federal courts confronted with analogous vertical restrictions have sought to limit its reach. In our view, the experience of the past 10 years should be brought to bear on this subject of considerable commercial importance. . . .

The market impact of vertical restrictions is complex because of their potential for a simultaneous reduction of intrabrand competition and stimulation of interbrand competition. Significantly, the Court in *Schwinn* did not distinguish among the challenged restrictions on the basis of their individual potential for intrabrand harm or interbrand benefit. . . .

Vertical restrictions reduce intrabrand competition by limiting the number of sellers of a particular product competing for the business of a given group of buyers. Location restrictions have this effect because of practical constraints on the effective marketing area of retail outlets. Although intrabrand competition may be reduced, the ability of retailers to exploit the resulting market may be limited both by the ability of consumers to travel to other franchised locations and, perhaps more importantly, to purchase the competing products of other manufacturers. None of these key variables, however, is affected by the form of the transaction by which a manufacturer conveys his products to the retailers.

Vertical restrictions promote interbrand competition by allowing the manufacturer to achieve certain efficiencies in the distribution of his products. . . . Economists have identified a number of ways in which manufacturers can use such restrictions to compete more effectively against other manufacturers. . . . For example, new manufacturers and manufacturers entering new markets can use the restrictions in order to induce competent and aggressive retailers to make the kind of investment of capital and labor that is often required in the distribution of products unknown to the consumer. Established manufacturers can use them to induce retailers to engage in promotional activities or to provide service and repair facilities necessary to the efficient marketing of their products. Service and repair are vital for many products, such as automobiles and major household appliances. The availability and quality of such services affect a manufacturer's goodwill and the competitiveness of his product. Because of market imperfections such as the so-called "free-rider" effect, these services might not be provided by retailers in a purely competitive situation, despite the fact that each retailer's benefit would be greater if all provided the services than if none did. . . .

Although the view that the manufacturer's interest necessarily corresponds with that of the public is not universally shared, even the leading critic of vertical restrictions concedes that *Schwinn*'s distinction between sale and nonsale transactions is essentially unrelated to any relevant economic impact. . . .

The question remains whether the per se rule stated in *Schwinn* should be expanded to include nonsale transactions or abandoned in favor of a return to the rule of reason. We have found no persuasive support for expanding the per se rule. . . . Accordingly, we conclude that the per se rule stated in *Schwinn* must be overruled. In so holding we do not foreclose the possibility that particular applications of vertical restrictions might justify per se prohibition. . . . But we do make clear that departure from the rule of reason standard must be based upon demonstrable economic effect rather than— as in *Schwinn*—upon formalistic line drawing.

In sum, we conclude that the appropriate decision is to return to the rule of reason that governed vertical restrictions prior to *Schwinn*. When anticompetitive effects are shown to result from particular vertical restrictions they can be adequately policed under the rule of reason, the standard traditionally applied for the majority of anticompetitive practices challenged under §1 of the Act. . . .

Affirmed.

Since the *Sylvania* decision, the clear trend in the lower courts has been to uphold most vertical nonprice restraints under the rule of reason. A significant factor in the analysis is the market size of the firm establishing the vertical restraint. If its market share is low, or if it is a relatively new competitor, the restraint generally will be viewed as reasonable. Also, the courts consider the intensity of competition among the product brands. The greater the number of competitors and the greater the degree of interchangeability among the brands, the more likely it is that the vertical restraint will be upheld. The courts, in addition, investigate other characteristics particular to the industry, such as the need for servicing, the importance of point-of-purchase information, the complexity of the product, and the significance of advertising by the distributor.

In 1985 the Department of Justice released its *vertical restraint guidelines*, which publicly report the conditions under which it will presumptively consider vertical nonprice restraints to be reasonable. These guidelines focus greatly on market-share statistics as a proxy for industry characteristics that make vertical restraints reasonable. For instance, the department will not challenge a restraint imposed by a supplier that has 10 percent or less of its market. Also, the department uses a complex statistical approach based on market shares to analyze the degree of interbrand competition in an industry. If a market is sufficiently competitive according to these statistical methods, the Justice Department will not challenge a nonprice vertical restraint. In the event that a restraint does not fall within these first stage "safe-harbors," the Justice Department will employ more comprehensive economic analyses based on ease of entry, possible efficiency benefits, and other factors.

The guidelines are useful to the business community, since they provide it with some certainty as to those vertical restraints the Justice Department likely will not challenge. However, be clear that the guidelines do not represent the law. Even though a restraint is reasonable under the guidelines, a private party still may sue for treble damages, and a court, using its version of the rule of reason, may find the restraint to be unreasonable. Similarly, state attorneys general may bring suits under the federal or state antitrust laws. Thus a business cannot rest comfortably upon the guidelines. Why, then, does the Department of Justice publicly announce its intentions? One consideration to keep in mind is their value in shaping antitrust thought according to the philosophy of the executive branch. The release of the guidelines stimulates attorneys to employ the guidelines approaches in their counseling and court arguments. Also, the guidelines serve as a springboard for widespread theoretical discussions. Together these forces may cause the court system to employ the approaches in its antitrust opinions. In this way the antitrust philosophy of the executive branch eventually may become dominant in the public policy forum.

VERTICAL PRICE AGREEMENTS

The legality of vertical price agreements is one of the most controversial topics in antitrust law. In the typical vertical price agreement, a retailer or dealer assures a manufacturer that it will not sell the manufacturer's product below a certain specified price. In other words, the retailer agrees that it will maintain the price above a requisite level. For this reason the practice is often called resale price maintenance. Vertical price agreements can take other forms, however, including promises to sell at or even below a specified price.

In 1911 the Supreme Court in *Dr. Miles Medical Co.* v. *John D. Park & Sons* held that vertical price agreements were illegal per se.[8] That case involved a resale price maintenance plan in which dealers agreed with a drug manufacturer that they would not sell the manufacturer's drug product below a certain price. The Court recognized this situation as a sham transaction to achieve a clearly unreasonable result.

Assume that the dealers did not wish to compete in selling Dr. Miles' product but rather wanted to form a dealers' cartel under which all agreed to sell the product at a designated high price. Such a horizontal conspiracy to fix prices certainly would be seen as unreasonable under the Sherman Act and thus would be unenforceable. Therefore, the dealers may have tried to hide their conspiracy by convincing Dr. Miles to dictate contractually to each of them that they must sell his product above the desired price. This arrangement would have achieved the objectives of the dealers' cartel with contracts that they believed would be enforced by the courts if any of the members attempted to cheat. However, the Supreme Court recognized that the purpose of the vertical price agreements was to benefit the dealers' conspiracy and, perceiving no countervailing reasonable explanations for vertical price relationships, announced that all such agreements would be automatically illegal.

Vertical price agreements are the subject of heated debates because many economists and business specialists believe that the Court, in reaching the illegal per se determination, did not consider potential benefits to the competitive system that such agreements might engender. Consider, again, the example in which the new company, Leesky, grants to Audio Fantasy the exclusive right to sell Leesky products on the central California coast. Remember that a possible valid rationale for this restraint on Audio Fantasy's competitors is that it might enable Leesky to compete better with major established brands by curing free-rider problems. Unfortunately, the territorial restriction by itself may be insufficient to rid Leesky totally of difficulties created by the free-rider effect. For instance, what is to stop a central coast resident, after being convinced by Audio Fantasy to purchase a Leesky, to drive to Los Angeles and purchase the desired model from a low-overhead discounter there? Or to make matters simpler, the shopper merely has to call discount houses around the country until he finds the lowest price and then request that the model be shipped. Obviously, if Audio Fantasy cannot make the Leesky sales on the central coast even with the territorial restraint, then it will cease to devote overhead to the promotion of the Leesky brand. As before, it will either discontinue the product or hope to free-ride off another dealer's investments. Consequently, Leesky's plan to compete with the major brands through territorial restrictions may be emasculated through long-distance shopping.

One possible solution to this remaining free-rider problem is for Leesky to require all retailers to sell its models above a certain price, no matter where they are located. Leesky would strive to establish this price at a high enough level for its full-service outlets, such as Audio Fantasy, to earn a reasonable return on their promotional investments while it is also low enough to compete with other brands. Consequently, any central coast shopper who now, thanks to Audio Fantasy's efforts, wanted a Leesky would be unable to find a significantly better deal, no matter where in the country she looked. Given this observance, the shopper would likely buy at Audio Fantasy, the most conveniently located outlet.

With this scenario as a perspective you should be seeing similarities to the discussion involving vertical nonprice restraints. Leesky's resale price-maintenance plan is damaging intrabrand competition because with it Leesky dealers are unable to compete on price. However, competition among Leesky and different brands might intensify because Leesky dealers are now willing to promote the Leesky name heavily. These are the same considerations that must be balanced with vertical nonprice restraints. Thus many business-policy makers, including those at the Justice Department, perceive no logical distinction between vertical price and nonprice restraints. Rather, they believe that both may work hand-in-hand to achieve efficient and pro-competitive goals of the manufacturers. Therefore, they argue that *Dr. Miles* should be overruled and that vertical price agreements henceforth should be appraised using the rule of reason. Indeed, the Justice Department has gone so far as to file amicus briefs in relevant Supreme Court cases requesting that the Court abandon the per se status. As we shall see, the Court has been sympathetic to its arguments and, to the dismay of many policy makers, has begun to cut back the reach of the per se rule in recent years.

For almost forty years Congress partially relaxed antitrust policy with regard to vertical price agreements. Beginning in the late 1920s some states were persuaded through their public policy processes to pass statutes declaring that vertical price fixing, under certain conditions, would be legal in the states' jurisdictions. Called fair trade laws, these state statutes allegedly were designed to relieve employment problems stemming from the Depression. However, these laws were ineffectual, since under the federal antitrust laws vertical price agreements were still illegal per se. In 1937 the Sherman Act, section 1, was amended so that vertical price agreements would be legal within a state if they were valid under state law. As with all changes in policy, you should consider who might have argued for this amendment and who might have been against it. Contemplate why the economic conditions of those times fostered the issue and nurtured it through the policy process. Also, recognize that fair trade laws fell into disfavor in the states soon thereafter. Why did the pendulum shift away from fair trade? Indeed, in 1975 the Sherman Act was again amended to remove the 1937 language that made price maintenance potentially legal in the first place. Again, you need to question why this step was taken at the federal level.

Although vertical price agreements have been illegal per se in many states since 1937 and in all states since 1975, manufacturers still devised a means to achieve the objectives of price maintenance without violating federal law. Such a technique was first conceived by Colgate & Company. Essentially, Colgate suggested to its retailers that they sell Colgate products at a specified price. Also, the retailers were made aware that if they did not charge the suggested price, Colgate, using its *independent* discretion, might choose to cease dealings with that retailer. Most retailers decided to charge the suggested price, and the Justice Department sued, claiming that this was vertical price fixing. The Supreme Court disagreed. It concluded that since Colgate was merely stating the terms under which it might deal with its retailers, and since there was no evidence that the retailers were asked to abide by or did agree to the suggestions, there was no violation of the Sherman Act, section 1, which requires either a contract, combination, or conspiracy.

This technique of suggesting prices has thereafter been known as the *Colgate doctrine*. The problems with the Colgate doctrine are multifaceted. First and foremost, the manufacturer cannot assure through enforceable contracts that its retailers will abide by resale price terms. The retailers must be free to use their independent judgment whether to follow the manufacturer's suggestions. Thus a plan such as Leesky's may be frustrated by its dealers. Also, any indication between the parties acknowledging acceptance of the terms may be considered evidence of agreement to maintain prices. For instance, what would be your judgment as a juror if a recalcitrant discounting retailer was cut off for a short period of time and then, after reinstatement, always charged the suggested price? Some juries, as you might suspect, have considered this sufficient evidence to prove that the retailer agreed it would charge the proper prices if it could get its supply back. Therefore, the manufacturer using the Colgate doctrine must be careful indeed.

An even more complicated problem arises when dealers who are abiding by suggested resale prices communicate disapprovingly to the manufacturer about the existence of competitors who are not conforming to the suggested level. What is the verdict if the manufacturer cuts off the supply to the discounting dealers after the information is received from the abiding outlets? Is this sufficient evidence to prove the existence of an illegal per se price-fixing conspiracy? What if the manufacturer goes so far as to agree explicitly with those complying retailers that the nonconforming discounter will be discontinued? As you might suspect, these are especially troublesome issues when the complaining dealers have established full-service facilities in response to legal vertical nonprice restraints and are having difficulty promoting the manufacturer's brand in the desired fashion because of free-riding by the discounter.

In *Monsanto Co.* v. *Spray-Rite Service Corp*, the Supreme Court considered the first issue about whether complaints from full-service dealers to the manufacturer about a discounting competitor, followed by the discontinuance of that discounter, might be sufficient in and of itself to prove that the complaining dealers had conspired with the manufacturer to maintain the price level. In this 1984 case the Supreme Court held that the answer is no. The Court explained this conclusion in the following way:

> [An] important distinction in distributor-termination cases is that between concerted action to set prices and concerted action on nonprice restrictions. The former have been per se illegal since the early years in national antitrust enforcement. The latter are judged under the rule of reason. . . . But the economic effect of all the conduct described above—unilateral and concerted vertical price-setting, agreements on price and nonprice restrictions—is in many, but not all, cases similar or identical. . . . For example, the fact that a manufacturer and its distributors are in constant communication about prices and marketing strategy does not alone show that the distributors are not making independent pricing decisions. A manufacturer and its distributors have legitimate reasons to exchange information about the prices and the reception of their products in the market. Moreover, it is precisely in cases in which the manufacturer attempts to further a particular marketing strategy by means of agreements on often costly nonprice restrictions that it will have the most interest in the distributors' resale prices. The manufacturer often will want to ensure that its distributors earn sufficient profit to pay for programs such as hiring and training additional salesmen or demonstrating the technical features of the product, and will want to see that "free-riders" do not interfere. Thus the manufacturer's strongly felt concern about resale prices does not necessarily mean that it has done more than the *Colgate* doctrine allows. Nevertheless, it is of considerable importance that independent action by the manufacturer, and concerted action on nonprice restrictions, be distinguished from price-fixing agreements, since under present law the latter are subject to per se treatment and treble damages. . . . Permitting an agreement to be inferred merely from the existence of complaints, or even from the fact that termination came about in response to complaints, could deter or penalize perfectly legitimate conduct. . . . Such complaints, particularly where the manufacturer has imposed a costly set of nonprice restrictions arise in the normal course of business and do not indicate illegal concerted action. . . . Thus something more than evidence of complaints is needed.

There must be evidence that tends to exclude the possibility that the manufacturer and nonterminated distributors were acting independently.[9]

The Justice Department filed an amicus brief with the Supreme Court in *Monsanto* asking the Court to overrule the precedent set in *Dr. Miles* and thereby evaluate all vertical agreements, whether about price or nonprice marketing aspects, under the rule of reason. Obviously, given the above-quoted language, the Supreme Court was very sensitive to the Justice Department's arguments. However, it was not willing to change the policy course completely in this particular lawsuit for technical procedural reasons.[10]

The responses to *Monsanto* by the various public-policy institutions were varied. The Justice Department, confident with the forgiving language of that case, indicated in its 1985 vertical restraint guidelines that it would pursue vertical price agreements only in very limited situations. It announced that although such agreements still are illegal per se, it would be careful not to characterize a restraint as resale price maintenance simply because price is affected. After all, even nonprice restraints will affect price. Thus the guidelines state that "if a supplier adopts a bona fide distribution program embodying non-price restraints [the rule of reason related in] these Guidelines will apply unless there is direct or circumstantial evidence (other than effects on price) establishing an explicit agreement as to the specific prices at which goods or services would be resold."

Congress reacted sharply to this policy directive issued by Justice. In 1985 it passed a law expressing the "sense of Congress" that the guidelines "are not an accurate expression of the federal antitrust laws or of congressional intent with regard to the application of such laws to resale price maintenance and other vertical restraints of trade." It declared that the guidelines "shall not be accorded any force of law or be treated by the courts of the United States as binding or persuasive."[11] Congress also debated numerous bills to retard any change in resale-price-maintenance policy. For example, Congress considered legislation designed to prevent the Justice Department from further spending funds to advocate use of the rule of reason by courts in vertical price cases. In addition, Congress debated legislation that would have overturned *Monsanto* by specifying that evidence of competitor complaints followed by the cutoff of the discounter raises an inference of a conspiracy. Finally, and most dramatically, bills were introduced in both houses to codify that vertical price fixing is illegal per se.[12]

In the face of Congressional hostility toward its decision in *Monsanto* the Supreme Court granted certiorari in a case that allowed it to answer the second question posed earlier—whether an explicit agreement between a dealer and a manufacturer to eliminate a discounter constitutes illegal per se price fixing. Various special-interest groups watched this case with great anticipation, for the direction taken by the Court obviously would have an impact on their efforts with the other policy makers. As expected, the Court continued its course toward the efficiency goals of antitrust and in 1988 resolved this controversy, to the detriment of the discounter. How Congress will respond to this policy action is open to speculation, but one can be sure that an exciting and electric policy showdown is forthcoming.

BUSINESS ELECTRONICS CORPORATION
v.
SHARP ELECTRONICS CORPORATION
United States Supreme Court
56 USLW 4387 (May 2, 1988)

BACKGROUND

Sharp Electronics manufactures calculators and sells them through retailers. Sharp publishes a list of suggested minimum retail prices, but its dealers are not obligated to observe them. Two retailers competed in the Houston, Texas, area—Business Electronics Corporation and Gilbert Hartwell. Business Electronics' prices were often below the suggested prices. Hartwell's prices also were at times below the suggested levels, although they were usually higher than Business Electronics' prices. There was some evidence that Hartwell provided more extensive presale educational and promotional services than did Business Electronics. In June 1973 Hartwell gave Sharp an ultimatum that it would terminate selling Sharp calculators unless Sharp ended its relationship with Business Electronics. Sharp terminated Business Electronics in July 1973.

Business Electronics sued in the District Court alleging vertical price fixing. The judge instructed the jury that if there was an agreement between Sharp and Hartwell to terminate Business Electronics because of its price cutting, then it must find that Sharp violated the Sherman Act. The jury determined that the agreement existed, and damages were awarded. The Court of Appeals reversed based on the jury instruction, and Business Electronics appealed.

OPINION

Justice Scalia

. . . Although vertical agreements on resale prices have been illegal per se since *Dr. Miles Medical Co.*, we have recognized that the scope of per se illegality should be narrow in the context of vertical restraints. In *Sylvania*, we refused to extend per se illegality to vertical nonprice restraints, specifically to a manufacturer's termination of one dealer pursuant to an exclusive territory agreement with another. . . . We concluded that vertical nonprice restraints had not been shown to have such a pernicious effect on competition and to be so lacking in redeeming value to justify per se illegality. . . .

Our approach to the question presented in the present case is guided by the premises of *Sylvania* and *Monsanto*: that there is a presumption in favor of a rule-of-reason standard; that departure from that standard must be justified by demonstrable economic effect, such as the facilitation of cartelization, rather than formalistic distinctions; that interbrand competition is the primary concern of the antitrust laws; and that the rules in this area should be formulated with a view towards protecting the doctrine of *Sylvania*. . . .

The District Court's rule on the scope of per se illegality for vertical restraints would threaten to dismantle the doctrine of *Sylvania*. Any agreement between a manufacturer and a dealer to terminate another dealer who happens to have charged lower prices can be alleged to have been directed against the dealer's "price cutting." In the vast majority of cases, it will be extremely difficult for the manufacturer to convince a jury that its motivation was to ensure adequate services, since price cutting and some measure of service cutting usually go hand in hand. Accordingly, a manufacturer that agrees to give one dealer an exclusive territory and terminates another dealer pursuant to that agreement, or even a manufacturer that agrees with one dealer to terminate another for failure to provide contractually obligated services, exposes itself to the highly plausible claim that its real motivation was to terminate a price cutter. Moreover, even vertical restraints that do not result in dealer termination, such as the initial granting of an exclusive territory or the requirement that certain services be provided, can be attacked as designed to allow existing dealers to charge higher prices. Manufacturers would be likely to forgo legitimate and competitively useful conduct rather than risk treble damages and perhaps even criminal penalties.

We cannot avoid this difficulty by invalidating as illegal per se only those agreements imposing vertical restraints that contain the word "price," or that affect the "prices" charged by dealers. Such formalism was explicitly rejected in *Sylvania*. As the above discussion indicates, all vertical restraints, including the exclusive territory agreement held not to be per se illegal in *Sylvania*, have the potential to allow dealers to increase "prices" and can be characterized as intended to achieve just that. In fact, vertical nonprice restraints only accomplish the benefits identified in *Sylvania* because they reduce intrabrand price competition to the point where the dealer's profit margin permits provision of the desired services. . . .

Finally, we do not agree with petitioner's contention that an agreement on the remaining dealer's price or price levels will so often follow from terminating another dealer "because of its price cutting" that prophylaxis against resale price maintenance warrants the District Court's per se rule. Petitioner has provided no support for the proposition that vertical price agreements generally underlie agreements to terminate a price cutter. The proposition is simply incompatible with the conclusion of *Sylvania* and *Monsanto* that manufacturers are often motivated by a legitimate desire to have dealers provide services, combined with the reality that price cutting is frequently made possible by "free riding" on the services provided by other dealers. . . .

In sum, economic analysis supports the view, and no precedent opposes it, that a vertical restraint is not illegal per se unless it includes some agreement on price or price levels. Accordingly, the judgment of the Fifth Circuit is Affirmed.

CONCLUSION

In this chapter we have reviewed how the public-policy process has dealt with a selected set of concerted activities. The important role that each institution can and has played in formulating antitrust policy should be clear. Also, you now have a somewhat sophisticated knowledge of some of the more important types of business transactions in terms of antitrust legality. As noted before, however, you have not covered all there is to know about antitrust and concerted arrangements. Franchise arrangements, refusals to deal, and information exchanges are just a few of the topics not treated in these pages. Nonetheless, you should have a feel for how policy might have been shaped for these common occurrences and what that policy currently might be.

In the next chapter the rapidly changing policy dynamics associated with monopolies and mergers will be investigated. This review will supplement your understanding of how the antitrust policy process has become increasingly favorable for the business activities of large corporations.

NOTES

1. 104 S. Ct. 1464, 1471 (1984).
2. *Standard Oil Co.* v. *U.S.*, 221 U.S. 1, 60 (1911).
3. 246 U.S. 231, 238 (1938).
4. 273 U.S. 392, 396–97 (1926).
5. 441 U.S. 1 (1979).
6. The Circuit Court for the District of Columbia recently used the rule of reason to decide a horizontal restraint case that would have been illegal per se under the *Topco* case. *Rothery Storage & Van Co.* v. *Atlas Van Lines, Inc.* 792 F. 2d 210, 226 (D.C. Cir. 1986).
7. 388 U.S. 365 (1967).
8. 220 U.S. 373 (1911).
9. 465 U.S. 752 (1984).
10. Since the defendant did not argue in the District Court that the rule of reason should be used or raise the issue on appeal, the Supreme Court refused to consider the question.
11. Public Law no. 99–180, sec. 605, 99 Stat. 1169 (December 13, 1965).
12. Examples include the Freedom from Vertical Price Fixing Act of 1987, H.R.

CHAPTER SIX
Antitrust Policy:
Monopolies and Mergers

INTRODUCTION

We have seen that there has been a radical shift in antitrust policy over the last two decades from one that emphasized the sanctity of small business units to one that now focuses on operational efficiency. It should not be surprising that this attitudinal shift has had a marked effect on policies dealing with the growth and practices of big business. In particular, the permissible activities of large organizations have expanded under section 2 of the Sherman Act. In addition, and much more controversial, restrictions on mergers based on antitrust concerns have been significantly relaxed over this period.

This chapter is designed to introduce you to the major public-policy concepts regarding monopolies and mergers. In approaching these topics concentrate not only on the current status of the law but also on the dynamics of the public-policy process. Be especially sensitive to how antitrust policy is adapting to an increasingly competitive world market. This consideration will be important when you analyze the future of the large corporation in the final chapter of this book.

MONOPOLIZATION

Section 2 of the Sherman Act provides that every person who monopolizes or attempts to monopolize or conspires to monopolize any part of commerce among the several states or with foreign nations is guilty of an antitrust violation. Although there are three offenses defined by the act, we will focus on monopolization, the most important of the three.

You probably learned in your introductory economics course that a company is a monopoly when it has no competitors in its field. Thus you might conclude that a firm could be guilty of a Sherman Act, section 2, violation only if it controlled 100 percent of its market. However, the courts to date have never interpreted the act to have such limited scope. Rather the courts have long held that *monopoly* means that a firm has such a predominant share of the market that it has the power to control prices or exclude competition. Therefore, the first prerequisite for a Sherman Act violation is simply that a firm be "too big." What size is too big? The answer depends on the circumstances existing in the particular industry, but market shares under 50 percent rarely constitute a size that is big enough for monopolizing violations.

Note that the act does not state that monopolies are illegal. Instead, it provides that to monopolize is illegal. Thus something more than just being a monopoly is required to run afoul of the act. As will be shown later, what that additional required element is has changed significantly over the last forty years. Currently, though, a company can be guilty of monopolizing only if it has achieved or maintained its size by engaging in business practices that cannot be justified on efficiency grounds or are otherwise not normal for that industry. In sum, then, there are two necessary conditions for a firm to be guilty of monopolizing:

1. The firm must be "too big", and
2. The firm must attain or maintain that size by nonnormal business practices.

We will now investigate these two prerequisites in more detail.

Determination of Market Share

Suppose a lawsuit is brought against Sperry alleging that it has monopolized the "topsider" market. The plaintiff claims that Sperry is the only maker of Topsiders and thus has 100 percent of the market. According to the plaintiff, its only task, then, is to prove that Sperry attained or maintained that size using unjustifiable business practices. Sperry in its reply argues that the market consists of more products than Topsiders. It suggests that all makers of deck shoes must be included in the market-share calculation as well as manufacturers of casual loafers, tennis shoes, aerobic shoes, running shoes, and formal shoes. Considering all these producers of shoes, Sperry's market share is below 5 percent, and consequently is much too low for a monopolization charge. How should a court determine what are the relevant products in the market? The basis for constructing this so-called *relevant product market* is critical since the presence or absence of liability may be based on it.

Consistent with both lines of antitrust philosophies, but emphasized to a greater extent today, is the fear that large firms that face few if any competitors might have the power to raise their prices without significantly losing their customers. The possession of market power in terms of price, then, must be a central focus of any monopolization inquiry. Thus in appraising the market power of Sperry, one must assess what other products might attract its customers if it were to raise the price of Topsiders by a small amount. In the eyes of consumers these alternative products are somewhat interchangeable with Topsiders, given the typical uses for Topsiders, and serve as competition for Sperry in the sale of Topsiders. Therefore, these products should be included in the relevant product market, and the firms that make them should be factored into the market-share determination.

In economic terms goods to which customers will readily shift when a product price rises are said to have a high *cross-elasticity of demand* with that product. The Supreme Court dealt with the question of how to determine the relevant product market and the importance of cross-elasticity of demand to this analysis in the following classic monopolization case.

UNITED STATES
v.
E. I. DU PONT DE NEMOURS & CO.
United States Supreme Court
351 U.S. 377 (1956)

BACKGROUND

The Justice Department sued under section 2 of the Sherman Act contending that Du Pont had monopolized the cellophane market. Du Pont produced approximately 75 percent of the cellophane sold in the United States, which constituted about 17.9 percent of all flexible packaging material sales. The District Court found that the relevant product market was all flexible packaging materials and ruled in favor of Du Pont. The government appealed directly to the Supreme Court.

OPINION

Justice Reed

. . . The Government asserts that cellophane and other wrapping materials are neither substantially fungible nor like priced. For these reasons, it argues that the market for other wrapping materials is distinct from the market for cellophane and that the competition afforded cellophane by other wrappings is not strong enough to be considered in determining whether Du Pont has monopoly powers. . . . Every manufacturer is the sole producer of the particular commodity it makes, but its control, in the above sense of the relevant market, depends upon the availability of alternative commodities for buyers: i.e., whether there is cross-elasticity of demand between cellophane and other wrappings. This interchangeability is largely gauged by the purchase of competing products for similar uses considering the price, characteristics and adaptability of the competing commodities. . . .

If cellophane is the "market" that Du Pont is found to dominate, it may be assumed it does have monopoly power over the "market." Monopoly power is the power to control prices or exclude competition. It seems apparent that Du Pont's power to set the price of cellophane has been limited only by the competition afforded by other flexible packaging materials. . . .

Determination of the competitive market for commodities depends on how different from one another are the offered commodities in character or use, how far buyers will go to substitute one commodity for another. For example, one can think of building materials as in commodity competition, but one can hardly say that brick competed with steel or wood or cement or stone in the meaning of Sherman Act litigation. The products are too different. . . . On the other hand, there are certain differences in the formulae for soft drinks, but one can hardly say that each one is an illegal monopoly. . . .

Because most products have possible substitutes, we cannot . . . give "that infinite range" to the definition of substitute. Nor is it a proper interpretation of the Sherman Act to require that products be fungible to be considered in the relevant market. . . .

But, despite cellophane's advantages, it has to meet competition from other materials in every one of its uses. . . . [C]ellophane furnishes less than 7% of wrappings for bakery products, 25% for candy, 32% for snacks, 35% for meats and poultry, 27% for crackers and biscuits, 47% for fresh produce, and 34% for frozen foods. Seventy-five to eighty percent of cigarettes are wrapped in cellophane. . . . Thus, cellophane shares the packaging market with others. The over-all result is that cellophane accounts for 17.9% of flexible wrapping materials, measured by the wrapping surface. . . . Moreover, a very considerable degree of functional interchangeability exists between these products. . . . [E]xcept as to permeability to gases, cellophane has no qualities that are not possessed by a number of other materials. . . .

An element for consideration as to cross-elasticity of demand between products is the responsiveness of the sales of one product to price changes in the other. . . . The court below held that the "[g]reat sensitivity of customers in the flexible packaging markets to price or quality changes" prevented Du Pont from possessing monopoly control over price. . . .

We conclude that cellophane's interchangeability with other materials mentioned suffices to make it a part of this flexible packaging material market.

Affirmed.

Although the term *cross-elasticity of demand* is highly technical, the courts have been somewhat sketchy on how to apply the concept. How high should the hypothesized increase in price be? How many customers must switch to another product before it is considered in the product market? The

Justice Department in pertinent guidelines contemplates a 5 percent price increase and includes in the product market those alternatives to which a significant percentage of buyers shift. However, the courts are not so precise in their use of the cross-elasticity-of-demand approach. Rather they use it as a guide in conjunction with a number of other indices to derive the relevant product market. For instance, courts often consider, along with cross-elasticity of demand, industry and public recognition of the competitive market and the uses, characteristics, and distribution channels of the product as compared with other products.

Recently the Justice Department advocated that two other factors be considered in determining the relevant product market, and not surprisingly, these serve to greatly expand that market. One is the concept of *cross-elasticity-of-supply*. To understand this term assume that there is only one manufacturer of screws and that in terms of the above customer-demand factors, there are no substitutes for screws. This firm, then, under the approach just outlined, would have 100 percent of the relevant product market. However, also assume that there are fifty manufacturers of nails. Given the characteristics of nail-manufacturing plants, these nail producers could begin making and selling screws with minimal financial outlay if they thought that such actions would be sufficiently profitable. Here nails are said to have high cross-elasticity of supply with screws because their production facilities can be retooled so easily to manufacture screws. Under these circumstances does our sole screw outlet have the market power to raise its screw prices and increase its profitability without significantly losing its customers? The answer is probably no, since the nail manufacturers would likely begin making screws as soon as they perceived the supranormal profit potential of the product. For this reason current antitrust policy makers at the Justice Department and in a few courts would include the fifty nail manufacturers in the relevant product market. In this way the product market would fall from 100 percent to an insignificant percentage.

Ease of entry is an associated consideration gaining prominence among the new breed of antitrust policy makers. Theoretically, if the costs for new firms to begin producing a product are relatively low, then from a market efficiency perspective, there is little to fear from even dominant businesses because the exercise of any market power will swiftly lead to competition from the new entrants. For example, if there were one dominant trucking firm, the modern antitrust theorists would probably ignore it since any attempt by it to increase profitability would be met with a host of new truckers. After all, essentially one needs only to buy a truck to enter the industry. As with cross-elasticity of supply, entry considerations are explicitly regarded by the Justice Department and have been considered by the courts in recent cases.

Once the product market has been defined, there remains one more step before the market share can be determined. Suppose we determine that grocery stores are a product market. There is only one grocery establishment within 20 miles of your house, but there are 15 stores in a 25-mile radius, and

50 stores within a 50-mile radius. Does the store in your area meet the first prerequisite of being too big? Now change the facts a little. Assume that audio component retailers are a product market. Again, there is one store within 20 miles, but 15 stores within 25 miles and 50 stores closer than 50 miles. Is your judgment different here?

Given the typical shopping patterns of consumers, a lone grocery store in a 20-mile radius would face little competition. When was the last time you traveled 20 miles to buy groceries? Most people will travel only a few miles for foodstuffs. Thus in determining the market share of stores competing in the grocery product market, one must include stores only within a *relevant geographic region of competition*. In this situation, given a relevant geographic range of 10 miles or so, the local grocery store would have a 100 percent market share. The shopping patterns for stereo equipment are much different, however. Now we are considering big-ticket items that are purchased infrequently. Most audio merchandise buyers will investigate prices at stores many miles away before being content with a purchase decision. Twenty-five miles is probably not out of the question for most stereo enthusiasts, and many will travel much farther for their equipment. Thus the local stereo store faces competition from at least 20 other stores, based on the buying patterns of typical consumers. Its market share, therefore, falls well short of monopoly status.

In sum, before a market share can be determined one must define a relevant product market and a relevant geographic area. The former is defined using cross-elasticity of demand and other measures of product substitutability as well as cross-elasticity of supply and ease of entry. The latter is based on the buying patterns of the typical consumer, given the product in question. Once these parameters are established, a firm's market share may be determined as a ratio of its size in relation to all others selling the relevant products in the relevant area. Here size may be represented by assets, sales, capacity, or other measures. As mentioned before, only market shares over 50 percent likely will meet the first requirement of a monopolizing violation.

Anticompetitive Conduct

Since the Sherman Act prohibits firms from monopolizing, something more than monopoly size is required. Because of the changes in antitrust policy, that additional element is more substantial today than it once was.

In a landmark case involving Alcoa in 1945 a court of appeals, acting by special statute as the Supreme Court for the controversy, interpreted the word "monopolize." The court explained:

> [Congress] did not condone "good" trusts and condemn "bad" ones; it forbade all. Moreover, in so doing, it was not necessarily actuated by economic motives alone. It is possible, because of its indirect social or moral effect, to prefer a system of small producers, each dependent for his success upon his own skill and character, to one in which the great mass of those engaged must accept the direction of a few.[1]

It emphasized that unchallenged economic power deadens initiative and that one could be guilty of monopolizing without making more than a fair profit. Thus the court clearly stated that large size alone can bring a firm within the prohibitions of the Sherman Act. The court confused the issue slightly by noting that "monopolize" is a verb and declared that therefore the large size must be obtained or retained by some anticompetitive action rather than by virtue of superior skill, foresight, or industry. However, it then proceeded to rest liability on actions taken by Alcoa that could be classified as little else but as skillful and insightful.[2] Therefore, this case set a precedent for almost twenty years for large size alone to be sufficient for a section 2 violation.

Since the late 1960s the courts have increasingly demanded anticompetitive business practices along with large market share before liability attached. Today firms must have obtained or maintained their large size by commercial activities that are not customary in their industry or are otherwise not justifiable on efficiency grounds. Often liability is premised on refusals by large firms to deal. For instance, a newspaper with a mass-media monopoly in a region responded to the advent of a new radio station by refusing to accept advertisements from businesses that also advertised on that new station. Such an action was deemed an illegal maintenance of its monopoly.[3] Also, "predatory pricing" has been viewed as a nonnormal business practice, although economists and recently the Supreme Court have brought this concept into disrepute by questioning whether a rational firm realistically would attempt to permanently exclude competitors by using this means.[4] The following case presents a recent example of what is required to constitute a monopolizing violation.

ASPEN SKIING COMPANY
v.
ASPEN HIGHLANDS SKIING CORPORATION
United States Supreme Court
105 S. Ct. 2847 (1985)

BACKGROUND

Aspen is a destination ski resort with a reputation for super powder, a wide range of runs, and an active night life. Aspen Skiing Company (Ski Co.) owns three of Aspen's four mountains: Ajax, Buttermilk, and Snowmass. Aspen Highlands (Highlands) owns the fourth mountain. Until 1977 the two companies jointly offered a six-day "around-the-neck" pass, which entitled its purchaser to ski at any of the four mountains. Usage of the pass was statistically monitored, and the receipts from pass sales were divided between the two companies according to usage at their respective mountains. Besides offering the around-the-neck pass, each company individually offered various mixes of one-day, three-day and six-day passes for use at its own mountains. The around-the-neck pass was most popular, and Highlands's share of ticket revenues was between 13.2 percent and 18.5 percent from 1973 to 1977.

In 1977 Ski Co. demanded that Highlands accept a fixed 15 percent of the around-the-neck revenues. Highlands reluctantly agreed. In 1978 Ski Co. announced that it would not continue the pass unless Highlands agreed to a fixed 12.5 percent of the revenues. This was too low a figure for Highlands to accept, and the around-the-neck pass was dead. Ski Co. then altered its advertising to suggest that Aspen had only three mountains and promoted its three-mountain, six-day pass. Also, it eliminated its individual three-day pass. In addition, it refused to accept Adventure Pack vouchers issued by Highlands equal in value to daily lift tickets at Ski Co. even though they were guaranteed. Highlands's share of the Aspen ski market declined from 20.5 percent in 1977 to 11 percent in 1981, and its revenues sank dramatically.

Highlands sued Ski Co. alleging that Ski Co. monopolized in contravention of section 2 of the Sherman Act. The lower courts found that Ski Co. had monopoly power: The product market was defined as downhill skiing at destination ski resorts, and Aspen was the relevant geographic area. They also determined that Ski Co. used anticompetitive practices and awarded Highlands $7.5 million plus attorneys' fees. In addition, it entered an injunction requiring a four-mountain pass.

OPINION

Justice Stevens

. . . The question whether Ski Co.'s conduct properly may be characterized as exclusionary cannot be answered by simply considering its effect on Highlands. In addition, it is relevant to consider its impact on consumers and whether it has impaired competition in an unnecessarily restrictive way. If a firm has been attempting to exclude rivals on some basis other than efficiency, it is fair to characterize its behavior as predatory. . . .

The 4-area attribute of the ticket allowed the skier to purchase his 6-day ticket in advance while reserving the right to decide in his own time and for his own reasons which mountain he would ski on each day. It provided convenience and flexibility . . . . [T]he evidence supports a conclusion that consumers were adversely affected by the elimination of the 4-area ticket. . . .

Ski Co. did not persuade the jury that its conduct was justified by any normal business purpose. . . .The jury may well have concluded that Ski Co. elected to forgo . . . short run benefits because it was more interested in reducing competition in the Aspen market over the long run by harming its smaller competitor. That conclusion is strongly supported by Ski Co.'s failure to offer any efficiency justification whatever for its pattern of conduct. . . .[T]he record in this case comfortably supports an inference that the monopolist made a deliberate effort to discourage its customers from doing business with its smaller rival. The sale of its 3-area, 6-day ticket, particularly when it was discounted below the daily ticket price, deterred the ticket holders from skiing at Highlands. The refusal to accept the

Adventure Pack coupons in exchange for daily tickets was apparently motivated entirely by a decision to avoid providing any benefit to Highlands even though accepting the coupons would have entailed no cost to Ski Co. itself, would have provided it with immediate benefits, and would have satisfied its potential customers. Thus the evidence supports an inference that Ski Co. was not motivated by efficiency concerns and that it was willing to sacrifice short run benefits and consumer good will in exchange for a perceived long-run impact on its smaller rival. . . .
Affirmed.

The Justice Department currently is in a state of inactivity in terms of policing monopolizing activities. Possibly this is because its members view most aspects of the U.S. economy as competitive or potentially competitive. Also, most practices undertaken by businesses are seen as efficient responses to market forces. Its two landmark cases of the 1970s, the IBM and ATT litigations, ended by dismissal and consent decree, respectively. We suspect that until there is a president with a significantly different concept of antitrust enforcement in the United States, there likely will be little attention given to the Sherman Act, section 2 by this executive-branch agency.

Similarly, the FTC has not directed its resources lately toward pursuing monopoly-based cases under section 5 of the FTC Act. This again reflects the influence of the executive branch over that independent agency. As you might suspect, however, this agency has not always been so docile toward business behavior conducted by large firms. For instance, in 1972 the FTC filed a celebrated complaint against four cereal companies alleging that their business actions were so similar in pricing, brand proliferation, and other ways that they, in essence, were an uncompetitive "shared monopoly." The cereal companies challenged the complaint, and a hearing was conducted before an FTC administrative-law judge. In 1981 the judge found that the companies engaged in intense and uncoordinated competition, and the FTC thereafter discontinued the case. Under the Reagan administration the concept of "shared monopoly" was not resurrected, and it is doubtful that we shall see it again for some time.

As *Aspen Highlands* demonstrates, you should not assume that section 2 is totally dormant just because the federal administrative agencies have a relatively low level of interest in it. Private lawsuits alleging monopolization under section 2 continue to be brought with some frequency, and their disposition depends on the antitrust philosophies of the judges sitting on the respective courts. As we have seen, appointments by President Reagan may have reduced the likelihood that a plaintiff will be successful in a monopolization suit. However, there still remain a great number of justices who have not joined the economic-efficiency bandwagon. Whether section 2 remains viable obviously depends on the future philosophical composition of the courts. This in turn will be strongly dependent on the antitrust objectives of future presidents and senators.

MERGERS

Introduction

The area of antitrust reform that has received the most public attention involves the rapidly changing standards for merger enforcement. Whereas in the 1960s, mergers between very small competitors often raised eyebrows at the government agencies and were struck down by the courts, today, in what some have termed an anything goes atmosphere, mergers are rarely challenged. Rather, under today's criteria most mergers are viewed as efficient and procompetitive. Even when there are concerns with pending mergers, the agencies still usually approve the mergers if certain trouble spots are ironed out. Only rarely, as when Coca-Cola Company bid for Dr. Pepper Company and PepsiCo, Inc. proposed to purchase Seven-Up Company, have the agencies blocked mergers wholesale. Such permissiveness clearly has fueled the takeover fever of the 1980s. Also, it has raised a public furor by those who advocate a return to the antitrust policies of the 1960s. As always, the future course will be determined by the dynamics of the public-policy process.

Mergers are governed by the Clayton Act, section 7, which essentially provides that mergers or acquisitions that may have the effect of substantially lessening competition are illegal. As discussed in Chapter 4, government enforcement is shared for the most part by the FTC and the Justice Department. However, a small set of mergers do fall under the jurisdiction of other agencies. For instance, mergers involving transportation media, such as between airlines, are evaluated by the Department of Transportation.

Unlike with the Sherman Act in which private parties have a significant role, the responsibility of policing the Clayton Act, section 7 lies almost exclusively with the administrative agencies. That is because a competitor lacks standing to sue under the Clayton Act unless it can establish that the merged firm will likely injure it through anticompetitive behavior such as below-cost predatory pricing. Thus the policy objectives of these agencies are of paramount importance to firms considering merger activity. However, on rare occasions merger suits have been brought by state attorneys general and by target firms in hostile tender-offer situations.

Since 1976 with the passage of the Hart-Scott-Rodino Act (codified as the Clayton Act, section 7A), mergers or acquisitions involving large entities have been subject to a *waiting period* before the transaction may be consummated. The purpose of the statute is to provide the antitrust agencies sufficient information and time to enable them to scrutinize proposed combinations and to seek preliminary injunctions, if necessary, before the mergers or acquisitions take place. This process in turn reduces the likelihood that assets of consummated mergers will have to go through a costly unscrambling process.

Under the act large companies, defined in terms of sales or assets, must notify the FTC and the Justice Department thirty days in advance of a merger or fifteen days in advance of a cash tender offer.[5] Accompanying the notification, the companies are required to file significant amounts of industry and economic data. The statute empowers the FTC to make rules, using the notice-and-comment rule-making procedure, establishing the appropriate types of information to be submitted. The required content of such information reports, developed through a series of FTC rule-making actions, can be found in Chapter 16, section 803, of the Code of Federal Regulations. The act also provides the FTC the power, through rule making, to exempt classes of transactions that are not likely to violate the antitrust laws. The FTC has undertaken notice-and-comment rule-making actions in this regard that have resulted in a set of exemptions, reported in Chapter 16, section 802, of the Code of Federal Regulations. In creating such exemptions, the FTC may even redefine the size of companies subject to the terms of the act. If you guessed that the FTC has passed rules altering the threshold size limits, you were correct, and unless there are changes in the antitrust-policy dynamic, you should expect the commission to propose and possibly promulgate further exemptions in this regard.[6]

Mergers can be analyzed with reference to three structural forms: horizontal mergers, vertical mergers, and conglomerate mergers. Horizontal mergers are those between competitors, vertical mergers are between firms in buyer-supplier relationships, and conglomerate mergers consist of all other arrangements. This chapter will now proceed to investigate the policy considerations raised by each form of merger and current developments within each area. Note that mergers between highly integrated companies, such as oil or steel companies, may involve components of each of these structural forms. This does not change the basic analytical frameworks, however.

Horizontal Mergers

Horizontal mergers are mergers of direct competitors. For instance, assume that there are six pizza parlors in your vicinity: Domino's, Pizza Hut, Woodstock's, Angelo's, Shakey's, and Armand's. If Domino's were to acquire Pizza Hut, this would be a horizontal arrangement, since before the merger these two companies directly competed for pizza consumers.

Why might these companies go through the trouble of undertaking this merger? Most often the simple and correct answer is that they envision higher profit potential from the merged firm. This increased profitability in turn may result from one or a combination of two effects. First, the merged entity may be able to create and distribute pizzas at lower cost, which combined with existing retail market prices for pizza, will yield a higher profit margin. Possibly the joint enterprise can take advantage of volume discounts in purchasing or more efficient uses of equipment, personnel, and management. In other words, the merger may create various beneficial synergistic effects. Such a result is socially useful since fewer of society's resources are expended on pizza manufacturing. Thus mergers that demonstrate substantial potential for synergies should be encouraged, barring contrary economic, political, or social reasons for discouraging them.

The foregoing formula for increasing profits was by way of lowering production costs. However, the merged firm may also raise profits if the competitive environment after the merger is more conducive to higher pizza prices. Unquestionably, it is difficult for firms guided by self-interest to maintain prices above the competitive level. However, such cartel behavior will more likely be successful with certain market structures than with others. For example, the potential for price leadership (or hidden collusive activities) obviously is eased when there are only a few competitors that must follow the lead. In our example a pricing program probably could be maintained with the six firms existing before the merger but would certainly be more feasible if there were only five firms. Also, a merger that yields a dominant firm might enable that firm to control prices through its own production reductions or otherwise make the market more conducive to price leadership. These potential results would be harmful to consumers and society because of the higher prices and their consequent market allocation inefficiencies.

When considering horizontal mergers in terms of an economic perspective, then, the analytical goal is to differentiate those mergers likely to decrease costs from those that might create a market structure conducive to higher prices. The former should be permitted while the latter constrained. Both the courts and the administrative agencies make at least a preliminary judgment as to this distinction by reviewing the market shares of the firms competing in the industry. As demonstrated in the next case, *United States* v. *Philadelphia National Bank*, courts investigate both the resultant size of the merged firm and the merger's effect on the concentration of the industry in terms of market shares. Thus a precondition to evaluating a merger is that market shares be determined. Just as with monopolies, this determination requires proper definition of the product market and the geographic market.

The techniques for deriving the product and geographic markets with mergers are the same as used for monopolies. Thus cross-elasticity of demand, product characteristics, distribution-channel behavior, ease of entry, and cross-elasticity of supply are relevant. These issues are no less difficult in the merger context than with monopolies. For example, when considering the proposed merger between Republic Steel Corporation and LTV Corporation in 1984, the Justice Department had to determine not only what kinds of steel competed with each other but also if steel competed with other products, such as hard plastics. In addition, the scope of the geographic market was a vexing issue. Without question, those who use steel will purchase that steel from any manufacturer in the world. Thus the geographic market, defined by the typical customer-supplier relationship, should consist of the entire globe. However, steel imports from many countries are subject to quotas. How then should steel companies in these countries be included in market-share calculations? Should we include only that amount of steel permissible by the quota, or should we include the total capacity of those companies in spite of the quota? Does your answer change by considering that foreign steel can be manufactured into component parts or other finished equipment before importation into the United States, thereby allowing the foreign steel to compete indirectly with steel from U.S. companies without being subject to the steel quota? Does it matter that companies in foreign countries that are restricted by U.S. import quotas may possibly avoid those quotas by selling to middlemen in countries that are not subject to restrictions?

These issues have not yet been fully resolved. In the LTV situation the Justice Department, although it finally approved the merger, seemed to take a restrictive position as to both market definitions, especially the geographic market. However, under the fire of hostile statements from the president, members of his cabinet, and heavy industry, the Justice Department subsequently revised its merger guidelines, specifying that foreign production sources would be scrutinized more closely in terms of actual competitive abilities. This ruling reflected the Reagan administration's permissive policies toward the growth of American business to counter the impacts of foreign competition.

The following case illustrates the basic concepts used by courts to handle horizontal merger litigations.

UNITED STATES
v.
PHILADELPHIA NATIONAL BANK
United States Supreme Court
374 U.S. 321 (1963)

BACKGROUND

The Justice Department sued to enjoin the proposed merger between Philadelphia National Bank and Girard Trust, arguing that it would violate the Clayton Act, section 7. The District Court, by defining the geographic market as the northeastern United States, found for the defendants. The U.S. appealed directly to the Supreme Court.

OPINION

Justice Brennan

. . . The Philadelphia National Bank and Girard Trust Corn Exchange Bank are, respectively, the second and third largest of the 42 commercial banks with head offices in the Philadelphia metropolitan area, which consists of the city of Philadelphia and its three contiguous counties in Pennsylvania. The home county of both banks is the city itself; Pennsylvania law, however, permits branching into the counties contiguous to the home county, and both banks have offices throughout the four-county area. . . . Were the proposed merger to be consummated the resulting bank would be the largest in the four-county area with (approximately) 36% of the area banks' total assets, 36% of deposits, and 34% of net loans. It and the second largest (First Pennsylvania Bank and Trust Company, now the largest) would have between them 59% of the total assets, 58% of deposits, and 58% of the net loans, while after the merger, the four largest banks in the area would have 78% of total assets, 77% of deposits, and 78% of net loans.

The present size of both PNB and Girard is in part the result of mergers. Indeed, the trend toward concentration is noticeable in the Philadelphia area generally, in which the number of commercial banks has declined from 108 in 1947 to the present 42. . . .

(T)he District Court held that . . . the four-county Philadelphia metropolitan area is not the relevant geographic market because PNB and Girard actively compete with other banks for bank business throughout the greater part of the northeastern United States. . . .

We have no difficulty in determining the "line of commerce" (relevant product or services market) and "section of the country" (relevant geographic market) in which to appraise the probable competitive effects to appellees' proposed merger. . . . The cluster of products (various kinds of credit) and services (such as checking accounts and trust administration) denoted by the term "commercial banking, . . ." composes a distinct line of commerce. Some commercial banking products or services are so distinctive that they are entirely free of effective competition from products or services of other financial institutions; the checking account is in this category. . . .

We part company with the District Court on the determination of the appropriate "section of the country." . . . This depends upon "the geographic structure of supplier-customer relations." . . . In banking, as in most service industries, convenience of location is essential to effective competition. Individuals and corporations typically confer the bulk of their patronage on banks in their local community; they find it impractical to conduct their banking business at a distance. . . . We think that the four-county Philadelphia metropolitan area . . . is a more appropriate "section of the country" in which to appraise the instant merger . . . .

Having determined the relevant market, we come to the ultimate question under section 7: whether the effect of the merger "may be substantially to lessen competition" in the relevant market. . . . It requires not merely an appraisal of the immediate impact of the merger upon competition, but a prediction of its impact upon competitive conditions in the future; this is what is meant when it is said that the amended section 7 was intended to arrest anticompetitive tendencies in their "incipiency." . . .

[The] intense congressional concern with the trend toward concentration warrants dispensing, in certain cases, with elaborate proof of market structure, market behavior, or probable anticompetitive effects. Specifically, we think that a merger which produces a firm controlling an undue percentage share of the relevant market, and results in a signifcant increase in the concentration of firms in that market, is so inherently likely to lessen competition substantially that it must be enjoined in the absence of evidence clearly showing that the merger is not likely to have such anticompetitive effects. . . .

> Without attempting to specify the smallest market share which would still be considered to threaten undue concentration, we are clear that 30% presents that threat. Further, whereas presently the two largest banks (First Pennsylvania and PNB) control between them approximately 44% of the area's commercial banking business, the two largest after the merger (PNB-Girard and First Pennsylvania) will control 59 percent. Plainly, we think this increase of more than 33 percent in concentration must be regarded as significant. . . .
>
> We are clear . . . that a merger the effect of which "may be substantially to lessen competition" is not saved because, on some ultimate reckoning of social or economic debits and credits, it may be deemed beneficial. . . . Congress determined to preserve our traditionally competitive economy. It therefore proscribed anticompetitive mergers, the benign and the malignant alike, fully aware, we must assume, that some price had to be paid. . . .
>
> Reversed.

Under current court policies mergers that create firms of undue size and significantly increase the concentration of firms in concentrated markets are presumed to be illegal but subject to a rebuttal that the market-share statistics do not reflect actual competitive conditions. To determine concentration courts usually assess the combined market share of the largest four firms in the industry (the *four-firm concentration ratio*), although in some cases only the top two or three firms are considered. Recent cases indicate that the relevant thresholds are met when the combined market share of the merging firms is around 11 percent and the four-firm concentration ratio exceeds about 63 percent.[7] Such standards of presumptive illegality far exceed those that existed in the 1960s when the philosophical foundations of antitrust relied on different values. For instance, in 1962 the Supreme Court blocked a merger in the highly competitive and fragmented shoe industry that would have resulted in the largest firm but one controlling only 5 percent of the relevant market. The Court stated: "[W]e cannot fail to recognize Congress' desire to promote competition through the protection of viable, small, locally owned business. Congress appreciated that occasional higher costs and prices might result from the maintenance of fragmented industries and markets. It resolved these competing considerations in favor of decentralization."[8]

The Justice Department and the FTC in their merger guidelines rely, as do the courts, somewhat on market-share statistics. However, evidence of actual competitive effects in terms of ease of entry, supply elasticity, and other criteria take a much more prominent role. Also, market-share evidence is scrutinized under a much different framework from the four-firm concentration ratio. Rather, the agencies use the *Herfindahl-Hirschman Index* (HHI), a statistic based on the market shares of all competitors in the relevant market. The HHI is calculated by squaring the market shares of all relevant firms and summing those squares. Thus the "premerger HHI" represents the sum of the squares of the firms before the merger, and the "postmerger HHI" is the projected sum if the merger is allowed to occur. According to the Justice Department guidelines, it is unlikely that a merger which produces a postmerger HHI of under 1000 will be challenged. If the postmerger HHI is between 1000 and 1800, the department still is not likely to challenge the merger when the postmerger HHI exceeds the premerger HHI by less than 100 points. However, if the HHI increase exceeds 100 points, the department will analyze the merger more closely in terms of competitive factors such as ease of entry. When the postmerger HHI exceeds 1800, the same criteria apply except that the pertinent increase in the HHI is 50 points.

The guidelines approaches, by using the HHI, elevate the confidence of merging firms as to the potential legality of their contemplated transactions. Court standards, which are based on terminology like "undue size" and "substantial increase," present only hazy guidance in relation to the more precise tripartite system of the guidelines discussed above. Of course, most courts still employ those *Philadelphia National Bank* concepts, and thus merging firms that end up in court likely will face them. However, as previously mentioned, merger cases are only rarely litigated unless the federal agencies bring the action. Consequently, firms whose contemplated mergers satisfy the guidelines criteria currently have little to fear. However, businesses still must be ever mindful that the guidelines are subject to change by future administrative agency personnel. Also, there is a growing concern by state attorneys general that the federal agencies are not adequately policing the antitrust laws.[9] If such concern rises to the point of definitive action, then the court criteria again will rise in importance.

Vertical Mergers

Vertical mergers are combinations of firms in buyer-supplier relationships. Thus a merger between a flower grower and a flower retailer would be a vertical merger. The major concern of such a merger is that the grower, who previously may have sold to many retailers, now will sell predominantly to the merging retailer. If several of these retailers have depended on this grower for their supplies, then their competitive existence may be jeopardized by the merger. In effect, the merger may "foreclose" them from necessary supplies to stay in business. Or alternatively, the retailer may have been the major customer of several flower growers before the merger. If that retailer after the merger buys exclusively from the merging grower, these other growers may experience a competitive squeeze. In this case the merger may foreclose the competitive growers from sufficient purchasers necessary for them to remain in business. Thus as with exclusive dealing relationships under the Sherman Act, section 1, vertical mergers are scrutinized as to potential competitive effects related to possible foreclosures. The following case demonstrates the concerns of foreclosure.

UNITED STATES
v.
DU PONT & CO.
United States Supreme Court
353 U.S. 586 (1956)

BACKGROUND

The Justice Department sued Du Pont in 1949 under the Clayton Act, section 7, challenging its acquisition of 23 percent of General Motors stock. The District Court dismissed the claim, and Justice appealed directly to the Supreme Court.

OPINION

Justice Brennan

. . . The primary issue is whether Du Pont's commanding position as General Motors' supplier of automotive finishes and fabrics was achieved on competitive merit alone or because its acquisition of the General Motors' stock, and the consequent close intercompany relationship, led to the insulation of most of the General Motors' market from free competition . . . .

We hold that any acquisition by one corporation of all or any part of the stock of another corporation, competitor or not, is within the reach of the section whenever the reasonable likelihood appears that the acquisition will result in a restraint of commerce or in the creation of a monopoly of any line of commerce. . . .

Determination of the relevant market is a necessary predicate to a finding of a violation of the Clayton Act. . . . The record shows that automotive finishes and fabrics have sufficient peculiar characteristics and uses to constitute them products sufficiently distinct from all other finishes and fabrics to make them a "line of commerce" within the meaning of the Clayton Act. . . .

General Motors is the colossus of the giant automobile industry. It accounts annually for upwards of two-fifths of the total sales of automotive vehicles in the Nation. In 1955 General Motors ranked first in sales and second in assets among all United States industrial corporations and became the first corporation to earn over a billion dollars in annual net income. In 1947, General Motors' total purchases of all products from Du Pont were $26,628,274. . . . Expressed in percentages, Du Pont supplied 67% of General Motors' requirements for finishes in 1946 and 68% in 1947. In fabrics, Du Pont supplied 52.3% of requirements in 1946, and 38.5% in 1947. Because General Motors accounts for almost one-half of the automobile industry's annual sales, its requirements for automotive finishes and fabrics must represent approximately one-half of the relevant market for these materials. . . . The Du Pont Company's commanding position as a General Motors supplier was not achieved until shortly after its purchase of a sizable block of General Motors' stock . . . . The inference is overwhelming that Du Pont's commanding position was promoted by its stock interest and was not gained solely on competitive merit. . . .

The statutory policy of fostering free competition is obviously furthered when no supplier has an advantage over his competitors from an acquisition of his customer's stock likely to have the effects condemned by the statute. We repeat, that the test of a violation of section 7 is whether, at the time of the suit, there is a reasonable probability that the acquisition is likely to result in the condemned restraints. The conclusion upon this record is inescapable that such likelihood was proved as to the acquisition. . . .

Reversed.

As the Du Pont case demonstrates, one must define the relevant market before determining the potential foreclosure. Here the relevant market of purchasers for fabrics and finishes was defined as automobile manufacturers. This definition has been criticized because there were many other possible buyers of fabrics and finishes besides auto companies. If these sources had been recognized as relevant, then the foreclosure would have been very small. In other words, even if GM had been "locked-up" by Du Pont, competing sellers of fabrics and finishes might have found sufficient other buyers for their wares outside the auto industry to remain in competition.

Vertical mergers are rarely litigated today. The federal agencies take a dim view of the foreclosure theory by focusing on other competitive factors such as the ease of entry into the allegedly foreclosed market. Thereby, competitive markets usually are defined so broadly that long-term potential foreclosures seem minimal. Also, the courts require a more significant showing of possible foreclosure than they once did. For example, in the early 1960s, foreclosures of under 2 percent of the market were considered competitively dangerous.[10] Today that figure is somewhat higher.

Conglomerate Mergers

A conglomerate merger is a catch-all category, consisting of mergers between firms that do not compete and are not in a buyer-supplier relationship. Conglomerate arrangements can be subdivided further into three conceptual categories, although each is accorded the same analytical treatment under the Clayton Act. A *product-extension merger* is the acquisition of a company whose product before the merger was not offered by the acquirer but was a natural extension of its product line. The *Procter & Gamble* case, described below, in which Procter & Gamble purchased Clorox, is an example of such a conglomerate merger. A *geographic-extension merger* is between two companies offering the same product but in different regions of the country. A merger between Leinenkrugal, which makes and sells beer in the Midwest, and Anchor Steam, which markets beer in the West, would be an example of a geographic-extension merger. A *pure conglomerate merger* consists of all other arrangements, such as a merger between Shakey's Pizza and L. L. Bean.

Given that there is no competitive relationship between the merging firms before the merger, how might such a merger substantially lessen competition? For conceptual ease assume that beer is a product market and San Francisco is a geographic market. There are six beer companies selling in the San Francisco market: *A, B, C, D, E,* and *F.* The San Francisco beer companies believe that company *G,* located in Fresno, is the only brewer that might enter their market in the foreseeable future. Suppose that *G* proposes a merger with *A.* Are there any ways this geographic-extension merger may substantially lessen competition in the San Francisco beer market?

The easiest way to think of a negative competitive effect is to hypothesize that *G,* if the merger were prevented, would enter the San Francisco market on its own. Then rather than just six firms competing in the area, there would be seven. However, courts as yet have been unwilling to enter such speculation and have not blocked conglomerate mergers based on this argument.

Another possibility is more complex but has gained favor with the courts and the administrative agencies. Given that there are only six firms in San Francisco, the climate opens the possibility for price leadership or collusive activities. However, these six firms may be unwilling to increase price or allocate outputs collusively because of their fear that *G* might be attracted to the market by the supranormal profits. In other words, *G* may be perceived by the San Francisco firms as a potential competitor looking in from the fringe of the market and waiting for sufficiently profitable conditions to merit entry. It is possible that *A–F* would rather retain the status quo than risk the entry by a new competitor that might not adhere to the current San Francisco marketing practices. However, if *G* were to purchase *A,* then there would still be only six firms in San Francisco. Thus the San Francisco beer market would not change in terms of the possibilities for market-power influences. Now, though, there would be no companies on the fringe of the market perceived by the San Francisco firms as potential entrants. Thus they could freely raise their prices. With this scenario it might be better to block the merger, thereby leaving *G* on the fringe to keep the San Francisco prices down. Then if *G* still wishes to enter the San Francisco market, it will have to do so on its own. Although this would leave no firms on the fringe of the market, at least there would be seven firms in San Francisco rather than six.

In order for this so called *potential-entrant doctrine* to work, there are a number of prerequisites that must be satisfied. First, the relevant market has to have sufficiently few competitors that collusive activities are feasible. Obviously, if San Francisco had twenty competing beer sellers, there would be little fear of market power, with or without potential entrants. Second, the acquiring firm must have been perceived by existing firms as a potential entrant before the merger. If the firm was not exercising an influence on pricing decisions before the merger, then its acquisition of *A* could have no market effects. Finally, the acquiring firm must be one of only a very few perceived potential entrants. If there were many firms on the edge of the San

Francisco market, then the acquisition by *G* of *A* would have little effect, given that all those other firms would still merit sufficient concern by the six San Francisco firms for them to keep prices down. If you are convinced that these conditions rarely coexist, you are correct. Thus conglomerate mergers almost never raise antitrust concerns. However, as *Procter & Gamble* demonstrates, it is not impossible.

FTC
v.
PROCTER & GAMBLE CO.
United States Supreme Court
386 U.S. 568 (1967)

BACKGROUND

Procter & Gamble purchased Clorox in 1957, and soon thereafter the FTC filed a complaint against Procter & Gamble alleging that the merger violated section 7 of the Clayton Act. After over a year of hearings before an FTC administrative-law judge, in 1960 the judge found for the FTC and ordered divestiture. Procter & Gamble appealed to the full commission, and the commission set aside the administrative-law judge's order. In 1962, after a second hearing, an FTC administrative-law judge again determined that the acquisition violated the Clayton Act. On appeal by Procter & Gamble the full commission, this time, affirmed the decision and issued a formal divestiture order in 1963. Procter & Gamble appealed the order to the federal court of appeals. In 1966 the court determined that the FTC order was not based on the substantial evidence produced at the hearing and reversed the FTC decision. The FTC appealed to the United States Supreme Court.

OPINION

Justice Douglas

This merger may most appropriately be described as a "product-extension merger." . . . It is agreed that household liquid bleach is the relevant line of commerce. . . . It is a distinctive product with no close substitutes. . . . The relevant geographical market is the Nation . . . .

At the time of the acquisition, Clorox was the leading manufacturer of household liquid bleach, with 48.8% of the national sales. . . . Its market share had been steadily increasing for the five years prior to the merger. Its nearest rival was Purex, which manufactures a number of products other than household liquid bleaches, including abrasive cleaners, toilet soap, and detergents. Purex accounted for 15.7% of the household liquid bleach market. The industry is highly concentrated; in 1957, Clorox and Purex accounted for almost 65% of the Nation's household liquid bleach sales, and, together with four other firms, for almost 80%. . . .

Since all liquid bleach is chemically identical, advertising and sales promotion are vital. In 1957, Clorox spent almost $3,700,000 on advertising, imprinting the value of its bleach in the mind of the consumer. In addition, it spent $1,700,000 for other promotional activities. The Commission found that these heavy expenditures went far to explain why Clorox maintained so high a market share despite the fact that its brand, though chemically indistinguishable from rival brands, retailed for a price equal to or, in many instances, higher than its competitors. . . . In 1957, Procter was the nation's largest advertiser, spending more than $80,000,000 on advertising and an additional $47,000,000 on sales promotion. . . .

Prior to the acquisition, Procter was in the course of diversifying into product lines related to its basic detergent-soap-cleanser business. Liquid bleach was a distinct possibility since packaged detergents— Procter's primary product line—and liquid bleach are used complementarily in washing clothes and fabrics, and in general household cleaning. . . .

Section 7 of the Clayton Act was intended to arrest anticompetitive effects of market power in their incipiency. The core question is whether a merger may substantially lessen competition, and necessarily requires a prediction of the merger's impact on competition, present and future. . . . All mergers are within the reach of section 7, and all must be tested by the same standard, whether they are classified as horizontal, vertical, conglomerate or other. . . .

The anticompetitive effects with which this product-extension merger is fraught can easily be seen: (1) The substitution of the powerful acquiring firm may substantially reduce the competitive structure of the industry by raising entry barriers and by dissuading the smaller firms from aggressively competing; (2) the acquisition eliminates the potential competition of the acquiring firm. . . .

The acquisition may also have the tendency of raising barriers to new entry. The major competitive weapon in the successful marketing of bleach is advertising. . . . Thus, a new entrant would be much more reluctant to face the giant Procter than it would have been to face the smaller Clorox.

Possible economies cannot be used as a defense to illegality. Congress was aware that some mergers which lessen competition may also result in economies but it struck the balance in favor of protecting competition. . . .

The Commission also found that the acquisition of Clorox by Procter eliminated Procter as a potential competitor. . . . It is clear that the existence of Procter at the edge of the industry exerted considerable influence on the market. First, the market behavior of the liquid bleach industry was influenced by each firm's predictions of the market behavior of competitors, actual and potential. Second, the barriers to entry by a firm of Procter's size and with its advantages were not significant. There is no indication that the barriers were so high that the price Procter would have to charge would be above the price that would maximize the profits of the existing firms. Third, the number of potential entrants was not so large that the elimination of one would be insignificant. Few firms would have the temerity to challenge a firm as solidly entrenched as Clorox. Fourth, Procter was found by the Commission to be the most likely entrant. . . .

Reversed.

As discussed in *Procter & Gamble*, the courts have also considered a "deep-pocket" theory in assessing the effects of conglomerate mergers. That is, there may be concern that a powerful firm with access to capital may enter an industry through merger and then either bully the existing smaller competitors into noncompetitive conduct, or frighten away potentially new competitors. This deep-pocket rationale is falling into disfavor today as the "small-is-beautiful" climate erodes. In particular, the federal agencies in their guidelines totally ignore it as a principle of analysis.

The Merger Environment

The Reagan administration took the position that big business can increase the welfare of American citizens, as long as it functions within competitive parameters. Indeed, in light of pressures from foreign business concerns, the executive branch supported measures that would further the competitiveness of U.S. concerns. In its view, therefore, efficiency had to take the driver's seat in formulating antitrust policy. With this focus most mergers were perceived as beneficial rather than with a suspicious eye.

It is not surprising then that Reagan administration officials supported the efforts of large American businesses to grow further through mergers. In fact, President Reagan's secretary of commerce, Malcolm Baldridge, publicly and forcefully urged for the repeal of the Clayton Act, section 7. He stated:

> Government must view antitrust relative to today's world—a world where U.S. goods face severe foreign competition at every turn. More than 70% of our products face some kind of import competition and the range and variety are changing. . . . Antitrust policy is an issue of domestic and international competitiveness that affects jobs throughout the U.S. economy. As part of our review of antitrust issues, I am urging repeal of one section of the Clayton Act—namely Section 7 . . . American firms now find that their principal foreign competitors that export to the U.S. are very large multinational corporations, backed in many instances by their governments—not the small or medium-sized firms that Clayton 7 sought to preserve in large numbers.[11]

Baldridge noted that the administrative agency's guidelines published under the Reagan administration recognized the competitive pressures from overseas and enforced antitrust policy consistent with his view. However, he correctly pointed out that the guidelines are not the law and that future administrations can change them.

Although the Reagan administration never formally asked Congress to repeal section 7, it did introduce legislation to significantly amend the language of the provision.[12] The aim of the Merger Modernization Act of 1987 was to amend section 7 of the Clayton Act in three ways. First, the "may be" language of the statute, designed to nip potentially harmful mergers in their incipiency, was to be replaced with a standard of "significant probability" that a merger would be harmful. Second, the act would have substituted the words "substantially increase the ability to exercise market power" for the current "substantially to lessen competition." Specifically, such market power was to be defined as the "ability of one or more firms profitably to maintain prices above competitive levels for a significant period of time." Third, the measure required courts to evaluate "all economic factors relevant to the effect of the acquisition in the affected markets" to determine whether there was a significant probability that a merger would increase the ability to exercise market power. The act listed seven factors that courts must consider in this evaluation, which included the ease of entry by foreign and domestic firms, the ability of smaller firms to increase production in response to attempts to increase market power, and efficiencies derived from the acquisition. Obviously, such an amendment would have substantially crystalized the Reagan administration's antitrust legacy beyond the suggestions of the current guidelines. However, the proposal stalled in Congress, and prospects for future consideration seem to be waning.

The federal antitrust agencies have furthered the administration's goals by acquiescing in almost all merger proposals. The sheer size of business is no longer a factor; rather, the likelihood that the merger will result in the exercise of market power is the key. To this end even mergers that have certain dangerous components are permitted as long as the areas of concern are addressed.

For instance, in 1984 the proposed merger of Republic and LTV raised a number of problems in the eyes of the Justice Department. The most acute concern centered on the potential for market power in certain sheet-steel products. To overcome this situation Justice approved the merger on the condition that two of Republic's steel-sheet plants be sold to competitors. In addition, because one of these plants relied on Republic for raw materials, the merged company agreed with the government to supply this plant with necessary raw materials for ten years. Such a pledge was designed to take care of potential foreclosure effects resulting from the vertical aspects of this merger.[13]

In a similar fashion the FTC in 1984 cleared the merger of Texaco and Getty based on the sale of certain properties. In particular, the horizontal effects of the merger would have given Texaco a high share of gasoline assets in the Northeast and the Middle Atlantic states. Thus Texaco agreed to shed nine Getty wholesale gasoline terminals and 1900 gasoline stations in the Northeast, as well as all of Getty's gasoline marketing assets in the Northeast and Middle Atlantic states. Also, Texaco agreed to continue supplying crude oil for five years to about seventeen independent refineries in California that had been Getty crude-oil customers before the merger. Five years was deemed sufficient to account for any possible foreclosure effects because of the expectation that crude oil discovered off the West Coast would be available by the end of the 1980s.[14]

The Department of Transportation has also engaged the "fix-it" approach to mergers in its routine approvals of airline mergers. For instance, Texas Air's proposed acquisition of Eastern Airlines raised significant antitrust concerns based on the horizontal effects in the heavily traveled Northeast corridor. However, this merger was approved once Texas Air announced that certain of its gates and takeoff-and-landing rights at three congested northeastern airports would be sold to Pan Am Corporation, a competitor.[15]

You should not assume that the Reagan administration's permissive attitude toward antitrust enforcement has been universally accepted. Senator Howard Metzenbaum, the chairman of the Senate Judiciary subcommittee which has jurisdiction over antitrust, has contended that the Reagan administration's "antitrust record is a disaster." He noted that the agency policies have encouraged companies "to attempt massive mergers that would never have made it past the corporate board room ten years ago."[16] Similar attitudes are shared by other members of Congress who have drafted legislation to impose more stringent antitrust constraints on combinations in the airline, oil, and other industries.

You should consider what interest groups might be advocating this congressional backlash to the Reagan administration's antitrust policies. Also, think about whether an appeal to Jeffersonian ideals might benefit a candidate for a congressional seat. What are the chances that the current course of antitrust policy will be aborted or reversed? How will foreign competition, especially from the Japanese, be factored into the public-policy process? Changes in attitude by government toward big business will dramatically affect the future social and economic course of this country. Antitrust policy will be an important battleground for such changes.

CONCLUSION

You now have completed a somewhat thorough public-policy analysis of antitrust. Our evaluation of antitrust demonstrated the depth of inquiry required to fully appreciate the various facets underlying any policy. As you have seen, an appropriate public policy analysis demands that you have a sophisticated understanding of the many intricate details that comprise the policy. Only with such a solid foundation can you totally comprehend the motivations behind the various forces applied to the policy process, and the impacts which might result from them.

It seems unlikely that the overall antitrust policy course established by the Reagan administration will be appreciably altered under President Bush. Although one cannot be sure at this early point in his presidency, we anticipate that George Bush will continue to favor the efficiency approach to antitrust. His nominations to the federal enforcement agencies, therefore, are likely to share this philosophy, thereby preserving the status quo there. In addition, most of his nominees to the federal courts probably will interpret the antitrust statutes in light of efficiency principles. This will strengthen even further the significant impact that President Reagan made on this policy making branch of government during his tenure. Thus, Congress is the only policy institution which is not predictably predisposed to pushing the antitrust pendulum further in its current direction.

Of course, you are now fully aware that the public-policy process is much more complicated than simply analyzing the make-up of government players. The social influences which affect their decisions can change markedly and unexpectedly. For instance, special interest groups pleading for antitrust protections may attract broad support. Possibly a substantial economic event with widespread deleterious effects will lead to a reconsideration of the benefits accruing from current antitrust philosophies. Also, while the overall trend may be based on efficiency, that does not foreclose particular antitrust policies from favoring small business interests. Antitrust remains an important policy force in this country, and it will continue to be an exciting and hotly contested area of public policymaking in the future.

NOTES

1. 148 F. 2d 416, 427 (2d Cir. 1945).
2. For instance, the Court noted that Alcoa increased its production capacity to meet anticipated increases in demand. For a thorough economic analysis of *Alcoa* read Dominick T. Armentano, *Antitrust and Monopoly* (New York: John Wiley & Sons, 1982), pp. 100-112.
3. *Lorain Journal* v. *U.S.*, 342 U.S. 143 (1951).
4. *Matsushita Elec. Ind. Co.* v. *Zenith Radio Corp.*, 106 S. Ct. 1348 (1986).
5. To be subject to premerger notification the acquisition must essentially meet two tests:
   (i) The "size of the person" test requires that one company have annual net sales or total assets of $100 million or more and the other party to the transaction, net sales or assets of $10 million or more;
   (ii) The "size of the transaction" test requires that the acquiring company hold 15 percent or more of the acquired company or hold over $15 million in securities and assets of the acquired company.
   The waiting periods may be extended by the FTC or the assistant attorney general for up to an additional twenty days for mergers or ten days for cash tender offers.
6. 16 CFR 802.20. The FTC by rule has exempted certain transactions wherein over 15 percent of a company is acquired. The FTC in recent rule-making proceedings considered expanding this exemption and also evaluated comments to raise the $15 million threshold to $50 million, but it deferred action in these regards as part of its final rule-making order, effective April 10, 1987. (*Federal Register* 52 [March 6, 1987], 7066.)
7. William T. Lifland, "Monopolies, Acquisitions and Joint Ventures," *28th Annual Antitrust Law Institute* (New York: Practising Law Institute, 1987), p. 149.
8. *Brown Shoe Co.* v. *U.S.*, 370 U.S. 294, 344 (1962).
9. "Horizontal Merger Guidelines of the National Association of Attorneys General," *CCH Trade Reg. Report No. 800*, Part II (March 16, 1987).
10. *Brown Shoe Co.* v. *U.S.*, 370 U.S. 294 (1962).
11. *Wall Street Journal*, October 15, 1985, sec. 1, p. 28.
12. Merger Modernization Act of 1987, S. 539, H.R. 1155 (1987).
13. *Wall Street Journal*, March 22, 1984, sec. 2, p. 35.
14. *Wall Street Journal*, February 14, 1984, sec. 1, p. 3
15. *Wall Street Journal*, May 21, 1986, sec. 1, p. 6.
16. *Wall Street Journal*, February 4, 1987, sec. 2, p. 64.

CHAPTER SEVEN
The Future
of the Business–
Government Relationship

INTRODUCTION

In this chapter we examine the relationship between the large corporation and government. We emphasize the forces currently at work in American society that are likely to influence this relationship and explore its future course. A closer, more cooperative link between the large corporation and government may serve to enhance America's international competitive position and reflect societal expectations of corporate social responsibility, but it also raises the possibility of an excessive concentration of economic and political power. On the other hand, an arm's-length relationship in which the large corporation sees its purpose as the purely economic one of maximizing profits and increasing economic efficiency may no longer be viewed by society as granting the corporation sufficient legitimacy. Such an economic role may also lead to excessive government regulation, which in turn may unduly interfere with managerial freedom and flexibility in operating the corporation. In this chapter we point to the increased expectation of corporate social responsibility and the growth of global economic competition as two of the major forces affecting the future of the business-government relationship.

As you read the topics covered in this chapter, consider how they relate to subject areas covered in the earlier chapters. The links between business-government relations, public-policy making, and institutions like the administrative agencies are real, and it is important that you think about and attempt to integrate these subject areas. For example, the large corporation in seeking to maintain and enhance its legitimacy and avoid the detrimental effects of excessive government regulation may determine that the benefits of social responsibility outweigh any associated economic costs. Thus the acceptance of the principle of corporate social responsibility may be one way to limit the number of regulatory public policies and administrative agencies affecting business.

There are also clear linkages between public-policy making, administrative agencies, and a business-government relationship that includes a limited industrial policy. The component parts of a limited industrial policy consist of specific public policies that would have to be implemented and coordinated by an administrative agency or agencies in cooperation with business and labor. As we shall see, the likelihood of a limited industrial policy affecting the future of the business-government relationship will depend in large part on the dynamics of the public-policy process.

When we speak of the business-government relationship in this chapter, we mean the interaction between the large corporation and the federal government. Our focus is on the large corporation rather than small business for two reasons. First, the large corporation is a highly visible and powerful institution in American society, affecting many different stakeholders including employees, investors, consumers, and the local communities and states where the corporation's facilities are located. Studies undertaken by committees of Congress and various economic organizations have consistently found that the five hundred largest industrial corporations account for more than 60 percent of total industrial sales, assets, and net income.[1] Although this level of concentration has not increased appreciably since the early 1950s, the data illustrate the importance of large corporations in the American economy. Second, unlike small business, which has always enjoyed strong support from American public opinion and has never had its legitimacy questioned, the large corporation has generally been cautiously regarded by the American public.[2] The implicit norms and standards of the American people, which we discussed in Chapter 1, have contributed to the small business institution and safeguarded its legitimacy. The right of a small-business person to work hard and succeed in building up a profitable enterprise has long been a central theme of American society. The large corporation, on the other hand, is a much newer institution, dating back to the 1870s. The American people have been unwilling to grant this institution the kind of blanket legitimacy they have accorded to small business. This lower level of legitimacy has made the large corporation more susceptible to government regulation and the potential loss of managerial freedom and flexibility.

It is paradoxical but nevertheless accurate to say that the one constant in the history of the business-government relationship has been change—a gradual evolution from a nation of shopkeepers, farmers, and small enterprises prior to the Civil War to rapid growth in the number and size of corporations after 1870; and then beginning in the 1950s to the recognition that the large corporation must be concerned with the social and political environment in which it exists as well as with its traditional goals of profit maximization and efficiency. In order to better understand the future of this relationship, it is helpful to think about how the relationship has evolved to its present state.

THE EVOLUTION OF THE BUSINESS-GOVERNMENT RELATIONSHIP

As we saw in Chapter 3, the interaction between business and government prior to the Civil War can generally be characterized as uncomplicated, arm's length, and not very extensive. The federal government was small and primarily concerned with national defense, foreign affairs, westward expansion, the postal system, and other traditional functions of a central government. The American free-enterprise system was made up of merchants, small-business people, and small-factory owners, who generally sold their products and services to nearby customers. The business enterprise and its customers were often located in the same town or region, and any commercial disputes could be handled informally by market forces (a business could not afford to antagonize local customers and jeopardize its goodwill in the community) or by resort to legal remedies in a local court. Most businesses took the form of sole proprietorships or small partnerships because capital requirements were not high, and the state laws allowing incorporation were often restrictive. There was little or no regulation of business by the federal or state governments during this early period.

Professor Irving Kristol in a penetrating essay entitled "Corporate Capitalism in America" labels the early role of small business in the American economy as *entrepreneurial capitalism*. He argues that this form of small business capitalism was closely linked to liberal democracy in early America. This linkage goes far in explaining the legitimacy of small business in American society. Kristol writes:

> The United States is the capitalist nation par excellence. That is to say, it is not merely the case that capitalism has flourished here more vigorously than, for instance, in the nations of Western Europe. The point is, rather, that the Founding Fathers *intended* this nation to be capitalist and regarded it as the only set of economic arrangements consistent with the liberal democracy they had established. They did not use the term "capitalism," of course; but, then, neither did Adam Smith, whose *Wealth of Nations* was also published in 1776, and who spoke of "the system of natural liberty.". . . But words aside, it is a fact that capitalism in this country has a historical legitimacy that it does not possess elsewhere. In other lands, the nation and its fundamental institutions antedate the capitalist era; in the United States, where liberal democracy is not merely a form of government but also a "way of life," capitalism and democracy have been organically linked. . . .

But one must also concede that both the Founding Fathers and Adam Smith would have been perplexed by the kind of capitalism we have in 1978. They could not have interpreted the domination of economic activity by large corporate bureaucracies as representing, in any sense, the working of a "system of natural liberty." Entrepreneurial capitalism, as they understood it, was mainly an individual—or at most, a family—affair. Such large organizations as might exist—joint stock companies, for example—were limited in purpose (e.g., building a canal or a railroad) and usually in duration as well. The large, publicly owned corporation of today which strives for immortality, which is committed to no line of business but rather (like an investment banker) seeks the best return on investment, which is governed by an anonymous oligarchy, would have troubled and puzzled them, just as it troubles and puzzles us. And they would have asked themselves the same questions we have been asking ourselves for almost a century now: Who owns this new leviathan? Who governs it, and by what right, and according to what principles?[3]

In the 1870s the large corporation began its rise to influence and power in American society. The modern corporation, characterized by a hierarchy of middle- and top-level salaried managers who monitor and coordinate the work of its various units and by an effective separation of shareholder ownership from the actual management of the business, accounted for one-fifth of business expenditures in 1870, about one-third by 1890, and more than half by 1920.[4] Unlike small business, where the owners are also the managers, the large corporation vests decision-making power firmly in the hands of professional managers who are theoretically accountable to the directors and shareholders. In practice however, such accountability is at best indirect since top-level managers often make up a substantial minority of the board of directors and play a key role in selecting the remaining outside directors (that is, directors who are not corporate employees) who serve on the board. The thousands of shareholders who are the legal owners of the large corporation are too numerous and have too small an ownership share to affect the decisions of management significantly. Their only practical means of voicing dissatisfaction with the actions of top management is to sell their stock.

The great strength of the large corporation in our market economy has been its ability to effectively and efficiently provide most Americans with abundant goods and services and steady economic growth for much of its one-hundred-year history. During most of this period the corporation's goals have been clear: to maximize profit, operate efficiently, and comply with the law. Although the material abundance made possible by the large corporation has provided this major economic institution with a reasonable level of legitimacy, the corporation has also been the subject of suspicion and hostility in American society. In a sense it has been a bittersweet relationship. Americans appreciate and desire the material goods and jobs that the large corporation has been so successful in providing but are suspicious of the concentrated economic power and lack of accountability of the corporation and its management.

Professor Kristol has described the role of the large corporation in the American economy as *corporate capitalism* to distinguish it from the earlier era of entrepreneurial (or small-business) capitalism. Kristol, a leader of the neoconservative movement in America and a strong supporter of free enterprise and the modern corporation, offers the following explanation for the undercurrent of suspicion and distrust of the large corporation that is a part of our history:

> In the latter part of the last century, in all industrialized nations, the large corporation was born out of both economic necessity and economic opportunity: the necessity of large pools of capital and of technical expertise to exploit the emerging technologies, and the opportunity for economies of scale in production, marketing, and service in a rapidly urbanizing society. It all happened so quickly that the term "corporate revolution" is not inappropriate. In 1870, the United States was a land of small family-owned business. By 1905, the large, publicly owned corporation dominated the economic scene.
>
> But the corporate revolution was always, during that period, an unpopular revolution. It was seen by most Americans as an accident of economic circumstance—something that happened to them rather than something they had created. They had not foreseen it; they did not understand it; in no way did it seem to "fit" into the accepted ideology of American democracy. . . .
>
> The old hostility is based on what we familiarly call "populism." This is a sentiment basic to any democracy—indispensable to its establishment but also, ironically, inimical to its survival. Populism is the constant fear and suspicion that power and/or authority, whether in government or out, is being used to frustrate the "will of the people." It is a spirit that intimidates authority and provides the popular energy to curb and resist it. . . .
>
> In the case of the large corporation, we see a healthy populism and a feverish paranoia simultaneously being provoked by its sudden and dramatic appearance. The paranoia takes the form of an instinctive readiness to believe anything reprehensible, no matter how incredible, about the machinations of "big business.". . .
>
> Along with this kind of paranoia, however, populist hostility toward the large corporation derives from an authentic bewilderment and concern about the place of this new institution in American life. In its concentration of assets and power—power to make economic decisions affecting the lives of tens of thousands of citizens—it seemed to create a dangerous disharmony between the economic system and the political. . . . No one was supposed to have such power; it was indeed a radical diffusion of power that was thought to be an essential characteristic of democratic capitalism.[5]

By the 1960s top managers of large publicly traded corporations were becoming more aware of the social and political environment in which the corporation existed. Although the economic goal of profit maximization remained primary for the corporation, a new managerial ideology was developing that recognized the importance of social and political constraints on the actions of the large corporation. The main themes of this new socioeconomic ideology of the corporation were brought together in the 1950s and 1960s by a number of chief executive officers of America's largest corporations who participated in the McKinsey lectures, sponsored by the

Graduate School of Business at Columbia University. These annual lectures, later published in book form, were delivered between 1956 and 1967.

One of the major themes of the McKinsey lectures dealt with the corporation's obligation to use its power responsibly. In his 1963 McKinsey lecture Thomas J. Watson, Jr., then chairman of the board of IBM commented: "We all know that special power imposes special responsibilities on those who hold it. . . . Bigness itself is a relatively new phenomenon in our society. Even if nothing else had changed, the vast concentrations of power in our society would demand that businessmen reconsider their responsibilities for the broader public welfare."[6] This theme was again expressed in the 1964 McKinsey lecture by David Rockefeller, then president of the Chase Manhattan Bank, as follows:

> The old concept that the owner of a business had a right to use his property as he pleased to maximize profits has evolved into the belief that ownership carries certain binding social obligations. Today's manager serves as trustee not only for the owners but for the workers and indeed for our entire society. . . . Corporations have developed a sensitive awareness of their responsibility for maintaining an equitable balance among the claims of stockholders, employees, customers, and the public at large.[7]

By the 1980s the socioeconomic model of the large corporation had gained relatively wide acceptance. Although profit maximization and continued growth are central to its economic mission, the corporation cannot afford to lose sight of its responsibilities to society at large, on whom it depends both economically and politically for its continued existence.[8]

Barring a major economic collapse or unforeseen factors that would cause rapid social change, the relationship between the large corporation and government is likely to become more cooperative in the future, but the process will be incremental rather than characterized by rapid change. This movement toward greater cooperation and away from the adversarial relationship that characterized the period from 1870 to the 1960s is the result of two major forces affecting the large corporation in the last half of the twentieth century. First, there is a growing recognition that the large corporation is operating in a social and political environment that requires it to go beyond economic criteria in order to maintain its legitimacy as one of the major institutions in American society. This increased concern with legitimacy heightens the corporation's recognition of the importance of corporate social responsibility. Second, there is the expanding challenge of international economic competition, which has become increasingly important in many sectors of the economy since the 1970s. The need to compete successfully with countries such as Japan, West Germany, France, and South Korea, which promote cooperation between the central government and the large corporation, may induce a closer relationship in the United States as well. In the remainder of this chapter we will discuss the nature of these two forces and how they are likely to encourage a more cooperative relationship between the large corporation and government.

THE NEED FOR CORPORATE LEGITIMACY

Simply stated, no major institution in a democratic society can long endure if it does not derive political legitimacy from the society. As we noted in the last section, *legitimacy* is a political concept that refers to the justifications for an institution to rightfully possess power. The federal and state governments, for example, derive legitimacy via their respective constitutions from the consent of the governed—the people.

The concept of legitimacy is especially important for large and powerful institutions that are highly visible actors in society and affect peoples' daily lives. The large corporation, given that it is a recognizably important source of economic power, needs to be perceived as a legitimate institution by the American people in order to retain its freedom and flexibility as an economic enterprise. Thus it is vital for corporate managers to understand the sources of corporate legitimacy. Also, they must consider whether these sources are evolving such that the corporation will be required to modify certain of its goals and relationships in order to retain the confidence of the American people and maintain that level of legitimacy necessary for the corporation to remain free of excessive and burdensome government regulation.

The large corporation historically has been viewed with some suspicion and hostility in the United States. Its legitimacy, which has served to counteract this hostility, derives from a number of sources: (1) the fact that it is created or chartered by the state and must comply with the state's corporation law; (2) the idea of private property rights, which allows individuals to own shares in a corporation, large or small, just as they might own real property or a sole proprietorship; (3) the idea that the managers of a corporation are ultimately accountable for their actions to the shareholder-owners; (4) the efficient production of abundant goods and services for the American people; and (5) the corporation's important contribution to American economic growth and general prosperity during much of the twentieth century.

By the 1960s certain of the traditional sources of corporate legitimacy had begun to weaken. Chief among these was the idea of corporate accountability; namely, that the top managers of the large corporation were directly accountable to the shareholders. The trend toward control of the large corporation by its management rather than its shareholders had been identified considerably earlier by Berle and Means in their landmark study, *The Modern Corporation and Private Property.*[9] Their study concluded that because of the dispersion of stock ownership for large publicly traded corporations, a separation had occurred between the ownership and control of the large corporation.[10] This dispersion typically means that even large individual or institutional shareholders cannot hope to own more than 1 to 10 percent of the corporation's outstanding stock. As a result, most shareholders view themselves as passive investors rather than as owners of a corporation over which they exercise control. Control of the corporation is instead exercised by management, which solicits signed proxy statements from the shareholder-investors who authorize management to vote a shareholder's stock at the corporation's annual meeting for a slate of corporate directors selected by management. The direct link between private property and the ownership of a business becomes more tenuous and the legitimacy less clear when shareholders are perceived as having little practical control or power over the property they legally own.

Concurrent with the separation of ownership from the control and management of the corporation was the growing realization by better-educated and better-informed Americans that large corporations had a great impact on their daily lives. Since the 1960s Americans have become more aware of and concerned about social issues such as environmental pollution, consumer protection, workplace safety, and fair employment practices. The large corporation is directly involved with these issues. The increased concern about social issues has tended to weaken economic efficiency as a source of corporate legitimacy. To be sure, efficiency remains important to legitimacy, but it is no longer sufficient. Professor Kristol elaborates on this point in an article he wrote in the mid-1970s:

> It is fairly clear that the American corporation today doesn't really understand what has happened to it in these past decades. It doesn't understand that, whereas the American democratic environment used to perceive it as being a merely economic institution, it now sees it as being to an equal degree a sociological and political institution, and demands that it behave as such. As is usual, in retrospect that change has an air of inevitability about it. A democracy is not likely to permit huge and powerful institutions, with multiple "spillover" effects on large sections of the population, to define their interests in a limited way or to go about pursuing them in a single minded way. It insists that such institutions show a proper attentiveness to what is conceived to be, at any moment, "the public interest." Nor is it any kind of answer to say that, in the long run, the institution's single-mindedness will be for the good of all. In a democracy, large and powerful institutions, if they seek legitimacy in public opinion, must be visibly and currently attentive to the public interest.[11]

The large corporation of the 1980s understands that the issue of legitimacy has become more complex than at any time in its history. It recognizes that as we enter the last decade of the twentieth century, the legitimacy of the large corporation depends not only on its substantial economic attributes but also on being "attentive to the public interest" and behaving in a socially responsible manner. Such behavior not only will enhance the corporation's legitimacy but also is likely to move the large corporation into a closer, more cooperative relationship with government. The latter prospect, as we shall see, is not entirely without controversy.

THE DEBATE ABOUT CORPORATE SOCIAL RESPONSIBILITY

The concept of social responsibility is an important factor affecting the evolution of the business-government relationship. Since the 1960s much has been written about corporate social responsibility. While the idea was initially con troversial, most large corporations today understand that the social and political environment in which they do business requires them to be cognizant of the concept of social responsibility and how it applies to particular corporations and their various stakeholders.

Edwin Epstein of the University of California, Berkeley, a leading authority on the subject of corporate social responsibility, suggests that the concept can best be understood when viewed as both a *process* and the *product* of certain corporate behaviors or outcomes. Epstein defines the process of corporate social responsibility as

> ... a system of decisionmaking whereby corporate managers try to anticipate and consider the *total* consequences of business policies and operations before they act. What managers consider to be relevant to formulating and implementing corporate policy encompasses not only economic factors but also the social, political, environmental, and cultural consequences of corporate action. . . . It requires that the firm build into and utilize in key aspects of its normal operating practices (particularly areas unregulated by government), structure and practices that require it to consider decision criteria that were once thought "exogenous" or irrelevant.[12]

In similar fashion Christopher Stone suggests that the process of corporate social responsibility requires managers to apply the following principles in their decision making:

1. The responsible manager reflects upon the implications of a decision, and does not act impulsively.
2. The responsible manager takes into account the consequences and repercussions of his actions.
3. The responsible manager considers and weighs alternatives.
4. The responsible manager has a "moral inclination—a desire, probably as much internalized as conscious, to do the right thing."[13]

Epstein also defines social responsibility in terms of the products or outcomes of a corporation's decision making. Examples of socially responsible corporate behavior under the product approach include fair employment practices, concern about health and safety in the workplace, a commitment to producing safe and reliable products, an awareness of and commitment to environmental quality, and a commitment to ethical business practices. Epstein believes that "the Product or outcome analysis of social responsibility is both inherently dynamic and value laden. It reflects a society's stage of economic development, its most pressing societal needs, the specific configuration of its political economy and the interrelationship of its key institutions, prevalent ideologies, and cultural ethos."[14] Stone adds specificity to the desired outcomes or product of corporate social responsibility by setting forth the various roles the corporation plays in our society and suggesting examples of socially responsible conduct or attitudes for the corporation. Table 7-1 sets forth Stone's suggestions.

TABLE 7-1   Corporate Roles and Socially Responsible Conduct

THE CORPORATION AS CITIZEN

- To be concerned with obeying the laws (even if it can get away with law-breaking profitably)
- To aid in the making of laws, as by volunteering information within its control regarding additional measures that may need to be imposed on industry
- To heed the fundamental moral rules of society
- Not to engage in deception, corruption, and the like
- As a citizen abroad, to act decently to host country citizens and not inimically to U.S. foreign policy

---

THE CORPORATION AS PRODUCER

- To aim for safe and reliable products at a fair price

THE CORPORATION AS EMPLOYER

- To be concerned with the safety of the work environment
- To be concerned with the emotional well-being of its workers
- Not to discriminate

THE CORPORATION AS RESOURCE MANAGER

- Not to contribute unduly to the depletion of resources
- To manifest some concern for the aesthetics of land management

---

THE CORPORATION AS AN INVESTMENT

- To safeguard the interests of investors
- To make full and fair disclosure of its economic condition

THE CORPORATION AS NEIGHBOR

- To be concerned with pollution
- To conduct safe and quiet operations

THE CORPORATION AS COMPETITOR

- Not to engage in unfair competition, on the one hand, or cozy restrictions of competition, on the other

---

THE CORPORATION AS SOCIAL DESIGNER

- To be innovative and responsive in the introduction of new products and methods

---

Adapted from Christopher D. Stone, Where the Law Ends: The Social Control of Corporate Behavior (New York: Harper & Row, Publishers, 1975), pp. 231–32. Reprinted with permission.

There are many product outcomes of corporate social responsibility that can be achieved at little or no cost to the corporation. These outcomes require only that the corporation accept the concept of social responsibility as part of the management process or culture of the corporation. Examples of such socially responsible outcomes include personnel practices that are nondiscriminatory; awareness of health and safety hazards in the workplace, many of which can be corrected inexpensively; and concern about product quality and safety, which is not only responsible conduct but as the Japanese have demonstrated, also inures to the long-term profitability of the company.

Economic and competitive reality places certain constraints on how far an individual corporation can proceed in the direction of corporate social responsibility. For example, while a steel or chemical company may be aware of and concerned about air and water pollution caused by its manufacturing processes and those of its competitors, a company cannot be expected to spend tens of millions of dollars to clean up its pollution if its competitors are not required to do likewise. The socially aware company's costs would increase, since it would no longer be externalizing them, and soon it would be unable to compete with its polluting competitors. The same scenario applies to those health and safety hazards in the workplace that are very expensive to correct.

In both of the above examples and in similar cases where the cost of unilateral corporate action is too great, how should a socially responsible corporation proceed? The definition of social responsibility developed above suggests a number of approaches. First, the socially responsible corporation is at least aware of and concerned about the public health, social, and political consequences of environmental pollution. Second, while it may not be competitively feasible to act unilaterally, the corporation can encourage its competitors to adopt a coordinated industrywide program to solve the pollution problem whereby all companies contribute financially and otherwise to the solution.[15] Third, if a voluntary industry solution is not possible, the socially responsible companies in the industry can cooperate with Congress in adopting a public policy (for example, clean-air-and-water legislation) that requires all companies within the industry and perhaps across many industries to install pollution-abatement equipment and adhere to particular environmental standards. Such action not only may be in the public interest but also is in the corporation's interest, since cooperation with Congress is likely to lead to more efficient and less costly regulation.

The Arguments for Social Responsibility

The arguments supporting corporate social responsibility can be summarized as follows:

1. Evolving Public Expectations Public expectations of the large corporation have been changing over the past fifty years. While the corporation could justify its existence on purely economic grounds in the first half of the twentieth century, the public began to demand that large corporations become more socially aware as they grew in power and affected more and more people by their activities. The corporation relies on society for its legitimacy; therefore, if the expectations of society change, the corporation must adapt to the new environment or be threatened with extinction.

2. *Avoidance of Additional Government Regulation* As you learned in Chapter 3, the large corporation is substantially affected by government regulation. Much of this regulation has been in response to particular business conduct that the public considered unacceptable. One lesson to be learned from the past periods of regulation is that business may be able to avoid or at least moderate the severity of future regulation by being aware of changes in social expectations and by acting to meet its obligations as a major economic and social institution. Such a proactive approach should result in less regulation and more business freedom.

3. *Improved Public Image* If societal expectations of the role of business have changed, then a company, large or small, that responds to these new expectations will be viewed more favorably than one that does not. This favorable reception should result in more customers, better employees, higher sales, and increased profits for the company. Moreover, the enhanced public image of a company, especially when it is a highly visible large corporation, improves the legitimacy and standing of large corporations generally.

4. *It Is Morally Right* This argument asserts that socially responsible conduct by the corporation is simply the "right thing to do." Just as individuals are expected to abide by the prevailing ethical norms in society, so too should the large corporation, which is, after all, managed by individuals. Because the large corporation is a major institution in society, its managers have a responsibility to run the corporation in a manner consistent with society's ethical and moral standards.

5. *Power Implies Responsibility* This argument suggests that powerful institutions in a democratic society must be viewed as responsibly exercising their power if they are to retain the support of the public and maintain their legitimacy. Corporate decisions affect the environment, consumers, local communities, and many other areas of society. Society expects corporate power to be exercised in a responsible manner because its irresponsible exercise is contrary to the public interest. Epstein writes: "Power and responsibility are reciprocally correlated concepts in American society. The existence of the former inevitably raises issues concerning the character of the latter."[16]

6. Long-Run Self-Interest   This argument incorporates a number of the preceding arguments. It asserts that given the social and political environment in which the large corporation does business and is likely to do business in the future, the corporation will succeed in maximizing long-run profits by operating in a socially responsible manner. In this sense social responsibility is a constraint to which the corporation must adjust in pursuing its economic goal of maximizing profit. Although socially responsible conduct and expenditures may lower short-run profits, in the long run it is in the corporation's enlightened self-interest to behave in a socially ethical manner. The Committee for Economic Development (CED), a group of prominent corporate leaders, issued a policy statement in the early 1970s on the social responsibilities of business corporations. The statement concludes that

> .... it is in the enlightened self-interest of corporations to promote the public welfare in a positive way. . . . Indeed, the corporate interest broadly defined by management can support involvement in helping to solve virtually any social problem, because people who have a good environment, education, and opportunity make better employees, customers, and neighbors for business than those who are poor, ignorant, and oppressed.[17]

The Arguments against Social Responsibility

The arguments opposing corporate social responsibility can be summarized as follows:

1. The Classical View of Profit Maximization   The case against social responsibility is centered on the classical economic view of business and the corporation. The classical view is summarized here by Professor Milton Friedman, one of America's leading economists:

> The view has been gaining widespread acceptance that corporate officials and labor leaders have a "social responsibility" that goes beyond serving the interest of their stockholders or their members. This view shows a fundamental misconception of the nature of a free economy. In such an economy there is one and only one social responsibility of business—to use its resources and engage in activities designed to increase its profits so long as it stays within the rules of the game, which is to say engages in open and free competition, without deception or fraud. . . .
> Few trends could so thoroughly undermine the very foundations of our free society as the acceptance by corporate officials of a social responsibility other than to make as much money for their stockholders as possible. This is a fundamentally subversive doctrine.[18]

The classical view argues that the corporation and business generally make their greatest contribution to society when they strive to maximize profits in a competitive economy by efficiently producing goods and services. Such business conduct creates jobs, efficiently allocates resources, and provides material abundance to society. Business should be allowed to concentrate on what it does best rather than dividing its energies between economic goals and social responsibilities.

2. The Problem of Accountability   Managers have expertise in efficiently operating the corporation in order to maximize profits. However, they have no special expertise or authority from the shareholders to determine what is socially responsible conduct. Nor in most cases have the shareholders authorized management to spend shareholder money (that is, corporate profits) on socially responsible conduct.

Friedman asserts that managers who spend the corporation's money for social purposes behave as though they were government officials. But while government officials respond to the desires of the people and are accountable to them through the electoral process, corporate managers are only indirectly accountable to shareholders whose goals and motivations are economic, not social or political. Unlike government officials, managers who engage in socially responsible activities (which often affect the public) are not selected by the electorate or accountable to them, a situation that creates a distortion of the democratic process. Moreover, not only are such management activities not subject to the political control of the electorate, they are also not guided by market forces, which typically are the basis for most management decisions. Thus Friedman sees the exercise of social responsibility by corporate managers as lacking any clear guidance on the social goals to be pursued, and perhaps more important, as lacking accountability to both shareholders and the electorate.[19]

3. The Problem of Concentrated Power   Another major concern of the opponents to corporate social responsibility is that corporations that undertake socially responsible conduct will begin to cooperate too closely with government, which is itself pursuing many of the same social objectives. The present pluralist system encourages an arm's-length and almost adversarial relationship between major power centers in society such as the large corporation, the federal government, labor unions, and the media. We saw in Chapter 1 that the idea of fragmented or off-setting power blocs has long been important in American society. If the large corporation and the federal government begin to cooperate in solving some of the nation's major social and economic problems, there is a risk that the convergence of these two major sources of economic and political power will lessen individual liberty and freedom.

It is this concern about concentrated power and the consequent risk to individual liberty that leads Friedman to characterize corporate social responsibility as a "fundamentally subversive doctrine" in a free society.[20] Friedman and other supporters of the classical view believe that a strong free market and the separation of business and government are important to the preservation of individual freedom. He addresses the issues of concentrated power and the free market in his book *Capitalism and Freedom*:

Consequently, if economic power is joined to political power, concentration seems almost inevitable. On the other hand, if economic power is kept in separate hands from political power, it can serve as a check and a counter to political power. . . . The preservation of freedom requires the elimination of such concentration of power to the fullest possible extent and the dispersal and distribution of whatever power cannot be eliminated—a system of checks and balances. By removing the organization of economic activity from the control of political authority, the market eliminated this source of coercive power. It enables economic strength to be a check to political power rather than a reinforcement.[21]

An Assessment of the Corporate-Social-Responsibility Debate

Many commentators believe that the social and political environment of the large corporation in the late twentieth century requires that the corporation modify its traditional goal of profit maximization by adding the complementary goal of socially responsible behavior. Societal expectations and the need for corporate legitimacy make it in the corporation's enlightened self-interest to adopt the concept and practice of social responsibility. To be sure, not all corporations have accepted the concept of social responsibility, but the trend since the 1960s clearly has been in the direction of a greater awareness and practice of social responsibility.

It can be argued that the concept of social responsibility is *consistent* with the more traditional profit-maximizing role of the corporation. If, as most observers agree, society has changed the "rules of the game" to require corporations to be more socially responsible, then it is in the corporation's self-interest to factor social responsibility into the economic decision-making process. The goal of maximizing profits remains, but the means for achieving the goal have been modified by the constraint of social responsibility.

The self-interest rationale for accepting the concept of corporate social responsibility does not fully answer the objections of Professor Friedman and others who hold a classical view of the corporation. They are not likely to agree that a corporation's failure to exercise social responsibility will lead consumers, employees, and other affected groups to seek new government regulation. Rather, the classical view holds that absent a few exceptions (for instance, pollution control and protection against anticompetitive practices) where government regulation is desirable, the competitive forces in a free-market economy are sufficient to regulate corporate conduct. For example, if employees are unhappy with the health and safety conditions at their workplace, they are free to seek employment elsewhere. Eventually the company will lose too many good employees and be forced to remedy the workplace hazards in order to attract the quality of employee necessary to remain competitive. Similarly, if a company attempts to maximize profits by limiting quality-control expenditures, thereby producing too many defective or unsafe products, consumers will eventually stop buying the company's products and turn to its competitors. Here again, the forces of the free market should be adequate to modify the company's conduct.

The classical view of the corporation and the free market does not, however, reflect society's expectations of the large corporation or the realities of the marketplace. While the free market is an important check on business and corporate conduct, it does not operate perfectly. For example, unskilled or semiskilled workers may not be able easily to shift employment from an unsafe to a safe workplace. This imperfection in the labor market may be caused by a number of factors, including, for example, a high unemployment rate, a low demand for unskilled workers, the difficulty of transferring pension benefits, or the difficulty of uprooting families from one section of the country in order for them to seek employment in another part of the country.

Another assumption of the free market is that consumers have adequate information upon which to evaluate competing products or services. But if consumers lack adequate information because of insufficient education, inability to evaluate information, lack of access to information, or the inability to afford the cost of information, they are not able to impose discipline on sellers in the way free-market theory would suggest.

The imperfections in the free market account for much of the government regulation of business described in Chapter 3. The corporation may be able to reduce the risk of excessive regulation in the future by mitigating the effects of such imperfections through the exercise of social responsibility.

Professor Friedman's concern that the large corporation's adoption of social responsibility may lead to a dangerous concentration of economic and political power is a serious one. It must be carefully considered as corporations begin to cooperate with government in their efforts to meet society's expectations of responsible conduct. However, for the corporation to disregard the public interest and avoid the concept of social responsibility invites those groups adversely affected by corporate action or inaction to petition their elected representatives for greater government regulation. The prospect of such additional regulation runs the risk of involving government to an increasing degree in corporate decision making, thereby limiting managerial freedom.

Thus the concerns that arise from a cooperative relationship between the large corporation and government are as likely to result from increased regulation as from social responsibility. There is, however, one major difference between these seemingly similar outcomes. A more cooperative relationship forced on the large corporation by increased regulation will do harm to the legitimacy of the large corporation, whereas greater cooperation premised on the concept of social responsibility should increase the corporation's legitimacy as a major institution in American society. While the concern about concentrated power attends both outcomes, the latter outcome is to be preferred since it reflects society's expectations, enhances corporate legitimacy, and holds the promise of continued managerial freedom and flexibility in running the corporation.

Finally, we must be careful not to exaggerate the risk of concentrated power resulting from corporate social responsibility. The degree of involvement by large corporations in socially responsible activities is likely to be limited relative to their primary economic goals of profit maximization and operating efficiency. Even in an environment of corporate social responsibility most business decisions will continue to focus on economic criteria and free-market forces. Although the concept of social responsibility does lead to more cooperation between business and government, it is not likely to be so substantial and pervasive as to raise a dangerous risk of concentrated power.

BUSINESS-GOVERNMENT RELATIONS AND THE CHALLENGE OF INTERNATIONAL ECONOMIC COMPETITION

We have discussed how the increased recognition of social responsibility is one factor suggesting a more cooperative relationship between the large corporation and government. We turn now to a more recent development that also suggests an increased level of cooperation between business and government; namely, the challenge of international economic competition.

The Challenge to American Competitiveness

During much of the twentieth century America's economic power and its ability to compete in the world went unchallenged. Many factors contributed to this agreeable state of affairs, including abundant natural resources, the free-market system, American inventiveness, a relatively low level of class conflict in American society, and the absence of war on American soil and the related social and economic disruption that results from war.

The competitive challenge to American economic power did not begin until the early 1960s. That it did not begin earlier was due largely to the severe social dislocation and economic destruction visited upon our potential economic competitors in Western Europe as a result of World Wars I and II. Japan's ability to compete with the United States was similarly affected by World War II as well as by its relative political and economic isolation in the early years of this century. While much of the industrial base of Germany, France, and Japan was destroyed during World War II, the United States was fortunate to escape fighting and destruction on its own territory. In fact, American industrial capacity and efficiency increased greatly during World War II in the drive to supply the Allied war effort in Europe and the Pacific.

Following World War II American industrial power was preeminent. Foreign markets were open to American industrial and agricultural products not only because those products had a reputation for quality but also because they had few real competitors following the war. America helped to rebuild the shattered economies of Western Europe and Japan with large grants of foreign economic aid (notably, the Marshall Plan in Europe) and substantial infusions of foreign investment by American corporations. The efforts at economic assistance proved to be remarkably successful. By the early 1960s the economies of West Germany, Japan, and France, energized by a new industrial base put in place after World War II, began to experience rapid economic growth and became increasingly competitive in world export markets.

It can be argued that the American economy was not seriously tested in terms of foreign economic competition until the late 1960s. Since that time various studies have documented increasing competitive pressure on the American economy by foreign imports from Japan and Western Europe.[22] By the mid-1970s significant additional competition was coming from South Korea, Taiwan, Hong Kong, and Singapore, the so-called four tigers of Asia.

One measure of the increased pressure of foreign competition on the American economy is the U.S. Merchandise Trade Balance (the difference between the value of U.S. exports and imports measured on an annual basis) with the rest of the world. In 1975 the U.S. had a merchandise trade surplus of approximately $2 billion. By 1980 this surplus had become a trade deficit of approximately $25 billion, increasing to $122 billion in 1985, and reaching $160 billion by 1987. The merchandise trade deficit for 1988 is expected to be approximately $121 billion.[23] The decline in the deficit for 1988 is due in large part to a devaluation of the dollar (via floating exchange rates), cheaper oil prices, and productivity/efficiency improvements by many U.S. business firms. Over half of this trade deficit represents an imbalance of trade (the fact that we import more products than we export) with Japan, South Korea, Taiwan, Hong Kong, and Singapore. Much of the remaining deficit is with Western Europe and the OPEC oil countries.

In 1985 the Harvard Business School sponsored a conference entitled "U.S. Competitiveness in the World Economy." The research papers presented at that meeting analyzed and evaluated America's changing competitive position in the world economy. The conference organizers summarized its findings and conclusions as follows:

1. For some fifteen years the United States has been losing its capacity to compete in the world economy. This loss is particularly serious as the nation's dependence on international trade increases. The effects can be seen particularly in the manufacturing sector.

2. Declining U.S. competitiveness is evident in the performance patterns of several measures: a shift from decades of trade surpluses to substantial deficits, eroding market shares in almost all sectors, and declining profitability since the late 1960s. In addition, real after-tax earnings of American workers have been declining since they peaked in 1972.

3. The principal competitive challenge comes not from our traditional rivals in Western Europe, but from a new group of competitors in East Asia: Japan, South Korea, Taiwan, Singapore, and Hong Kong.

4. The competitive thrust of these new challengers comes not from favorable endowments of natural resources but from coherent national strategies through which each country mobilizes and shapes its productive capabilities to achieve economic growth and global competitiveness. These strategies emphasize work, saving, and investment to build a higher standard of living through increased productivity in existing activities, and through accelerating the shift toward activities that promise above average growth and/or technical change.

5. The United States and most of the West European industrial democracies suffer by comparison from increasingly less competitive strategies. Although generally not explicit, their strategies emphasize more secure and equitable distribution of current income at the expense of increased market rigidities, and current consumption at the expense of investment for long-term benefits.

6. Unless the United States reexamines and modifies its basic economic strategy, it cannot expect to generate the performance necessary to finance its simultaneous commitments to leading the Western Alliance, increasing the domestic standard of living, and improving the distribution of income.[24]

The Importance of Dynamic Comparative Advantage

In analyzing the economic strategy of our major trade competitors, the Harvard study found that many of these countries (especially those in Asia) have developed a national strategy whereby business, government, and labor cooperate in implementing the economic concept of dynamic comparative advantage. The study suggests that the United States also should adopt a national strategy of international competitiveness premised on the concept of *dynamic comparative advantage.* Pursuit of such a strategy would require greater cooperation among business, government, and labor than we have experienced in the past.[25]

The traditional, or static, view of comparative advantage holds that a country should produce and export those goods in which it has the greatest economic advantage and import from other countries those goods in which it has the least economic advantage. A country may have an economic advantage over another country (that is, a comparative advantage) in producing certain goods because of abundant and available natural resources, good climate, or perhaps a preferred geographic location. In simplified form the theory suggests that a country's exports are determined by its fixed natural resources.

The theory of dynamic comparative advantage asserts that a country can adopt development strategies, often in the form of public policies enacted by government, that can move a country's comparative advantage beyond its fixed natural resources. For example, a country can adopt a national development strategy that encourages savings and capital investment, a strong educational system, the development of a skilled labor force, and investment in research and development to encourage new-product development and the improvement of existing manufacturing processes. Government can adopt policies and create institutions whose purpose it is to receive input from business and labor in order to develop a consensus on accelerating the development of new sectors of the economy and hastening the abandonment of sectors or industries where the country no longer holds a comparative advantage. In short, the advocates of dynamic comparative advantage believe that a country's economic development is not constrained by its fixed natural resource base. Rather, it can be shaped by strategic planning and the development of a national consensus that identifies those sectors of the economy (steel, computer technology, fiber optics, biotechnology, aerospace, and so on) that should be encouraged to develop on a fast track.

The exercise of dynamic comparative advantage has been a major element in the development of a national competitive strategy, often referred to as an industrial policy, by countries such as Japan, South Korea, France, and to a lesser extent West Germany. One of the major issues on the public-policy agenda in the United States is whether and to what extent America will move in the direction of an industrial policy in order to meet the international competitive challenge. Will American policy makers conclude that in certain industrial and high-technology sectors of the economy, traditional free-market forces need to be supplemented by a set of coordinated policies involving cooperation among business, government, and labor? The answer to that question is not yet apparent as the decade of the 1980s draws to a close. What is clear, however, is that a decision to seek even a limited industrial policy would lead to a closer relationship between business and government than has existed in the past.

Meeting the Competitive Challenge

In the remainder of this chapter we develop two scenarios that the United States may choose to pursue in meeting the challenge of international economic competition. As will become apparent, the second scenario, which we believe is more likely to occur, implies a closer, more cooperative relationship between business and government in the years to come.

1. *The Economy Continues on Its Present Course*   The more conservative scenario is that America continues its current reliance on free-market forces (and limited protectionism) supplemented by government macroeconomic policies designed to encourage economic growth and increased American competitiveness. Effective macroeconomic policy requires the careful coordination of budgetary, tax, and monetary policy by the executive branch, Congress, and the Federal Reserve Board. Examples of such macroeconomic policies include a budgetary policy that reduces the massive federal budget deficits of the 1980s that have been partially responsible for the very high U.S. trade deficit; federal tax policy that encourages an increased level of individual savings and increased capital investment by corporations; and a monetary policy (for instance, lower interest rates) that pursues the important but difficult task of encouraging economic growth while at the same time guarding against excessive inflation in the economy.

This scenario calls for American companies to become more competitive by keeping their operating costs under control. Companies must set priorities, raise productivity, eliminate marginal employees, and develop more cost-effective operating and manufacturing processes. The attention to cost control and efficiency has been partially responsible for the wave of mergers and acquisitions that have occurred in the 1980s. Many of these mergers are intended to consolidate and streamline businesses that operate in sectors of the economy characterized by excess capacity, inefficient operating methods, and outmoded plant and equipment.

This scenario is also consistent with many of the implicit norms and standards of American society discussed in Chapter 1; namely, the preference for fragmented power, decentralized government, and a free-enterprise economy. While it is apparent that these norms and standards have been somewhat compromised in contemporary American society, they are nevertheless favored as general principles and continue to provide support for a quasi-free-enterprise economy in which government plays a limited, albeit increasing, role. The macroeconomic policies discussed above involve government in such a limited role. For the most part they can be implemented by the relevant administrative agency (for instance, the Internal Revenue Service or the Federal Reserve Board) without requiring detailed intervention or regulation of the economy.

The economy is likely to continue on its present course so long as government macroeconomic policies and efforts by American companies to improve productivity and competitiveness prove adequate to offset the increased competitive pressure from abroad. If, however, the United States finds itself continuing to lose world market share in important product areas (aerospace, semiconductors, computers, biotechnology, consumer electronics, machine tools, autos, steel, and so on) to competitors like Japan, West Germany, France, and South Korea, and the trade deficit figures do not improve significantly, then we are likely to see some compromise in the implicit norms and standards discussed above, which will allow for the enactment of public policies establishing a limited industrial policy.

2. The Prospect of a Limited Industrial Policy The advocates of a limited industrial policy argue that more specific and coordinated policies are needed to supplement the traditional workings of the market system and government's existing role in influencing economic performance through the use of macroeconomic policy. Its supporters believe that free-market forces acting alone will be too slow in restructuring those sectors of the American economy that are no longer competitive and promoting those sectors that are competitive or can be made to be so in the future. They believe that America's major economic competitors are better able to shape and respond to the forces of international competition because they have implemented industrial policies through which business and government cooperate more effectively than in the United States.

Chalmers Johnson, who has written extensively about Japanese industrial policy, defines *industrial policy* as

> . . . . A summary term for the activities of government that are intended to develop or retrench various industries in a national economy in order to maintain global competitiveness. . . .

By industrial policy I mean the government's explicit attempt to coordinate its own multifarious activities and expenditures and to reform them using as a basic criterion the achievement of dynamic comparative advantage for the American economy. Such an industrial policy would work on the supply side and would be long term in outlook. It would seek to produce aggressive investment behavior by reducing risks, providing information, promoting R & D, removing irrational antitrust barriers (joint research by American auto makers in developing emission-control technology would have saved millions but was prevented by governmental regulations), and encouraging the appropriate education and reeducation of the labor force.[26]

A somewhat similar definition speaks of the objectives and means of industrial policy in this way:

What then is industrial policy? The most generally accepted definition today is that it is whatever the government does vis à vis private industry or individual firms to achieve a variety of objectives. These objectives include promoting the nation's economic development and growth, accelerating the structural transformation of domestic industry in a desired direction, improving the international competitiveness of designated products, encouraging the development of new technologies, smoothing the phasing out of chronically depressed industries, assisting the rationalization and reorganization of a weakened industry that is judged to have a chance of recovery, protecting domestic employment, and programing regional development. The means to achieve these ends may be tax incentives, subsidies, special government procurement, grants, low-interest loans, government-guaranteed loans, tariffs, quantitative import restrictions, administrative guidance, and the like.[27]

At its core, then, industrial policy involves the coordination and targeting of government programs in cooperation with business and labor in an effort to improve American global competitiveness.

Any move in the direction of an American industrial policy would be limited. That is because of the implicit norms and standards of American society as well as the realization that in a complex economy, with literally thousands of different products and services, the invisible hand of the market is generally to be preferred over the difficulty of administering and coordinating government programs to assist business and the economy. It is likely, however, that the increasing assistance, cooperation, and planning that characterize the business-government relationship of America's most important international economic competitors will require a somewhat similar strategy in the United States.

Government support for particular industrial sectors is not a new development in the relationship between American business and government. We noted in Chapter 3 that Congress provided generous assistance to the railroads in order to encourage the construction of a transcontinental railway system in the nineteenth century. Congress also has provided substantial assistance to American agriculture through federal programs administered by the Departments of Agriculture and Interior. American higher education and indirectly the American economy benefited greatly from Congress's enactment of the Morrill Act in 1862, which provided support for the establishment of a system of land grant colleges and universities in the United States. In more recent years Congress has appropriated billions of dollars for research and development in the fields of aerospace, computer technology, and fiber optics, to name but a few. While much of this research has focused on the needs of the military and NASA, it has also generated spin-off products and benefits for the civilian economy. This effect is especially apparent in many of the high-technology industries where American corporations have long been recognized as leading the way.

However, a recent report issued by the Business Roundtable notes that research and development (R&D) spending for defense-related programs has fewer commercial advantages than R&D spending by corporations and government for commercial purposes. The Roundtable report states:

> In 1986, more than 70 percent of the United States' R&D funding was directed to defense projects. Total federal R&D funding has doubled since 1980, but almost all of the increase has gone to defense R&D. West Germany and Japan have traditionally spent less than 10 percent of their total R&D funding on defense.
>
> The devotion of almost three-quarters of our government R&D resources to defense affects the competitive position of U.S. firms. Compared to other industrial economies, the United States has extracted far less commercial benefit from a much larger R&D budget.[28]

In the area of research and development funding, the challenge for the United States is to maintain adequate levels of R&D spending for defense programs while at the same time increasing federal R&D funds for commercial purposes and coordinating better with industry.

In the past government support for particular sectors of the economy has been uncoordinated and at the behest of special-interest groups rather than designed with the objective of meeting international competition. Of course, one reason is that international economic competition was not a serious concern for the United States prior to the 1970s. Supporters of a limited industrial policy argue that existing and future governmental programs to strengthen particular sectors of the economy must be better planned and coordinated to achieve the objective of improving American competitiveness.

An important question arises as we approach the 1990s: Will the increased challenge of international competition lead American business and labor to conclude that it is in their respective self-interests to cooperate more fully with each other and with government in developing a national strategy for a more economically competitive America? If such a strategy is adopted, it will probably consist of joint initiatives by business and labor as well as packages of governmental programs or public policies (often supported by both business and labor interest groups) whose objective would be the promotion of dynamic comparative advantage in the American economy.

While such packages of public policies might be termed a limited industrial policy, it is the substance of the policies rather than the label attached to them that is important. It may be that for ideological or political reasons the term industrial policy has become too controversial, since to some it connotes too much government planning and cooperation with the private sector. Therefore, the president and Congress may prefer to promote and justify such a set of policies by describing it as a program to enhance American competitiveness or perhaps as a program in the national security interests of the United States, in the sense that the United States, as the leader of the free world, must preserve, protect, and strengthen its defense-related industries.[29] The important point to remember is that whatever the justification or label applied to such policies, if adopted they would move the business-government relationship in the direction of increased cooperation.

The Business Roundtable in its 1987 report on international competitiveness outlines a program of public and private initiatives to advance American competitiveness. Although the report does not advocate an American industrial policy, it does suggest that improving America's international competitive position will require a joint effort by both the public and private sectors. The report states: "Both government and the private sector have a role to play, but much of the responsibility will fall upon business and private initiative."[30] Significantly, a number of the recommendations included in the report call for a cooperative effort between business and government. These proposals and others are discussed below.

In response to the growing competitive challenge, Congress in recent years has enacted a number of public policies that can be characterized as elements of a limited industrial policy. Other proposals remain on the public-policy agenda. Examples of such policies and proposals include:

1. The 1986 Tax Reform Act, which among other things, lowered the marginal tax rates of individual taxpayers and corporations in an effort to encourage an increased level of savings and investment. Economists hope that the increased level of savings available for investment will be channeled into new and more productive plants and equipment. Although the Tax Reform Act is an example of a macroeconomic policy proposed in the first scenario discussed above, it also is supported by the advocates of a limited industrial policy. They believe that macroeconomic policy complements and must be coordinated with other public- and private-sector programs to strengthen and restructure particular sectors of the economy.

2. Congress has enacted legislation on a limited scale to fund the reeducation and retraining of American workers who become unemployed as a result of plant closings or cutbacks caused by international competition. The purpose of this legislation is to improve labor mobility and to encourage the phasing out of noncompetitive firms or industries.

The Business Roundtable in its 1987 report on international competitiveness recognized the continuing need for cooperation between business and government in improving labor mobility and assisting displaced workers. The report states:

For many years to come, problems of worker adjustment will be among the most difficult challenges facing all countries. Cushioning dislocation to facilitate change is a desirable response. . . .

The public-policy issue is how to mitigate the serious dislocations generated by such changes without slowing the dynamics of a growing American economy.

The private sector frequently is in a good position to help respond at the local level. In its 1984 report, *Strategy for a Vital U.S. Economy,* the Business Roundtable recommended that the private sector offer training, retraining, job search assistance and income support wherever possible to displaced employees in order to qualify them for new existing jobs.

In many instances a corporation will be unable to retrain an employee or to play a significant role in gaining the individual reemployment. For these cases, good public programs that help prepare the individual to move quickly into new employment should be available. The wide variety of ad hoc laws now dealing with certain classes of displaced individuals (and not others) do not respond to the nature of the problem or the magnitude of the need.[31]

3. In 1987 Congress enacted legislation that calls upon the federal government to help fund a research-and-development consortium made up of leading firms in the U.S. semiconductor industry. The federal government will provide approximately $100 million per year over a four-year period with the participating firms contributing an equivalent amount. Other legislation being considered would over the next five years almost double the budget of the National Science Foundation, the government agency that finances much university research.

The Business Roundtable has expressed support for a cooperative effort between business and government to ensure that sufficient research-and-development funding is available to meet the challenge of international competition. In a recent report the Roundtable explained:

Where the search for new technology requires large investments in basic research with very long commercial lead time and no certainty of result, few companies can justify the expense. Although the benefits may be great, one company may find it impossible to assume the cost and risks when it is clear that the knowledge gained will quickly become the property of its competitors at relatively low cost. As R&D and application costs soar, the private market may forgo projects that would return important benefits overall — but not to any single investor. In cases such as these, there is a legitimate role for government.[32]

4. In 1988 the Office of Technology Assessment, a research arm of Congress, issued a draft report warning that Japanese companies are poised to commercialize superconductor technology well ahead of their U.S. rivals, despite the U.S. lead in basic research. The draft report recommends that the federal government establish a Commercial Technology Agency, with an annual budget between $100 million and $500 million, to assist private corporations in conducting high risk research and solve technical problems hindering U.S. efforts to commercialize new technologies. The report suggests that the new agency be modeled after the Defense Department's Defense Advanced Research Projects Agency, which explores next-generation technology that might aid the military.[33]

5. A number of liberal and conservative economists have recommended that the merger provisions of the Clayton Antitrust Act be relaxed by amending the act to provide that actual and potential international competition be taken into account when analyzing the anticompetitive effects of a proposed merger between two

American companies. Legislation to amend the merger provisions of the Clayton Act was introduced in Congress during 1987. It remains to be seen whether this legislative proposal will succeed in becoming the latest addition to antitrust public policy.

Some economists and business leaders have also urged relaxing the antitrust restrictions on competitor corporations that wish to engage in joint research-and-development projects. Congress responded positively in 1984 when it enacted the National Cooperative Research Act. It is likely that such legislation was passed because of congressional concern about the increased level of international economic competition.

CONCLUSION

We began this chapter by raising a speculative question about the future relationship between government and the large corporation. In addressing this question we reviewed the historical development of the business-government relationship, discussed the importance of the political concept of legitimacy for the large corporation, and suggested that two major forces, corporate social responsibility and international economic competition, will be important in developing a more cooperative relationship between the large corporation and government in the years to come.

Corporate social responsibility is defined in terms of the product or conduct that one would expect from a socially responsible company as well as the process of internal decision making that helps encourage responsible corporate behavior. Arguments are developed for and against the practice of social responsibility by the large corporation. Today most corporations accept the idea that society expects them to be economic institutions that are also aware of their obligations to consumers, investors, employees, and the communities in which they do business. The corporation's recognition and acceptance of the concept of social responsibility, what some have called the socioeconomic model of the corporation, indicates the development of a more cooperative relationship between the large corporation and government.

The chapter also suggests that the increased level of international economic competition between the United States, Japan, West Germany, France, and the so-called four tigers of Asia is likely to encourage greater cooperation among business, government, and labor. In this regard the theory of dynamic comparative advantage urges that the United States move in the direction of a limited industrial policy (although it may not be labeled as such) that combines macroeconomic policies with government programs and private-sector initiatives to strengthen particular sectors of the economy.

In a broader sense this chapter serves as the last link in a series of interrelated topic areas covered in this book. Recall that in Chapters 1 and 2 we began with a discussion of the public-policy process and the major institutions involved in the making of public policy. We saw in Chapter 3 that the task of implementing public policy has been delegated by Congress to the administrative agencies. The discussion in Chapter 3 analyzes the reasons for the rise of administrative agencies and government regulation of business. Most important, it focuses on the substantial powers of agencies and the effectiveness of legal and political checks on agency power and suggests how business firms can effectively interact with agencies.

The discussion of the antitrust laws in Chapters 4, 5, and 6 provides an excellent example of how administrative agencies enjoy substantial discretion in the implementation of particular public policies (for example, the antitrust statutes). The chapters demonstrate how a public policy can evolve over time because of varying levels of enforcement, often caused by an evolving political and/or economic philosophy in the executive branch and sometimes by modifications legislated by Congress. Of equal importance is the more detailed analysis of particular statutory provisions and their application to specific business practices.

In Chapter 7 we conclude our discussion of business, government, and public policy by focusing on two important forces that are likely to affect the relationship between the large corporation and government in the years to come. Both forces, social responsibility and international economic competition, are linked to earlier topics covered in this book. In part, the large corporation has been attracted to the concept of social responsibility in order to minimize the creation of additional regulatory public policies affecting business. The growing challenge of international economic competition raises questions concerning the necessity and desirability of enacting new public policies (for example, a limited industrial policy including some reforms of the antitrust laws) to assist in restructuring and strengthening particular sectors of the economy. The implications of such policy proposals for the business-government relationship and their ability to negotiate the hurdles of the public-policy process are likely to be important topics of national debate in the 1990s.

NOTES

1. Philip I. Blumberg, *The Megacorporation in American Society* (Englewood Cliffs, N.J.: Prentice-Hall, 1975), p. 25. See also F. M. Scherer, *Industrial Market Structure and Economic Performance* (Boston: Houghton Mifflin Co., 1980), chap. 3.
2. Legitimacy is a concept taken from political theory and refers to the justifications for a person or institution to possess political or economic power in a society. This concept will be explored more thoroughly later in the chapter.
3. Irving Kristol, "Corporate Capitalism in America," in *Two Cheers for Capitalism*, ed. Irving Kristol (New York: Basic Books, 1978), pp. 3–5.
4. Neil H. Jacoby, *Corporate Power and Social Responsibility* (New York: Macmillan, 1973), p. 23.
5. Kristol, "Corporate Capitalism in America," pp. 5–8.
6. Thomas J. Watson, Jr., *A Business and Its Beliefs* (New York: McGraw-Hill Book Co., 1963), p. 80.
7. David Rockefeller, *Creative Management in Banking* (New York: McGraw-Hill Book Co., 1964), pp. 22–23.
8. Business Roundtable, *Statement on Corporate Responsibility* (New York: Business Roundtable, 1981), pp. 12, 14.

See also Committee for Economic Development, *Social Responsibilities of Business Corporations* (New York: CED, 1971), pp. 11, 25.

9. Adolph A. Berle, Jr., and Gardner C. Means, *The Modern Corporation and Private Property* (New York: Macmillan Co., 1932).

10. The stock of the large corporation is owned by thousands of individual shareholders and by large financial institutions such as pension funds, insurance companies, and private foundations.

11. Irving Kristol, "The Corporation and the Dinosaur," in *Two Cheers for Capitalism* (New York: Basic Books, 1978), pp. 74–75.

12. Epstein, "Societal, Managerial, and Legal Perspectives on Corporate Social Responsibility—Product and Process," *Hastings Law Journal* 30 (1979), 1287, 1303–04.

13. Christopher D. Stone, *Where the Law Ends: The Social Control of Corporate Behavior* (New York: Harper & Row Publishers, 1975), pp. 113–14.

14. Epstein, "Perspectives on Corporate Social Responsibility," p. 1300.

15. In pursuing this approach a prudent corporation should first discuss its plans with the Antitrust Division of the Department of Justice in order to seek its advice on whether such a coordinated program would pose any antitrust problems under the Sherman Act. The Justice Department would likely balance the potential environmental benefits against the risk, if any, of a lessening of competition among the companies involved.

16. Ibid., p. 1295.

17. Committee for Economic Development, *Social Responsibilities of Business Corporations* (New York: CED, 1971), pp. 25–26.

18. Milton Friedman, *Capitalism and Freedom* (Chicago: University of Chicago Press, 1962), p. 133.

19. Milton Friedman, "The Social Responsibility of Business Is to Increase Its Profits," *New York Times Magazine*, September 13, 1970, p. 33.

20. Ibid., p. 126.

21. Friedman, *Capitalism and Freedom*, pp. 15–16.

22. Bruce R. Scott and George C. Lodge, eds., *U.S. Competitiveness in the World Economy* (Boston: Harvard Business School Press, 1985). See also Business Roundtable, *American Excellence in a World Economy* (New York: Business Roundtable, 1987).

23. Joint Economic Committee, U.S. Congress, *Economic Indicators*, October, 1988, p. 36.

24. Scott and Lodge, *U.S. Competitiveness*, pp. 1–2.

25. Scott, "National Strategies: Key to International Competition," in *U.S. Competitiveness*, chap. 2.

26. Chalmers Johnson, "Introduction: The Idea of Industrial Policy," in *The Industrial Policy Debate*, ed. Chalmers Johnson (San Francisco: ICS Press, 1984), pp. 7, 11.

27. Robert S. Ozaki, "How Japanese Industrial Policy Works," in *The Industrial Policy Debate*, p. 48.

28. Business Roundtable, *American Excellence*, p. 31.

29. Paul Seabury, "Industrial Policy and National Defense," in *The Industrial Policy Debate*, chap. 10.

30. Business Roundtable, *American Excellence*, p. 1.

31. Ibid., pp. 28–29.

32. Ibid., p. 31.

33. Bob Davis, "U.S. Agency Sees Japanese Firms Ready to Win Superconductor Projects Race," *Wall Street Journal*, June 20, 1988, p. 2. See also Stephen K. Yoder, "Japan Plans Speedy Superconductor Ships: It Hopes to Lead in Commercializing New Technology," *Wall Street Journal*, August 17, 1988, p. 18.

INDEX

Entries in italics refer to tabular matter or dates.